The Blackademic Life

The Blackademic Life

*Academic Fiction, Higher Education,
and the Black Intellectual*

✦

Lavelle Porter

NORTHWESTERN UNIVERSITY PRESS
EVANSTON, ILLINOIS

Northwestern University Press
www.nupress.northwestern.edu

Copyright © 2020 by Northwestern University Press.
Published 2020. All rights reserved.

10 9 8 7 6 5 4 3 2 1

ISBN 978-0-8101-4099-8 (paper)
ISBN 978-0-8101-4100-1 (cloth)
ISBN 978-0-8101-4101-8 (ebook)

Cataloging-in-Publication data are available from the Library of Congress.

*To the Reverend Archie L. Porter and Mrs. Ivria J. Porter,
who set me on my path to The Blackademic Life*

*Train up a child in the way he should go: and
when he is old, he will not depart from it.*
—*Proverbs 22:6*

CONTENTS

Acknowledgments ix

Introduction: Blackademic Lives Matter 3

Chapter 1
The Overeducation of the Negro: On Reading Black Academic Fiction 15

Chapter 2
Educating and Uplifting the Race, 1876–1919 45

Chapter 3
The New Negro, 1919–1954 69

Chapter 4
Integration and Nationalism, 1954–1980 95

Chapter 5
Culture Wars and Capitalism, 1980–Present 125

Conclusion: Blackademics On Screen 167

Notes 175

Bibliography 189

Index 197

ACKNOWLEDGMENTS

In the formal conventions of the "Acknowledgments" page in academic monographs, the author usually thanks a long list of foundations for their generous support in completion of the book. But this book was not completed with lucrative fellowship support from prestigious foundations. This work was subsidized by the copious amounts of teaching and service I did while working as a full-time tenure-track assistant professor at a teaching-intensive institution. That means this book was written while I was actively engaged in teaching full classes of twenty-five to thirty (or more) students, many of them first-generation college students from working-class backgrounds. The students at the New York City College of Technology, CUNY, work hard. Many of them juggle the duties of parenting and employment while attending classes. The majority of them are from immigrant families hailing from various countries across the globe. And they are completing their educations while having to listen to government officials attack their families as thugs and criminals who do not belong in this country. I listened to them as they spoke about being harassed in the streets in the hostile postelection environment of 2016. Together we've read about the history of immigration in New York City, and I've read their writings about their families' struggles and triumphs. If this country has any future at all, it will be because of these bright and beautiful people who make New York City the great city that it is and who will give this country any greatness that it can lay claim to. I am grateful to the hundreds of City Tech students who came through my classroom during my completion of this book, who indulged me while I rambled on about this strangely neglected topic. Their thoughtful engagement with the works of Ralph Ellison, Chimamanda Adichie, W. E. B. Du Bois, Paule Marshall, and Samuel R. Delany have reminded me why I'm doing this work and whom I am writing for.

    I also want to recognize our union, PSC-CUNY, which remains engaged in ongoing struggles for fair pay for adjunct faculty, who make up the majority of CUNY's instructional staff. PSC-CUNY has also fought for reassigned time for new full-time faculty, which opened up some time for me to finish this book. I want to acknowledge the CUNY Faculty Fellowship Publication Program for a course release in the spring of 2017 that allowed me time to get the manuscript in shape for peer review, and I'm especially thankful to the fellow members of my workshop for their thoughtful comments on an early draft of this book. I would also like to thank my colleagues at City Tech and other CUNY campuses for their encouragement and interest in my scholarly work and for their collaborations on various other scholarly endeavors. I spent many hours in libraries throughout the CUNY system, and I have to give a big thank you to our CUNY librarians, work-study students, and custodial staff, who are all vital parts of our instructional program.

My professors at the CUNY Graduate Center helped me start this book project, and this work was formulated in conversation with many of my Graduate Center teachers and classmates. Big thanks to my adviser, Robert Reid-Pharr, who supported my research interests ever since I first emailed him about the possibility of studying at the Graduate Center. Ammiel Alcalay was a huge help in the job search that eventually landed me at City Tech. This work is a testament to the legacies of Jerry G. Watts and Jon-Christian Suggs, two members of my dissertation committee who were both enthusiastic supporters of my research ideas. Their scholarly fingerprints are all over the pages of this book. I also acknowledge the memory of Dr. Alton Hornsby Jr., the chair of the history department at Morehouse College, who set me on my academic journey and who ushered many Morehouse Men into the academic profession. And I want to thank all my professors at Morehouse, who introduced me to the blackademic life, and the classmates and alumni who encouraged me along the way.

I want to thank the many friends and colleagues who have listened to and engaged with this work at various academic conferences over the years, including those of the American Studies Association, Modern Language Association, and African American Intellectual History Society. Special thanks to Dr. Barbara Ching and the members of the Iowa State University English Department, who graciously invited me out to Ames to lecture on my project in April 2017. Thanks to Jeffrey J. Williams, who read an early version of the manuscript and gave me valuable notes on its structure. Thanks to my reviewers, whose thoughtful comments helped to strengthen this book.

Thank you also to my editor at Northwestern University Press, Gianna Mosser, who believed in this book from the beginning and helped me to see it through, from the first embarrassing and incomplete drafts to this slightly less-embarrassing finished volume.

Of course, I cannot put down every name that deserves to be here, but I have to thank my friends, who listened to me talk about this work, who have read and shared my writing, and who have cheered me on as I put this book out in the world. Thank you to my wife, Dr. Deborah Gambs, for putting up with my long days and nights in the library after classes and on weekends. And a thank you to my sisters, Carol and Melinda, and my nephews, Isaac, Jonathan, and Anthony, for all their love and support through the years.

The Blackademic Life

Introduction

✦

Blackademic Lives Matter

It would be only fair to the reader to say frankly in advance that the attitude of any person toward this story will be distinctly influenced by his theories of the Negro race. If he believes that the Negro in America and in general is an average and ordinary human being, who under given environment develops like other human beings, then he will read this story and judge it by the facts adduced. If, however, he regards the Negro as a distinctly inferior creation, who can never successfully take part in modern civilization and whose emancipation and enfranchisement were gestures against nature, then he will need something more than the sort of facts that I have set down.

But this latter person, I am not trying to convince. I am simply pointing out these two points of view, so obvious to Americans, and then without further ado, I am assuming the truth of the first. In fine, I am going to tell this story as though Negroes were ordinary human beings, realizing that this attitude will from the first seriously curtail my audience.
—W. E. B. Du Bois, *Black Reconstruction*

Black intellectual life is ripe with heroic possibilities.
—Jerry Watts, *Heroism and the Black Intellectual*

I didn't know it then, but I began building *The Blackademic Life* years ago, in my hometown of Meridian, Mississippi, where I was born and raised by two Mississippi Valley State College graduates who instilled in their three children a missionary fervor for education. I graduated from high school and then continued building this project as a history major (and football player) at Morehouse College, an institution defined by manhood, uplift, and respectability. It was there at Dear Old Morehouse that I was introduced to the academic profession by my mentors in the history department, who took me and my fellow students to academic conferences and groomed us for graduate school. As a graduate student in history at the University of Michigan I was assigned Paule Marshall's *The Chosen Place, the Timeless People* and absorbed Marshall's creative critique of social scientific knowledge production. Outside my program, I also discovered the work of a black queer science fiction writer named Samuel R. Delany, whose novel *The Mad Man*, about a black gay philosophy student in New York working on his dissertation, was my first intimation that there was such a thing as an "academic novel." *The Mad Man*'s scathing criticism of academia resonated with my own unpleasant experiences in graduate school, and I began to consider that maybe, just maybe, this noble, scholarly profession that I was working so hard to enter was really just a bastion of elitism, condescension, and selfish careerism. I left that program, moved to New York, and then, glutton for punishment, ended up back in graduate school a year later and eventually spent far too many years as an English Ph.D. candidate at the CUNY Graduate Center. The idea for a book about academic novels took shape there, and I decided to focus on novels by black writers, who seemed to be neglected in the critical literature on the subject. In 2008 I watched the ascent of a black law professor with the unlikely name of Barack Hussein Obama II, who miraculously became the forty-fourth president of the United States and, even more miraculously, got reelected in 2012.

This book has arrived during a uniquely turbulent moment in U.S. history. Indeed, for its most disenfranchised citizens, there has never been a time of "domestic tranquility." But the recent years leading up to my completion of this book have been a time of economic crisis; of unspeakable gun violence, with several of the worst mass shootings in U.S. history (and thousands more routine gun deaths every year); and of protest movements against police brutality (and other forms of social inequality) organized under the slogan Black Lives Matter. And as I'm putting the finishing touches on this work, the daily transgressions of Donald Trump's unfortunate presidency are so voluminous and chaotic that I am hesitant to make any further declarations in print about the situation since things change by the hour with each vulgar tweet, each insult, each unconstitutional threat, each baffling administrative appointment, each administrative firing, and each nonsensical public statement.

A few days after delivering the commencement address at Hampshire College on May 20, 2017, Keeanga-Yamahtta Taylor, an assistant professor of African American studies at Princeton University, found herself under an onslaught of threatening emails and social media messages. In her commencement speech, she had (correctly) referred to Donald Trump as a racist, sexist megalomaniac. Those words were picked up by online conservative platforms and eventually ended up on *Fox News*, and Taylor soon began receiving hateful messages threatening violence and murder. These messages were racist, sexist, and homophobic in nature. The messages referred to her as a "nigger," "bitch," "cunt," "dyke," "she-male," and "coon." In her statement responding to the attacks, Taylor shared these slurs to illustrate the vulgarity she was dealing with, and she linked these attacks on her to other incidents of white-supremacist violence around the country, including the murder of Bowie State University student Lt. Richard Collins III, an ROTC member who was stabbed to death by a white supremacist on the University of Maryland campus on the night of May 20, 2017, the very same day that Taylor had spoken at Hampshire.[1] Taylor joined a dubious fraternity of other black professors who have recently been targeted by racist trolls, including Zandria Robinson, Johnny Eric Williams, and Tommy Curry.

These incidents are not spontaneous eruptions of outrage on social media but are calculated, coordinated efforts emanating from racist fever swamps like Daily Caller, Breitbart, and Campus Reform. These platforms draw on tips from activists who monitor the social media of black scholars and even embed moles in their classrooms to catch them saying something controversial and then feed information to media platform producers, who are always on the lookout for rage clicks and views. And nothing brings the outrage quite like an uppity Negro professor who needs to be put in her place. The ultimate goal of these campaigns is to discredit black academics and destroy their careers, which the white supremacists do not see as legitimate in the first place.

But this was not the first time Taylor's name came up in a conservative attack. Just five years earlier, Taylor was among several graduates of a new Ph.D. program in African American studies at Northwestern University who were called out by Naomi Schaefer Riley in a *Chronicle of Higher Education* article, "The Most Persuasive Case for Eliminating Black Studies: Look at the Dissertation Titles." Riley surveyed and ridiculed the various dissertation topics from the inaugural graduating class (including Taylor's dissertation, "Race for Profit: Black Housing and the Urban Crisis of the 1970s"), referring to them as "a collection of left-wing victimization claptrap." Many people rightfully questioned how the article made it onto the site in the first place. The sociologist and public intellectual Tressie McMillan Cottom cut through the tired culture-wars rhetoric to ask some deeper questions about the piece, noting the role of attention economy in the architecture of the web and pointing out that these vulnerable black scholars were used as bait to lure in rage clicks to the site.[2] But as she also noted in a later Twitter conversation about social media and black scholars, "network based attacks on faculty predates technological efficiencies of scale."[3] There have been several social media campaigns targeting "liberal" professors, of various racial backgrounds, for controversial statements, but much of the analysis of this phenomenon fails to acknowledge that black scholars have been vulnerable to public attacks long before the invention of Twitter and Facebook.

So, what's the point of writing about a topic like the academic novel in a time like this? Aren't they the novels that are always about some horny straight white male professor at some elite East Coast college who is cheating on his wife with some buxom young student? Having read my share of academic novels, and seen my share of academic films, I have to say that this sordid reputation is unfortunately well-earned by the genre. But no, not all academic novels are like that. And no, that's not what this is about.

This study of fictional narratives on higher education includes an evaluation of a long history of racist discourses about black intellectuals in higher education. I reconstruct the specific ways that these discourses have been deployed against black academics and show how academic fiction is an essential form for understanding why the black academic is a lightning rod in contemporary American politics, and why white supremacists work so hard to undermine the legitimacy of black students and professors. But I also show how this field of literature goes beyond this narrative of victimization and embraces the full lives of black knowledge workers, showing what it means to choose this life that Vincent Harding referred to as "The Vocation of the Black Scholar."[4] This is a study of how black intellectuals crafted counternarratives in defiance of white supremacy and created their own academic and intellectual lives. Yes, the academic novel can be playful and melodramatic, satirical and vengeful, but it should also be read as a genre that addresses the meaning and purposes of the university and the place of black persons in it. Representations of higher education have the power to shape public perceptions of the university and the professoriat, and they often reveal who is seen as included and includable in the university, whether as students, professors, or administrators.

This is an ideal genre for making sense of culture-war debacles such as the attacks on Keeanga-Yamahtta Taylor and other black scholars. Taylor's 2016 book *From #BlackLivesMatter to Black Liberation* has already become a touchstone of this political moment, and the Black Lives Matter movement is connected to the struggle for black higher education. In the hands of black writers, the academic novel, so often used for dubious and frivolous purposes, has been used to show that Blackademic Lives Matter, by centering the lives and thought of black scholars and challenging the university's view of itself as an objective and disinterested center of knowledge production. These works also articulate the black intellectual's skepticism and reticence about academic institutionality and their inclusion in it. A serious assessment of the American university and its history requires an engagement with this group of scholars, whose place in the academy has always been precarious and contested.

Blackademic. Lives. Matter.

The name of the #BlackLivesMatter movement has galvanized a new era of student activism since it was first used by Alicia Garza, Patrisse Cullors, and Opal Tometi, three black women activists who coined the phrase and utilized social media to organize the first protests in the wake of the 2012 murder of unarmed seventeen-year-old high school student Trayvon Martin in Sanford, Florida, at the hands of a racist neighborhood-watch vigilante with a gun.

To read the bibliography of black academic novels is to reckon with the idea that Blackademic Lives Matter. Blackademics matter in these novels in a way that they do not in the rest of the genre, where black writers have largely been ignored and where black academic characters, if they exist at all, make only occasional appearances and are rarely essential to the narrative. In the rest of the genre, black professors are an afterthought, black institutions of higher learning barely exist, and the complexity of blackademic life is largely illegible. Black academic novels also respond to key ideas in black political discourse, addressing criticisms of higher education's conservatism and elitism. In the black academic novel one finds that despite the university's history of antiblack racism, the academic life can be a worthwhile endeavor and that the production and dissemination of knowledge that takes place in universities has been, and remains, an important battleground in black freedom struggles.

So what does it mean to say that Blackademic Lives Matter?

Blackademic: A portmanteau of "black" and "academic." My first literary encounter with the word was in Mat Johnson's academic novel *Pym*, but I'm sure he was not the first to use it. It is a word that has long been floating around the internet as a term of solidarity among black students and professors. We all understand that no matter where we are located, even on majority-black campuses, we represent only a small portion of the professoriat. According to a 2013 report from the U.S. Department of Education's National Center for Education Statistics, African Americans account for 6 percent of full-time faculty in America's postsecondary institutions (with black women accounting for half of that 6 percent).[5]

Though my focus is on formal higher education, I have strived toward a conception of the academic that is not an exclusionary one. The history of black scholarship is a history of independent black intellectuals working on the margins of an academy that was often hostile toward and dismissive of their work. Despite the gripes of conservatives in the culture wars—which Ishmael Reed satirizes in his 1993 academic novel *Japanese by Spring*—it hasn't really been that long since scholarship on African American literature, culture, and history has been taken seriously in academia. Black studies is hardly the dominant presence that culture warriors invent in their strident political screeds. I confess that there are times when maybe I conflate intellectual and academic more than I should, no matter how much I know I should contextualize the term with the help of Antonio Gramsci, bell hooks, Harold Cruse, and Jerry Watts. However, one thing that draws me to academic fiction is the way that this work affirms the importance of the college as a site for the institutionalization and dissemination of knowledge. Rather than retreating from the academy and declaring it a space for hopeless sellouts, these works constitute a documented record of how black intellectuals have brought the fight to the Ivory Tower and have insisted on making spaces for themselves, whether at black colleges or at white colleges that originally excluded them.

They show why the fight for the university is a worthy struggle, even as they may hold on to doubts about its political efficacy as a site for liberation.

Lives: Being neither a biologist, cosmologist, nor theologian, I won't claim to speak to the definition of life on those terms. But in the context of academia one finds in the literature various invocations of the term "the academic life." Cynthia Franklin's *Academic Lives: Memoir, Cultural Theory, and the University Today* is a study of the academic memoir, a genre very closely related to the academic novel (and some might say too closely related, since the dominant mode of "literary realism" in academic novels often means its authors use names of real professors and institutions, or use pseudonyms so thin they might as well be real names).[6] To me, the word "life" in this academic context involves ideas of intention, purpose, and mindfulness. What does it mean to devote one's energy and substance to this profession? What does it mean to make a choice to devote one's finite time in this earthly form to the purposes of scholarship and teaching? I think one of the most eloquent statements about the academic life comes from the terminally ill Dr. Vivian Bearing, the professor of English in Margaret Edson's academic play *Wit*, who speaks of "the contribution to knowledge" as the most profound act of her life.[7] In her case that contribution included her scholarship, her teaching, and even the very substance of her body, which she gives over as a sacrifice to medical research on the aggressive ovarian cancer that would eventually take her life. There are similarly poignant stories of sacrifice in black academic novels, of people who gave their lives to the cause of education and uplift, for whom academia was not just a profession but also a calling and a critical site in a multigenerational struggle for equality and liberation.

Matter: "To matter" is to make a difference, to have meaning and purpose. I am also thinking of "matter" and "life" in materialist terms related to the body and labor. The biopolitical history of America is one in which the black body is solely a material resource for white wealth extraction. In Thomas Jefferson's infamous Query XIV in *Notes on the State of Virginia* he argued that blacks were essentially born to be beasts of burden, that they didn't suffer in the heat, that they had animalistic sexual appetites, and that even if one of them, like the poet Phillis Wheatley, managed to become literate and attempt to write, at best her work could achieve only cheap imitation and never reach the intellectual accomplishment of imaginative literature.[8] When black bodies were shipped to the Americas as part of a massive project of capitalist profiteering, the enslaved were not considered persons at all but raw material in this enterprise. The university was also part of that capitalist slave economy, and Craig Steven Wilder's sobering 2015 book *Ebony and Ivy: Race, Slavery, and the Troubled History of America's Universities* has shown the extent to which universities in their early years were funded by the transatlantic slave trade and functioned as the ideological wing of a racial capitalist enterprise.[9] That raises the question—what does it mean to have black bodies in these same spaces that were built, in part if not in whole, for the perpetuation of racial capitalism? This is a concept that student activists are addressing now as they challenge their institutions to consider what it means to have their black students living and studying in buildings named for slaveholders and slavery apologists, such as the students of Middle Tennessee State University, who successfully protested to change the name of Forrest Hall, a building named for Nathan Bedford Forrest, a Confederate general and early leader of the Ku Klux Klan. Since the days of Olaudah Equiano and Phillis Wheatley, black writers have been writing against regimes of domination and dehumanization. Black academic novels not only participate in this tradition of using writing and education as tools of liberation but also call attention to the ways that practices of literary production have historically been bound up with racialized thinking.

In the pages that follow I show how and why Blackademic Lives Matter, why blackademic novels matter, and I share some of the lessons I've learned by spending time with these books. And to paraphrase something that the activists in the Black Lives Matter movement have argued, ceaselessly, against their most obtuse critics: to say that Blackademic Lives Matter does not mean these are the only lives that matter. I won't even dignify the foolish argument that focusing on black people means I'm being antiwhite. More importantly, I do not wish to reify an elitist vanguardism of "the talented tenth," an idea that privileges educated, respectable black people over other members of the group. Black academic novels deal with higher forms of education and therefore often deal with black people of academic achievement who move in elite spaces, but they also contain numerous criticisms of the respectability, elitism, and colorism that have afflicted black politics. One of the most valuable aspects of this project has been the opportunity to review the variety of strategies that black intellectuals have used to define their own political roles as intellectuals.

The Blackademic Life is an examination of those who have been the least protected in the university, whose place in the university is the most tenuous and precarious. The black academic novel shows what the picture of the institution looks like from their perspective. Black academics have often needed to play the role of advocates and representatives, as spokespersons on behalf of their "group," an idea that some blackademics have embraced while others have challenged and resisted. These works illustrate the black intellectual's complicated relationship to these concepts of responsibility and representation, and their complicated relationship with academic institutionality.

The Blackademic Fiction of W. E. B. Du Bois

I am taking an unconventional, but not entirely unprecedented, approach to the work of W. E. B. Du Bois through his fiction. Many scholars have questioned the quality of his fiction in comparison with his essays and his historical and sociological writing. I make a case for why we should read Du Bois as an academic novelist and show how he creatively used the novelistic form to fulfill his critical expectations for black art and to propagate representations of black intellectuals.

But I started this introduction with a Du Bois quote from one of his nonfiction works, the monumental 1935 historical study *Black Reconstruction*. I use this quote for three reasons. First, Du Bois's powerful introductory note resonates with the Black Lives Matter movement. Du Bois insisted upon the value of black life as a precondition for his scholarship, even as the white supremacists with whom he was surrounded viewed black minds as inferior and black bodies as disposable. The caustic defiance of his statement expresses a wise recognition of how deeply entrenched white-supremacist thought remains in American political discourse, an idea Derrick Bell echoed later in his 1992 collection *Faces at the Bottom of the Well*, with his radically pessimistic view that racism is permanent because it is baked into the ideology of America itself. There's an understanding in Du Bois's statement that there is no use trying to convince the "Pitchfork" Ben Tillmans or Strom Thurmonds or George Wallaces (or Donald Trumps) that black life is worthwhile, that black minds can be cultivated the same as any others, that given equal access to resources and opportunities, black people can thrive as well as any other people. And there's a recognition in Du Bois's words that the racist's strategy is one of distraction and dissemblance. One of the challenges of being a black intellectual in this contemporary moment is not to have one's time, effort, and energy wasted with the obtuse, diversionary tactics of white supremacists who insist that they will really, truly have an honest dialogue with you if only you can prove the basic humanity of black people first.

Second, I begin with that passage from Du Bois because this story that I want to tell about the blackademic life really begins with Reconstruction, when institutional black education began in earnest with the founding of black schools and colleges. As enslaved persons, African Americans were restricted from reading, though some managed to become literate. There were no institutional structures for black education, though a few free schools existed in the North. It was in the postslavery years that black schools appeared, when educators and philanthropists established institutions of higher education to train a black leadership class, including the teachers who would teach younger black children. These new colleges were designed to educate black students well beyond the basics of readin', 'ritin', and 'rithmatic, and they faced massive obstacles from some of America's most powerful white political leaders and educational policy makers. For as long as black higher education has existed it has been constructed by white supremacists as a dangerous and foolhardy proposition. As with all white supremacy, some educated blacks internalized those attitudes. In works of academic fiction one finds writers who recognized the consequences of this internalized hatred, and they turned to literature as a way to reckon with the psychologies of racism and to create literary works that nurtured and affirmed black life and black intelligence.

And last, related to the prior two points, I begin with Du Bois because he was a writer of academic novels. His creative approach to writing is what made his nonfiction work so richly evocative, but the creative writing itself also deserves critical attention (for reasons that I elaborate upon later in these pages). Du Bois is an underappreciated innovator in the genre of the academic novel, and his commentary on representations of educated African Americans in popular culture provides a nascent critical framework for thinking about this genre. Du Bois's archival record clearly indicates that he was aware of the genre, and in his novels he interrogates his own theories of higher education and black political progress. An evaluation of Du Bois's novels not only exposes his literary ambitions but also contributes to a better understanding of the academic novel itself, why it exists, where it came from, and why it has been a remarkably resilient genre despite its reputation as self-indulgent navel gazing.

The Blackademic Life

The second epigraph of this introduction comes from one of my graduate-school professors, Dr. Jerry Gafio Watts, a scholar of black intellectual history, an expert on Ralph Ellison and Amiri Baraka, a consummate scholar who somehow seemed to know about every black writer who had ever put pen to paper, a magnetic presence at the CUNY Graduate Center during my years there, and someone whom I was blessed to have as a member of my orals and dissertation committees. Jerry passed away in November 2015 before I could share with him the news that the project that he had enthusiastically supported was on its way to becoming a book. His work on black intellectuals inspired my own research. At his memorial service, on a cool, clear autumn evening at the Center for Ethical Culture on Sixty-Fourth Street and Central Park West in Manhattan, it seemed that every black professor in America (and beyond) was there, from graduate students and adjuncts to celebrity professors who regularly appear on television. I specifically noticed that there were many black women scholars in attendance whom he had encouraged, mentored, and ushered into the professoriat. Most of us will never be as charismatic as Jerry. But when I think of the heroic blackademic life I think of him, a scholar of prodigious reading whose office overflowed with a circulation of books that he would bring in and give away to students. Everyone seemed to come away from every meeting in his office with armfuls of new reading material. And as I listened to the ribald anecdotes people shared about him at the service, it occurred to me that these stories conveyed a warmth and intimacy that one can't get from reading his scholarly work, as lively as it is. The stories they were telling articulated what it meant to be a part of a community and how he went out of his way to welcome others into that community.

Black academic novels are all about expressing that meaning and intimacy. They are, like all novels, an attempt to get at some aspect of life in a way that rote information and data might not be able to do. We live by stories, these narratives that guide us through this weird, bewildering voyage between one existential darkness and another. These novels and other fictional works are a sampling of some of the stories that blackademics have lived by over the years, stories that they imagined, created, composed, and shared with others, stories that can still help us find meaning as we wander through this academic wilderness.

Knowing Watts, he'd never let me abide by such uncritical sentimentality. His book on Ralph Ellison is an exemplary analysis of the heroic narrative and a critique of how Ellison deployed it in his work. That said, I do think the story of black scholars in America is one shot through with heroism, mainly because these blackademic lives were never meant to happen. People who were brought here as chattel, who were dehumanized and disciplined by harsh regimes of labor, who were forbidden to read and write somehow, through pluck and subterfuge, managed to learn the language and have come to use that language in all sorts of inventive ways, from the sacred profanity of blues and hip-hop to the soaring oratory of the sermon, and yes, even in the formalized languages of scholarship.

But if these stories of blackademic life never went beyond a celebratory mode, they would be dull, and I would not be fulfilling my critical duty if I didn't also pay attention to the faults in them. What makes them vibrant and complex texts is that they take aim at the brutality and hypocrisies of white supremacy, while they also represent a sustained, candid analysis of black political thought. And, when necessary, they include criticisms of opportunistic and exploitative leadership. I'm interested in the politics of black intellectuals, how this group of artists and scholars have strategized and written about their existence in a society in which their inner lives have been constructed as nonexistent, a metaphysical impossibility, and for whom education has often been interpreted as dangerous, unnecessary, and counterproductive.

I think of the cumulative effort involved in the composition of these stories, that these writers and artists managed to put their hopes and dreams down on the page, or up on the screen. After all the logic and the theory, after all the "paradigms" and "frames" and "tropes," and after I've problematized and deconstructed it all, I hope that this text serves as an affirmation that blackademic lives matter, in all their contradictions and complexity, and that it provides a few explanations for why blackademic lives matter in this profession, and in this world.

Chapter 1, "The Overeducation of the Negro," surveys the literature on academic novels and introduces a critical framework for examining the black academic novel, and other forms of black academic fiction. In particular I show how the blackademic life is one that is circumscribed by discourses of overeducation, and in subsequent chapters I trace a literary history that demonstrates how black writers confronted these overeducation discourses in their work. With a roster that includes some of the most prominent African American writers, including Sutton Griggs, W. E. B. Du Bois, Nella Larsen, Ralph Ellison, Paule Marshall, and Alice Walker, among others, the academic novel is not an anomaly in black literature but is actually central to understanding this literature's confrontations with white-supremacist discourses on black intelligence and its expressions of black interiority. Chapter 2, "Educating and Uplifting the Race, 1876–1919," analyzes the earliest examples of black academic novels, including the first literary experiments of Du Bois and Griggs, and illustrates how Du Bois was specifically aware of the academic novel as a form and adopted it as a genre for his own writing. This chapter examines the roots of the black academic novel in the history of Reconstruction and post-Reconstruction black education and how the early novels paved the way for the New Negro ideology that followed. Chapter 3, "The New Negro, 1919–1954," traces the growth of the academic novel from the Harlem Renaissance through the first movements toward national integration of educational institutions, showing how the novels by Nella Larsen, Ralph Ellison, J. Saunders Redding, and others interrogated the politics of the black college and anticipated a forthcoming integration of black academics into majority-white institutions. Chapter 4, "Integration and Nationalism, 1954–1980," evaluates the black academic novel in the wake of the *Brown v. Board of Education of Topeka* decision of 1954 and how the influences of globalization, anticolonialism, black nationalism, and student protest were depicted in novels of the 1960s and 1970s. The chapter also addresses the consequences embedded in the institutionalization of black studies and the development of diversity initiatives. In this chapter I take a global approach to the black academic novel, placing the international vision of W. E. B. Du Bois and Paule Marshall in conversation with the domestic student protest novels by Gil Scott-Heron and Alice Walker. Chapter 5, "Culture Wars and Capitalism, 1980–Present," extends this conversation about institutionalization and neoliberal diversity and considers how academic novels of this period respond to culture-war debates and theories of multiculturalism. Notable novels from this period include Ishmael Reed's culture-wars satire *Japanese by Spring*, Samuel R. Delany's queer critique in *The Mad Man*, and Percival Everett's engagement with black literary theory in *Erasure*. In the "Conclusion" I address some of the most popular film and television depictions of the blackademic life, specifically *The Cosby Show* and *A Different World*, and discuss how blackademic images become a microcosm of larger debates about positive and negative images of black people in popular culture.

This journey into the blackademic life begins in the years after slavery as the first black schools were founded. From the very beginning, the existence of the black intellectual is constructed as a problem for white supremacy. The restrictions on literacy and the brutal physical violence needed to extract labor from the enslaved proved the bad faith inherent in white supremacy's beliefs about black intelligence. The black intellectual exists, despite white supremacy's insistence that she should not be possible. This is why, as Samuel Delany states, "transgression inheres, however unarticulated, in every aspect of the black writer's career in America."[10] For him, the context of that statement was his experiences of racism as a black writer in the communities of science fiction. Because racism is systemic and discursive, it is a topic that engulfs all the works that I have encountered in the process of writing this text. It is also something that I have confronted myself in many ways, large and small, on my own academic journey and in my everyday life. The blackademic novel defies this racism while also showing a commitment to life lived beyond bigotry's narrow imagination.

Chapter 1

✦

The Overeducation of the Negro

On Reading Black Academic Fiction

Much of the criticism on African American literature has been carried out under the auspices of universities: in college courses, on curriculum committees, in articles published by university-affiliated literary journals, and in monographs published by university presses. But what about higher education itself as a subject of African American literature? An evaluation of the black academic novel is an opportunity to understand the role of higher education in the history of black literary production and in the language of black literary and cultural theory. In their portrayals of the college experience in literature, black writers show the black intellectual's relationship to the university to be one that is defined by histories of institutional exclusion and by the persistence of racist ideas about black intelligence.

The history of America's universities is rife with antiblack racism at its most virulent, from the earliest universities and their financial entanglement with slavery, to universities serving as incubators for racist public policy, to their violent resistance against integration and antiracist activism. Even when these institutions begrudgingly included black students, they did so without examining their intrinsic racism, let alone thinking about how structural inequalities created the conditions for that exclusion in the first place. Today what we might call progress in the post-*Brown* era of integration is too often the cynical appropriation of black students and professors for diversity image making.

While my use of the term "exclusion" might seem to sidestep the histories of black colleges, where black students were welcomed and nurtured, academic novels reveal an ongoing conversation about how white-supremacist ideas were perpetuated within these black colleges, particularly in their curricula, and in their respectability politics. Inasmuch as we alumni of Historically Black Colleges and Universities (HBCU) are proud of our schools, many of which were built from the ground up with meager resources in a hostile post-Reconstruction America, we also understand that even the traditionally elite black colleges (Fisk, Atlanta, Morehouse, Spelman, Howard, Hampton) were never separate and equal institutions. All these colleges, white or historically black, were shaped from the beginning by educational policies rooted in white supremacy and were contained by fears of what an educated black populace might do to challenge the hierarchy of Jim Crow. Booker T. Washington's "Atlanta Compromise" speech was partly designed to calm white fears of overeducated Negroes running amok with their inflated self-regard and unwillingness to serve and respect white people. In the fiction about black college life—*Quicksand, Stranger and Alone, Invisible Man, Meridian, The Nigger Factory* among them—one finds writers criticizing the racial politics of the black college, showing that although the black college was a nominally separate institution for the uplift of black people, it was deeply influenced by the purse strings of white philanthropy and often infected with white-supremacist ideologies in the educational program that its professors imparted to their students. These novels of HBCU life show that the disciplinary regime of the black college was designed not only to train the students as fastidious professionals but also to train black bodies and minds to be acceptable to whiteness, and that this uplift project was one rooted in a problematic politics of respectability and assimilation based upon antiblackness and colorism.

For the black academic fiction writer the university cannot be an innocent, disinterested site of knowledge production. Rather, the university is repeatedly revealed to be an institution for reproducing white heteropatriarchal norms that either rejected black intellectuals as incapable of assimilating to such norms or included the black intellectual under a permanently provisional status in which her presence is always questioned and contested.

Despite this institutional precarity, black academic fiction is also a record of the continued engagement of black students and scholars with this problematic institution, and it shows them employing various strategies to navigate through and attempt to reform the institution, even as these students and professors sometimes questioned the efficacy of reformist ideologies.

I have crowded this study with my own analysis of black academic texts based upon their thematic content, but I also leave room in the conversation for the artists to speak for themselves and for all the divergent ideas that these writers have woven into their works. They allow their characters to speak openly about their fatigue with the race problem, to criticize racial orthodoxies, to explore other ideas beyond the black freedom struggle. I have written this book because I believe black academic fiction is an intelligible, coherent category with certain commonalities and theoretical strings that tie them together, but I also keep in mind that the category is a provisional one. What I have collected here is a diverse range of texts with varied themes, styles, topics, and rhetorical strategies, and they demonstrate the expansive possibilities that can exist under the rubric of black academic fiction.

Overeducated

For the white supremacist, the "overeducation" of the Negro essentially begins with the acquisition of basic literacy. From the first black poets, Jupiter Hammon and Phillis Wheatley, to the authors of nineteenth-century slave narratives such as Frederick Douglass, Harriet Jacobs, and Henry Bibb, black writers were used as examples in arguments, pro and con, about the intellectual possibilities of black persons. Their work was seen as evidence of black humanity (or inhumanity) and was read with and against an overwhelming discourse of black intellectual inferiority. Frederick Douglass poignantly articulates the relationship between knowledge and power when he explains how his slave master's wife taught him in secret how to read. Her husband discovered what she was doing and scolded her, and Douglass's rendition of what his enslaver said about teaching the young boy how to read is one of the most devastating statements about literacy and power anywhere in American letters.

> If you give a nigger an inch, he will take an ell. A nigger should know nothing but to obey his master—to do as he is told to do. Learning would spoil the best nigger in the world . . . if you teach that nigger how to read there would be no keeping him. It would forever unfit him to be a slave. He would at once become unmanageable, and of no value to his master. As to himself, it could do him no good, but a great deal of harm. It would make him discontent and unhappy.[1]

Later in the *Narrative*, Douglass essentially confirms his slaveholder's suspicions about education, that it had indeed made him discontent and restless. "I have observed this in my experience of slavery, that whenever my condition was improved, instead of its increasing my contentment, it only increased my desire to be free, and set me to thinking of plans to gain my freedom. I have found that, to make a contented slave, it is necessary to make a thoughtless one."[2]

From Douglass's narrative, and from similar stories about black literacy and resistance, we learn an important precept: For the white supremacist, any education of Negroes is already too much. The educated Negro is always already overeducated. This fundamental idea informs much of the dialogue around black education, and in reading the literature on black higher education, one sees this attitude encountered repeatedly, and the writers of academic novels particularly found it important to register their own encounters with such discourses.

To understand the importance of these novels involves an understanding of both their historical context and their literary intertextuality. To make sense of the black presence in the academy requires that one understand the extent to which that presence was met with vociferous resistance and that the black body on campus was constructed as a sign of disorder, even as black students and professors are exploited to tout the diversity of the corporate university.

My conception of "The Overeducation of the Negro" was inspired by Carter G. Woodson's *The Mis-Education of the Negro*. (And yes, it is also partly inspired by Lauryn Hill's award-winning, educationally themed album *The Miseducation of Lauryn Hill*, the soundtrack of my junior year in college). At the outset, I knew I needed to vet the phrase, and, of course, being a twenty-first century person, I turned to Google.

At the time, a Google search of the specific phrase "The Over-Education of the Negro" delivered two distinct hits that I actually found to be instructive for my topic. One was a quote by James Vardaman, a former governor of my home state of Mississippi and likely one of the most virulently racist governors in U.S. history (his name comes up in Du Bois's *The Black Flame* at one point in a passage about racist politicians in the South, along with South Carolina's Ben Tillman). The other hit was from Wilbur Thirkield, a white president of the historically black Howard University. This was just a simple Google search and not an exhaustive archival search for the term, but the hits seemed worthy of dissection, and I found them to be useful places from which to launch my discussion on this important discursive formation in black higher education. The first quote, by Vardaman, appears in a February 6, 1904, issue of the *Literary Digest*:

> **The over-education of the negro** is an evil certainly, but there is small danger that he will be over-educated in the average rural public school of the South. Education makes a criminal of the negro only when he is educated beyond that point which fits him for the state of life in which it hath pleased God to call him.[3]

The passage is reprinted from an article in the New Orleans *Times-Democrat* in which the governor is quoted, and both the *Times-Democrat* article and this one in the *Literary Digest* were reporting on the governor's comments about the prevalence of crime among the educated black population in Massachusetts. Vardaman used those dubious statistics as justification for the South's feeble educational program for black children and argued that further education could lead to disobedience and criminal behavior among black southerners, as it most assuredly had done in the North. By the way, this is the same Vardaman who once referred to the Negro as "a lazy, lying, lustful animal which no conceivable amount of training can transform into a tolerable citizen."[4]

The second hit for "the overeducation of the Negro" came from *The Negro Problem*, an anthology of articles on black social issues. In an article titled "The Higher Education of the Negro," the white Methodist minister and educator Wilbur B. Thirkield, who served as president of Howard University from 1906 to 1912, uses the term in rebuttal to racist arguments against black higher education:

> The capacity of the Negro for the higher education has been settled. We have learned, however, to distinguish between the intellectual capacity with which God has endowed all races, and the intellectual and moral equipment of a race which is the outcome of civilization and environment. The last danger is the over-education of the Negro. We have only touched the fringes of the race. His real education is a task of generations.[5]

As it turns out, these two quotes illustrate two complementary ideas about the overeducation of the Negro. The first, from a white-supremacist governor of a southern state, expresses a fairly typical attitude among white supremacists about the dangers of black education, that it will lead to insubordination toward their white superiors, and that it will lead to criminality because it encouraged a distaste for the kind of work that would keep black people obedient and contained. The statement by Thirkield, the white president of a black college, reaffirms his belief in the educability of blacks and his commitment to the project of black higher education, and he dismisses the idea that overeducation should be any concern for a population so starved for education in the first place. But his statement also reiterates just how much that idea of higher education as a danger was embedded in the thoughts of students and educators in the world of black higher education, and this concern is clearly corroborated in the pages of black academic novels.

Mostly my use of the term "the overeducation of the Negro" refers to this form of racist resistance to black education, but like all forms of domination, such discourses can also be internalized by those who are subjugated. For black Americans, overeducation discourses particularly resulted in fears that too much education could compromise one's employability, an idea Sutton Griggs eloquently addresses in *Imperium in Imperio*.

However, I must also note that under chattel slavery and into the postemancipation era with its subjugating regime of Jim Crow, African Americans did receive an education of sorts. It was a particular kind of education that taught them the skills of laborers and servants, and taught them to accept that this would be their permanent lot in life, and that their appropriate place was on the bottom of the social hierarchy. It was an education in which blacks were admonished with biblical references to slavery and obedience to masters. It was the discipline of the lash and the threats of violence that taught them that the only way for a black person to make peace with white supremacy was to stay in one's place and accept one's inferior status. Some enslavers even referred to the institution as a "school" that brought values and civilization to the pagan and uncivilized Africans. When in Du Bois's *The Quest of the*

Silver Fleece the character Dr. Boldish implores young Bles Alwyn to remember that the "slavery of your people was not necessarily a crime. It was a school of work and love. It gave you noble friends, like Mr. Cresswell here," Du Bois was articulating a common belief on the part of white supremacists that enslavement was a method of training and discipline that taught valuable skills and gave the enslaved a purpose in life.[6]

And this attitude that the discipline of hard labor was the appropriate school for unsophisticated people persisted after emancipation as an actual educational system began to develop. Even with the founding of schools, the curricula of such schools were constricted by what white educators and philanthropists wanted black students to learn and black teachers to teach, and any efforts to educate beyond the basics of reading and writing were considered foolhardy and wasteful. As the historian James Anderson reminds us in *The Education of Blacks in the South*, "both schooling for democratic citizenship and schooling for second-class citizenship have been basic traditions in American education."[7] This kind of education for second-class status was depicted in harsh terms in Sutton Griggs's *Imperium in Imperio* in his description of the racist abuse inflicted upon black children in southern schoolhouses. This type of white-supremacist education is perpetuated into later institutions of higher learning, and in J. Saunders Redding's 1950 novel *Stranger and Alone*, he shows how ideologies of black inferiority were passed on from a well-meaning white professor in a historically black college and taught as objective scientific truth. Redding's depiction is essential, because it illustrates the insidious nature of white supremacy, that white supremacy works as well as it does not because it merely reflects the attitudes of a few white people but because it is supported by the church, the state, and educational institutions, and it persists through an internalization of such beliefs by blacks themselves. In the postemancipation period, as black schools and colleges began to sprout up through the collective effort of southern blacks and white philanthropists, an anxiety develops about the Negro's educational advancement. In particular the idea of a classical education in the humanities becomes contentious, because it is an education that was seen by some as wasteful and ruinous to the work ethic of black laborers and as part of the ominous beginnings of a demand for equality.

Famously, W. E. B. Du Bois and Booker T. Washington debated over the proper educational curriculum for black advancement. Washington's 1901 autobiography, *Up from Slavery*, described his travels to black schools throughout the South, and in one striking passage Washington issues a cautionary tale about a young man trained in classical education but without practical skills of physical labor.

> It was also interesting to note how many big books some of them had studied, and how many high-sounding subjects some of them claimed to have mastered. The bigger the book and the longer the name of

the subject, the prouder they felt of their accomplishment. Some had studied Latin, and one or two Greek. This they thought entitled them to special distinction.

In fact, one of the saddest things I saw during the month of travel which I have described was a young man, who had attended some high school, sitting down in a one-room cabin, with grease on his clothing, filth all around him, and weeds in the yard and garden, engaged in a studying of French grammar.[8]

In this telling passage Washington deploys the pejorative image of the "scholar as buffoon" or the "educated fool." This caricature is targeted at black intellectuals like Du Bois who wanted black students to learn the classical tradition, even though there were few practical employment opportunities for black intellectuals beyond a few teaching positions.[9] And throughout *Up from Slavery*, Washington attempts to reassure his sympathetic white readers that black people who are interested in this sort of classical education are not representative of the race and that he intends to steer black students away from such foolish, wasteful, dangerous pursuits and toward a practical education with a strong foundation in farming and skilled labor. Washington's pragmatism does receive a fair hearing in black academic novels, most famously in Ralph Ellison's *Invisible Man*, where the college-educated protagonist absorbs Washingtonian ideals and later confronts labor issues head-on when he travels to New York, works in a factory, and gets involved in a Marxist political organization called the Brotherhood. The concerns about the employability of educated black people are real, and the idea was clearly on the minds of black writers.

An indicative example of this discourse of overeducation, and the challenges it presents for black intellectuals, comes from William S. Scarborough in one of the most important early black educational projects, the American Negro Academy. The collection of papers from the American Negro Academy is an important historical document in the history of black intellectuals, including essays by black male scholars such as Alexander Crummell, William Pickens, Arturo Schomburg, and W. E. B. Du Bois. (The lack of gender equity in the project must be noted.) William S. Scarborough was one of the earliest African American scholars in classics. A graduate of Oberlin College and president of Wilberforce University in Ohio from 1908 to 1920, he contributed an essay to the published collection of occasional papers from the American Negro Academy titled "The Educated Negro and His Mission," and in that essay he wrote, "The educated Negro is an absolute fact. The day is past when his ability to learn is scoffed at. But on the other hand is born that fear that he may go too far—excel or equal the Anglo-Saxon,—and that fear is a prime motive in the minds of many who seek to hedge the onward path of the race."[10] Scarborough's words resonate deeply with my reading of black academic novels, where the "fear that he may go too far" persists as a trope in the black educational narrative. However, Scarborough goes on to say that "this path will not be hedged. This educated class, though few in number, has been keeping for years the torch aloft for the race . . . For the good of the whole country this class must multiply, not decrease in number." In his essay Scarborough captures how this anxiety of overeducation both emanates from antiblack racists and gets internalized within black political discourse.

But perhaps the aspiration to join such institutions and be a part of that educated class is a problem in itself that cannot be solved by reform from the inside. This is a question that Carter G. Woodson raises in *The Mis-Education of the Negro*. As a Ph.D. graduate of Harvard University and a history professor at Howard University who founded the Association for the Study of Negro Life and History, Woodson was certainly a staunch advocate of black higher education. But in his classic text, Woodson also questions the efficacy of sending black intellectuals to be educated in institutions saturated in unchecked white supremacy and having them reproduce that ideology. Woodson was vigilant about how an educated class could become self-interested and exploitative betrayers of their community. In an oft-repeated paragraph from the preface of the book Woodson describes the indoctrination of white supremacy through the education system as it existed then: "The problem of holding the Negro down, therefore, is easily solved. When you control a man's thinking you do not have to worry about his actions. You do not have to tell him not to stand here or go yonder. He will find his "proper place" and will stay in it. You do not need to send him to the back door. He will go without being told. In fact, if there is no back door, he will cut one for his special benefit. His education makes it necessary."[11]

Indeed, this problem of the oppressive underpinnings of higher education is one that many scholars and activists continue to struggle with. What does it mean to be included in institutions that were founded on black subjugation and continue to produce racist, antiblack knowledge? Woodson's criticisms are still germane when it comes to the institutional histories of white supremacy and the content and disciplinary structures of academia.

Theorizing the Black Intellectual

Woodson's analysis of the educated black elite becomes an important marker in an ongoing conversation about the role of black intellectuals in leading the race and how they should use their education and influence. The academic novel is inextricably bound up with that conversation about the politics of black intellectuals. There have been many volumes written about the politics of the black intellectual since Woodson's *Mis-Education*, the most prominent of which is Harold Cruse's *The Crisis of the Negro Intellectual: A Historical Analysis of the Failure of Black Leadership* (1967). Cruse's groundbreaking work was a synthesis of decades of thinking about the role of the black intellectual, from writers such as W. E. B. Du Bois, Alain Locke, Langston Hughes, James Baldwin, and Lorraine Hansberry. Cruse's main intervention was to document that there was such a thing as a black intellectual culture and that it was one worthy of extensive critical attention and theorizing. Problems with the rather large and unwieldy book have been well noted, including the fact that the whole thing was essentially a polemical argument that black nationalism was the proper ideology of the black intellectual. There was also Cruse's tendency to divide black intellectuals into an overdetermined dichotomy of "integrationists" and "nationalists," as well as his nasty attacks on Caribbean intellectuals. Still, the book towers over the field and has maintained an enduring influence owing to Cruse's sharp and often biting analysis of black intellectuals as a group—whose members serve as spokespersons, gatekeepers, creators, and tastemakers, those who are often asked to speak on behalf of the race in the media and who possess the platforms and influence to be able to do so.[12]

Jerry Watts is among a cohort of post-Cruse scholars who expounded upon the politics of the black intellectual. In his book *Heroism and the Black Intellectual: Ralph Ellison, Politics, and Afro-American Intellectual Life*, Watts uses Ralph Ellison's life and work as an opportunity to theorize about the political thought of black intellectuals. Watts takes a "sociology of intellectuals" approach by evaluating this subset of persons called intellectuals, noting that "because of the language, analytical, and information-processing skills that intellectuals possess, they play certain key roles in the social order."[13] I engage this concept of intellectuals with the understanding that the designation will always be contested, but it remains an important designation for understanding political power and legitimation, because as Watts states, "the quality of the diversity of the roles intellectuals are allowed to assume has ultimately something to do with their political behavior as a group."[14] I am interested in the way that intellectuals as a group are producers of academic novels, as well as subjects in the novels, and the political roles that intellectuals can play are examined in these works, including the political restrictions that black intellectuals face. What Ralph Ellison accomplished so well with *Invisible Man* and his trope of invisibility was to create a metaphor that allowed him to examine the many ways that the black intellectual is pulled to and fro by competing groups that want to co-opt him as a symbol and fail to see him as an autonomous human being.

The intellectual, as Watts describes him in this passage, need not be a practicing academic, and the black literary tradition is full of autodidacts who operate outside academia as artists, teachers, archivists, and scholars. Again, given academia's racist history and the constrictions on black educational opportunity, many black scholars operated outside the mainstream white academy and even operated on the margins of historically black colleges and universities, which were sometimes reluctant to embrace trends in militant black thought.

In another of his books on black intellectuals, *Amiri Baraka: The Politics and Art of a Black Intellectual* (2001), Watts writes that "traditional Afro-American intellectuals, like all traditional intellectuals, have as one of their priorities the reproduction of themselves as intellectuals . . . Whatever provides the time and space to write or paint becomes a priority for intellectuals."[15] While the idea of the independent, free-floating "public intellectual," untainted by bureaucratic connections, is a seductive notion, and one taken up by writers like Russell Jacoby, who laments their demise in the American public sphere in his book *The Last Intellectuals* (1987), working as an academic can provide the intellectual with access to a steady salary, (sometimes) health insurance, and (sometimes) the occasional sabbatical to complete creative or critical work.

Despite its histories of exclusion, academia does play a fundamental role in the "how" of black intellectual practice. It has been, and continues to be, an attractive career for black intellectuals to sustain themselves. And now, with the collapse of newspapers, magazines, and book publishing under digitization, which dried up revenue streams for intellectuals who at one time could have lived frugally as nonacademic writers and speakers, it seems academia has become an even more important source of stable income for all practicing intellectuals in America. (Even the meager paycheck of the precarious adjunct professor can show up more regularly than the payments of freelance workers, who often have to spend time making sure that they are properly compensated for contract work.) Most of the writers covered in the main chapters of this study have spent significant time as university professors. As critics of academic novels have pointed out, some of the most active writers in the genre do not have doctoral degrees. Some critics have argued that the best academic novels come from the writers who have more professional experience as novelists than as professors. Presumably the experienced novelist has a better understanding of characterization, story structure, and the aesthetics of writing, as opposed to the professor, whose only novel is an academic novel written to satirize her institution and colleagues. When I look at my bibliography of academic novelists, there are the few like W. E. B. Du Bois and J. Saunders Redding who had a doctorate and worked as professors. But more common in that bibliography are writers such as Ralph Ellison, Chester Himes, Zadie Smith, Ishmael Reed, Percival Everett, and Mat Johnson who did not earn a Ph.D., have written mostly works of fiction, but who have also spent time as university professors.

Given the debates over black intellectual life and the academic profession, the black academic novel, featuring professors and students as characters, is an ideal laboratory in which to observe the politics of the black intellectual. I am drawn to black academic novels precisely because they confront this complex relationship between education and black identity. In black academic fiction one finds depictions of black scholars wrestling with the meaning of higher education and the expectations placed upon them, with or without their compliance, to be racial representatives and spokespersons. The writers of these novels acknowledge that the academy is only one site of intellectual production but reaffirm that it is an important one. I am attracted to these novels by the way they critically analyze the academy, and even because they tend to view it with some reticence and suspicion. While their focus is on institutions of higher education I believe that these novels represent some of the most productive thinking available about black intellectuals, whether those intellectuals work inside or outside the academy. By addressing topics of race, labor, color, representation, authenticity, gender, and sexuality, these works explore the potentials of black intellectualism and provide valuable lessons on the function and ethics of academic knowledge production and intellectual practice.

W. E. B. Du Bois, Black Academic Fiction, and the Politics of Representation

In February 1926, W. E. B. Du Bois took to the pages of *The Crisis*, the National Association for the Advancement of Colored People (NAACP) magazine that he founded in 1910 (and continued to edit until 1934) and addressed the state of black cultural production in seven rhetorical questions titled "Opinion of W. E. B. Du Bois: A Questionnaire." What Du Bois produced in this article is not only one of the most incisive critical statements on black media representation but also an important set of ideas with which to think about the origins, meaning, and purposes of black academic fiction.

1. When the artist, black or white, portrays Negro characters is he under any obligations or limitations as to the sort of character he will portray?
2. Can any author be criticized for painting the worst or the best characters of a group?
3. Can publishers be criticized for refusing to handle novels that portray Negroes of education and accomplishment, on the grounds that these characters are no different from white folk and therefore not interesting?
4. What are Negroes to do when they are continually painted at their worst and judged by the public as they are painted?
5. Does the situation of the educated Negro in America with its pathos, humiliation, and tragedy call for artistic treatment at least as sincere and sympathetic as "Porgy" received?
6. Is not the continual portrayal of the sordid, foolish, and criminal among Negroes convincing the world that this and this alone is really and essentially Negroid, and preventing white artists from knowing any other types and preventing black artists from daring to paint them?

7. Is there not a real danger that young colored writers will be tempted to follow the popular trend in portraying Negro character[s] in the underworld rather than seeking to paint the truth about themselves and their own social class?[16]

I have come to think of this piece as a trenchant set of observations on the topic of black academic fiction, and even an inaugural critical work on the subject. Du Bois concisely articulates what is at stake for the black writer who endeavors to depict black academics in her work. Even though Du Bois does not specifically use the term "academic novel" here, it is clear that he was interested in the diversification of black images in the media, and that he was particularly interested in seeing more representations of college-educated African Americans in popular culture. Every single author of every black academic novel has implicitly or explicitly addressed these very issues of representation, authenticity, and marketing that Du Bois defines here in this list. And I even find it instructive that Du Bois slips between "artist" and "author" in the queries. He is referring principally to the novel but seems to have other media representations in mind, including the theater (where DuBose Heyward's novel *Porgy* would be successfully adapted a few years later, in 1935), as well as the burgeoning medium of film, where the auteur Oscar Micheaux's early films incorporated educated black characters. Micheaux would initiate the presence of the black scholar on screen with the Harvard-educated protagonist Peter Siner in his 1939 film *Birthright* (adapted from the novel of the same name by white writer T. S. Stribling), which was made as a silent film in 1924 then revised as a sound version in 1939.

Certainly, Du Bois's first question about the "obligations or limitations as to the sort of character he will portray" was informed by the existing literary and theatrical representations of black life at that time, a cultural history rife with minstrel caricatures and degrading performances produced by white artists and sometimes performed by black artists themselves.

These questions were also informed by his context, living in New York, editing *The Crisis*, participating in the black cultural movement happening in the uptown Manhattan neighborhood of Harlem, and fully aware of the fraught relationship between racial representation and the marketplace in the literature, music, visual art, and drama of this movement. The plight of the black artist was bound up with the neighborhood itself, a black enclave where migrants from the South settled in the early years of the twentieth century, many of them working-class laborers who came for job opportunities, and some of them black performers, artists, and intellectuals who came for a chance to practice their craft and gain access to the city's influential culture industries.

White tourists ventured into the neighborhood to go "slumming," often at Jim Crow nightclubs like the infamous Cotton Club, where blacks performed but were not allowed in the audience. White tourists would partake of bootleg liquor in the Prohibition-era speakeasies of Jungle Alley, a stretch of One Hundred Thirty-Second Street that catered to white audiences. In the arts, white patrons were encouraging black artists to peddle images of blackness that would sell to white audiences, playing up the exoticism of black culture. And in the midst of this cultural flowering many black intellectuals wondered if this movement might be doing more harm than good. These images of Harlem appeared in black academic novels later, including Du Bois's *The Black Flame* trilogy, where he included an extensive dilation on the Harlem Renaissance (with literary excerpts included in the text) and theorized about the movement's significance.

In the seventh and final question, Du Bois voices his concerns about whether the artists who produced this work were downplaying the complexity of their own lives, that the images they were distributing about themselves and their communities did not match their lived experiences. For Du Bois, if his fiction was any indication, telling "the truth about themselves and their own social class" meant creating images of African Americans who were practicing scholars and intellectuals, who had attended at least some college if not gone on to earn advanced degrees, or had become licensed professionals in their fields.

Du Bois's analysis is significant also when we consider the implications of his dichotomy between "the worst" of their group and "the educated Negro." Reiterated in his formulation of "the talented tenth," this class dichotomy manifests as an intraracial class conflict that recurs throughout black academic novels, a conflict pitting the Negro bourgeoisie and its desires for upward mobility and Eurocentric sophistication against the uneducated black rural and urban poor. Many black writers perpetuate this attitude in their work, even as some of them challenge the classism of black intellectuals. In Nella Larsen's *Quicksand*, for instance, Helga Crane laments the way that Naxos College disciplines its rural black students into respectable dress and manners. Alice Walker's title character in *Meridian* also mentions the white gloves and dresses that the black women of Saxon College wore. (The names of their fictional colleges were clearly calling attention to assimilationism.) In both cases Walker and Larsen wrote protagonists who rebelled against and questioned these cultural norms, even though there are also instances in both novels where those same characters lapse back into chauvinistic and condescending attitudes toward the black poor and working class.

In effect, Du Bois wanted those black intellectuals who were fortunate enough to have attended a Fisk, Howard, or Hampton, or to have attended one of the few white colleges admitting black students at that time, to tell the truth about their experiences, and he wanted them to believe that the lives that they knew were just as worthy of fictionalized treatment as the images of the common folk and were just as representative of a "black experience." While it is reasonable to suspect that black academic novels probably reinforce this hierarchical gap between "the worst" and "the best" of the group, what actually happens with their authors who come about after Du Bois is they end up creating complex images of blackness that affirm and normalize the existence of educated African Americans but do not settle for being merely celebratory propaganda. The bibliography of black academic novels constitutes a diverse body of work that probes and challenges the many ways that elitism and classism manifested among educated blacks. One finds in these novels questions about the very project of higher education, whether it would lead to social improvements or only create a new class of H.N.I.C.'s. One finds these novelists questioning whether a college education was part of a resistance against racism or turned one into a servant of white supremacy.

Looking into Du Bois's creative work and the archival record of his early writing, it is apparent that he was well aware of novels about academic life in the years before this article was written, and that the academic novel informed his own early literary experiments. His first published work of fiction, "Tom Brown at Fisk," a serial story presented in three parts in the *Fisk Herald* between December 1887 and March 1888, takes its title from Thomas Hughes's college novel *Tom Brown at Oxford* (1861).[17] In 1892 Du Bois composed a sketch for a college novel under the working title "A Fellow of Harvard." That novel never came to fruition, but the presence of the sketch in his archive provides further evidence of his awareness of academic fiction and his desire to write novels about the academic life (in this case, the life of a white scholar who ends up teaching at a black college).[18] In *The Souls of Black Folk* (1903), Du Bois applied an engagingly lyrical style to his essays on race matters, a collection that included an academic short story, "Of the Coming of John." He then went on to publish his first novel, *The Quest of the Silver Fleece* (1911), which depicts the struggle for black education in the post-Reconstruction South, including the economic and political challenges of building higher education under the South's plantation economy and its need for black manual labor. In 1928, two years after the appearance of his questionnaire in *The Crisis*, he published *Dark Princess*, another novel featuring an educated black protagonist, the medical student Matthew Townes. And, toward the end of his life, in his late eighties, as he found himself with more years in old age than he had anticipated, he wrote and published *The Black Flame Trilogy*, a series of novels that includes *The Ordeal of Mansart* (1957), *Mansart Builds a School* (1959), and *Worlds of Color* (1961), an epic narrative that dramatizes the black freedom struggle through the life of a professor and college president named Manuel Mansart.

Some of the issues that Du Bois raised in that *Crisis* article and in his fiction would appear in the work of later academic novelists such as Percival Everett, whose novel *Erasure* (2001) addresses questions of racial authenticity and marketing in a story about a black novelist who is irritated that publishers want to publish only works about African Americans that emphasize the "sordid, foolish, and criminal." And Du Bois anticipates the intraracial class conflicts that would animate later depictions of black higher education, most famously in the TV shows produced by Bill Cosby *The Cosby Show* and *A Different World*, both of which were celebrated as groundbreaking depictions of educated, accomplished, dignified African Americans in a medium that favored buffoonish caricatures. The shows became a source of pride for college-educated African Americans but also revealed critical fissures along class lines, particularly as these shows became popular with white audiences and were wielded as examples of black respectability.

I have tried to follow the lead of these black academic novelists by centering the black intellectual's own thinking about black cultural production instead of deferring to white European theorists to validate and interpret their work as sufficiently intellectual. Black artists have often been constricted by the gaze of white audiences, and this is a subject that all black academic novelists confront and explore. What I find most compelling about their novels is the sense of interiority, that these writers offer us complex visions of what it looks like to operate within a framework where black intellectuals speak to one another. I am reminded of the Bechdel Test, cartoonist Alison Bechdel's idea from her comic strip *Dykes to Watch Out For*, in which a black woman character refuses to see a movie unless (1) the movie has at least two women in it, (2) who talk to each other, (3) about something besides a man.[19] Black academic novels often pass something like a black version of the Bechdel Test in depicting black folks talking to other black folks about something other than white folks. Recently, film critic Manohla Dargis suggested a DuVernay test, inspired by African American film director Ava DuVernay, which simply insists that "African Americans and other minorities have fully realized lives rather than serve as scenery in white stories."[20] Yes, many times the conversations in black academic novels are about the ways of white folk and other matters of race, gender, and identity, but just as often these novelists write about other things entirely—their craft as artists, their intellectual and academic disciplines, their beliefs, ideas, dreams, and aspirations beyond the race question. These works also subversively show black intellectuals who are engaged in the uplift and representation of black people but also express their fatigue with the whole race talk business, giving readers a window into what Elizabeth Alexander describes as "black life and creativity behind the public face of stereotype and limited imagination."[21]

These are certainly diverse works of art that depict many aspects of human experience, and writing about them together necessarily means making certain reductions and generalizations. I allow that to compose such a study I am engaging in what Barbara Fields and Karen Fields refer to as racecraft, racialized thinking that assumes the existence, truth value, and objective reality of racial categories.[22] But to borrow one of Ralph Ellison's favorite words, I always try to come down on the side of *complexity*. These are complex texts in terms of their themes and rhetorical strategies, and though I make certain strategically essentialist judgments about them as "black" texts, I keep emphasizing their complexity, because it is precisely the complex intellectual life that black people have been denied under regimes of white supremacy, which demand black simplicity and black obedience.

By tracing a literary history of the black academic novel, I show how this particular subset of novels relates to the larger genre, but diverges from it in important ways, particularly by addressing issues related to the politics of black intellectuals. I also take my cue from the existing critical literature on academic fiction in which scholars have used the term "academic fiction" as a way to explore creative representations of academic life in novels, short stories, plays, films, and television. The focus for much of this study is on the literary, on the long, written form of the novel and its theoretical underpinnings. But I also connect this form to other forms of fiction, including short stories, plays, and film. Indeed, connecting the novel to other artistic forms introduces some disciplinary and theoretical challenges, but the works themselves already contain some cross-disciplinary connections (novels influenced by films, films based on novels), so that it is worth thinking about how these works conform to and resist their genre conventions.

I am also interested in how black writers have used the academic novel (and other forms of academic fiction) to contest, undercut, and ridicule racist conceptions of black intelligence in higher education. I evaluate white supremacy not just as a belief system but also as "discursive" in the Foucauldian sense of a relationship between knowledge, institutions, power, and language. In "The Discourse on Language" he describes the will to truth and its social functions: "This will to truth . . . relies on institutional support: it is both reinforced and accompanied by whole strata of practices such as pedagogy—naturally—the book system, publishing, libraries, such as the learned societies in the past, and laboratories today."[23] *The Blackademic Life* draws from Foucault's theorization of discourse as a concept that is not individualized but rather is a complex and impersonal social formation dispersed across institutions, including the university and the state. The "truth" of white supremacy is not merely an expression of attitudes but also an exercise of power over black lives that is predicated on widely disseminated beliefs about black inferiority.

"The overeducation of the Negro" is a discourse in which black educability was questionable, black higher education was discouraged, and black people were conditioned to be wary of its effects on themselves. All these novelists and artists confront this discourse in one form or another, and by doing so they take what is usually seen as an insular literary genre and use it as a vehicle to disseminate dynamic representations of black intellectuals, thereby resisting stereotypes of blackness and challenging assumptions about who constitutes the typical university student or professor. Their novels aestheticize the black educational experience, daring to show the black intellectual life as a beautiful and heroic one while also leveraging criticism of the university in its various forms.

This Strangely Neglected Topic, or Who's Afraid of the Black Academic Novel?

Kingsley Amis's academic satire *Lucky Jim* (1954) remains one of the most widely read and influential academic novels. In Elaine Showalter's *Faculty Towers: The Academic Novel and Its Discontents* (2005), she writes, "Just as [C. P. Snow's] *The Masters* appeals to and addresses that side of the academic psyche that idealizes the ivory tower, Lucky Jim speaks to the academic spirit of rebellion and impatience, the feeling that life must be lived more intensely outside the walls."[24] Jim Dixon, the protagonist of Amis's novel, is a lecturer in history at a small British college, and the novel follows Dixon's progressive disenchantment with academic life. A feeling of dread overcomes Dixon as he is preparing a presentation when he reflects on the title of his paper, "The Economic Influence of the Developments in Shipbuilding Techniques, 1450 to 1485":

> It was a perfect title, in that it crystallized the article's niggling mindlessness, its funereal parade of yawn-enforcing facts, the pseudo-light it threw upon non-problems. Dixon had read, or begun to read, dozens like it, but his own seemed worse than most in its air of being convinced of its own usefulness and significance. "In considering this strangely neglected topic," it began. This what neglected topic? This strangely what topic? This strangely neglected what? His thinking all this without having defiled and set fire to the typescript only made him appear to himself as more of a hypocrite and fool.[25]

Many of us in the academic profession have at times felt a little like Jim Dixon, particularly on those long days and nights spent working on monographs and conference papers and journal articles that felt like little more than "pseudo-light" "upon non-problems." There are times when we are hounded by feelings of futility and question the relevance and value of the work we are doing. For Jim Dixon the existential questions about academia become too much for him, and by the end of the novel he has decided to leave academia altogether.

Like many readers, it seems, I discovered the academic novel around the same time that I was having feelings of ambivalence about the academy. Academic novels often satirize the worst aspects of academia, and they can feel downright cathartic when they describe things in academic life that aggravate us. These novels can be affirming precisely because they confirm that, yes, someone else must have experienced these frustrations—from stifling institutional bureaucracies to obnoxious, conniving colleagues—and has managed to render these experiences eloquently and forcefully on paper. And yet beneath all this parody and satire is often a reformer's spirit. Many of the authors of these novels were themselves academics and continued to be so even after publishing their novels.

To establish a critical framework for thinking about black academic fiction I am putting two fields of literary criticism in conversation with each other: First I briefly survey some of the existing literature on academic novels and academic fiction, defining the terms used in the genre and pointing to a few representative examples of the preexisting critical analysis in this field. And then I turn to some specific works in African American literary criticism, including Henry Louis Gates Jr.'s work on literacy and signification in black literature, to think about the history of black writing and black higher education. Fundamentally, the black academic novel participates in some of the same overall themes in this genre when it comes to the structures of the university, the educational experience, and the academic profession, but the black academic novel diverges from this field in the way that it necessarily addresses a distinct set of political concerns of the black intellectual as a representative figure and necessarily confronts a history of deeply ingrained racism in American culture directed at black literacy, intelligence, and educability.

The parameters of the genre have been explored in numerous book-length studies, such as Mortimer R. Proctor's *The English University Novel* (1957), John O. Lyons's *The College Novel in America* (1962), John E. Kramer's *The American College Novel: An Annotated Bibliography* (1981, expanded in 2004) and *Academe in Mystery and Detective Fiction* (2000), Ian Carter's *Ancient Cultures of Conceit* (1990), Janice Rossen's *The University in Modern Fiction* (1993), Kenneth Womack's *Postwar Academic Fiction* (2002), and Elaine Showalter's *Faculty Towers* (2005). The interest in academic novels remains strong, evidenced by a plethora of journal articles, bloggers writing about academic novels and academic films, and regular columns on academic fiction in venues such as the *Chronicle of Higher Education, Inside Higher Ed,* and *Times Higher Education.*

So what is an academic novel? There are several names used to describe this form of writing, including "the college novel," "the campus novel," and "the academic novel." As literary critic John Lyons stated in *The College Novel in America,* "I consider a novel of academic life one in which higher education is treated with seriousness and the main characters are students or professors."[26] This broad definition is more or less the basic definition that I come back to when all the subdivisions and critical disagreements become too complicated. This definition puts the focus on students and professors, thus a novel about someone who is an "intellectual" or "artist" but isn't a practicing student or professor wouldn't qualify for me. It also excludes novels where the character's status as a student or a professor is only incidental to the plot. For some critics and readers of novels about academic life, the aforementioned descriptors are used interchangeably. For other critics, such as Elaine Showalter, the terms "college novel" and "campus novel" refer to books about undergraduate campus life, while the "academic novel" originates in the 1950s with novels like Randal Jarrell's *Pictures from an Institution* and Mary McCarthy's *Groves of Academe*, which focus on the lives of professors and graduate students. Merritt Moseley, in his chapter "Types of Academic Fiction" in the edited anthology *The Academic Novel: New and Classic Essays*, provides a useful taxonomy of academic novels, dividing them into three categories of novels focused on (1) students, (2) administration, and (3) faculty and subdividing those categories based on recurring thematic tropes (while keeping in mind these boundaries are porous and that novels focusing on one type of academic character often include depictions of other types).[27] When it comes to my own take on the genre I tend to avoid the term "campus novel" since it is usually applied to coming-of-age comedies and dramas about the fleeting four years of undergraduate life, and because it nominally implies a campus setting. While many of the black academic novels I evaluate are actually set on college campuses, there are others that deal with the lives of academics but do not necessarily show the student and professor on campus for the entire novel.

In *Faculty Towers* Elaine Showalter uses the term "professorromane" to describe the novels that are about the lives of career academics (professors and graduate students).[28] While "professorromane" has its critical uses and applies to several of the novels included here, I don't divide the novels into works based on a faculty-centered or a student-centered focus. The main criteria I looked for is that the works are specifically about higher education and the lives of academics, as students or professors, and are not stories that feature a professor or a college student merely as a stock character whose life and experience have little to do with the academic profession, intellectualism, or higher education. This is why, for instance, I don't consider a book like E. Lynn Harris's *Invisible Life* (included in Kramer's bibliography) as a college novel, even though it does start on a college campus and features college-educated black professionals (as do many of Harris's other novels). *Invisible Life* certainly has other qualities worthy of critical attention—namely, that it was a groundbreaking depiction of black gay life in the 1990s and launched Harris's career as one of the most commercially successful black writers—but I do not consider it an academic novel. Likewise, the comedy film *The Best Man*, which depicts a group of college classmates in their postgraduate years and even contains flashbacks to their campus days, deals mostly with their romantic and professional lives beyond the academy and therefore doesn't provide material for thinking about higher education and intellectual labor.

While I include academic narratives that move beyond the campus, I do recognize the institutional space of the campus as an important concept in many of these novels, and one that other critics of academic novels have emphasized in their assessments. Descriptions of the architecture of the campus often correlate to its status in the hierarchy of institutions, from the ideal pastoral campus with its ancient Gothic buildings to the urban community college that functions inside a converted factory. Campuses are sites of engagement where administrators, faculty, and students encounter one another in hallways, offices, classrooms, and conference rooms, and these interior spaces can be sites of conflict and tension. The geography of the campus is particularly important in "town and gown" novels, which often have a built-in class conflict between the students and faculty, who are part of the privileged, enclosed college community, and the people who happen to live just outside the gates in college towns and may even be laborers who work on the campus itself. (Gus Van Sant's 1997 drama *Good Will Hunting* has become an iconic and widely familiar example of town and gown conflict in academic fiction.)

British critic George Saintsbury's 1898 *Macmillan's Magazine* article "Novels of University Life," one of the earliest studies of academic fiction, describes what makes student life an attractive subject for the fiction writer, and in the process he articulates the dominant image of what the "college student" looks like at the end of the nineteenth century.

> There can be, or should be, few passages in life with greater capabilities than that when a man is for the first time almost his own master, for the first time wholly arbiter of whatsoever sports and whatsoever studies he shall pursue, and when he is subjected to local, historical and other influences, sensual and suprasensual, such as might not only "draw three souls out of a weaver," but infuse something like a soul even into the stupidest and most graceless of boys.[29]

For Saintsbury, the default college student is a young man (presumably white and presumably wealthy) who is in his late teenage years and is living away from the bourgeois home for the first time. Though universities continue to be physical places where young people move to, and where they live away from home for the first time, the population of the college has evolved since Saintsbury's time. We can no longer assume that the college student is a white male, nor can we assume that the student is a young person who has no prior experience in the labor force. And now, with the rise of online education, we can no longer assume that the student actually attends classes on a physical campus. While I hope my study serves as evidence that some academic fiction reflects the demographic and institutional diversity of universities, this study is also partly about how that hegemonic image of the young white male coming of age on campus persists as the dominant representation of college life, and it's a representation that blackademic fiction directly confronts with its own counternarratives.

This study focuses on American higher education and its depictions, though I understand that the American university has British antecedents and carries other global intellectual influences, including the Germanic model of research and scholarship. The field of academic-fiction criticism shows a strong relationship between academic novels in England and those in the United States. Matthew Fullerty's 2008 dissertation on the British and American academic novel begins with an appropriate epigraph taken from George Bernard Shaw:

"England and America are two countries divided by a common language."[30] The English author David Lodge may be the most popular academic novelist, and his name has become virtually synonymous with academic satire. *Changing Places* (1975), one of his earliest and best-known academic novels, depicts an exchange program between one British and one American scholar who crisscross the Atlantic to teach at institutions in England and the United States, a device that allows Lodge to highlight the cultural differences between the United States and England (and Europe more broadly). Elaine Showalter identifies Kingsley Amis's *Lucky Jim* as an important influence on the development of the professorromane. *Lucky Jim* is also significant in this discussion because of its setting in a "redbrick" university, newer British institutions created in the twentieth century for working-class and nontraditional students, as opposed to the ancient bastions of wealth and privilege of Oxbridge, where many of the nineteenth-century college novels were set. The class tensions created by the expansion of higher education appear in many twentieth-century British and American academic novels. The scholarship on British college novels includes Proctor's *The English University Novel*, Carter's *Ancient Cultures of Conceit*, John Dougill's *Oxford in English Literature*, and Rossen's *The University in Modern Fiction* (which focuses mostly on England but includes novels from American writers).

Perhaps, then, it was inevitable that the academic novel in America would begin in New England. Nathaniel Hawthorne's *Fanshawe*, published in 1828, was his first novel and based on his experiences as a student at Bowdoin College in Maine. (Apparently Hawthorne hated the novel and tried to destroy all the copies. Alas, it remains in print in the Library of America's *Nathaniel Hawthorne: Collected Novels*.) Several of the nation's oldest colleges, including William and Mary, Princeton, and Harvard, began in former English colonies, and the common language and historical origins have persisted. Studies of the American college novel by Womack, Showalter, Kramer, and others have elucidated some of the distinctive features of the American college novel and how it differs from its English counterpart.

Hawthorne's *Fanshawe* was an early entry into the genre in the United States, and other authors, like Du Bois, experimented with the form in the late nineteenth century, but the academic novel really comes of age as an American phenomenon in the twentieth century. And as such it is framed by the economic growth and social dislocations that began in the late nineteenth century with industrialism and extended into the first decades of the twentieth.

Those social forces of the twentieth century would come to shape the black academic novel as well, social forces including the Great Migration, the two world wars, the expansion of new colleges, the opening of previously all-white and male colleges to women and ethnic minorities, and the growth of colleges as corporate entities. I have laid out my chapters here chronologically to chart some of the important political developments that have influenced the themes and contents of the academic novels evaluated here, including segregation and desegregation of schools, political changes in the attitudes of black Americans, and political discourses about the black presence in higher education.

Before turning to a discussion of black literary criticism, as a way to frame how black representations have been theorized historically I want to include a word about the allegedly "intramural" nature of this genre. For as long as critics have been writing about the "college novel" as a form, there have been skeptics who have questioned the absurd insularity of the practice: an academic writing a novel about academia. I am aware that this very book presents an even more ridiculous scenario, an academic critic writing about novels about academia. That criticism of the insularity of academic fiction has intensified in recent years as creative writing programs have grown and many more writers now work in academia, leading many to believe that the novelist in academia will only ever write about academia. Mark McGurl's *The Program Era: Postwar Fiction and the Rise of Creative Writing* (2011) is a welcome rebuttal to this claim. McGurl explores the history of writing programs, evaluates many novels produced in creative writing programs, and argues that the actual fiction produced by these programs includes a plethora of topics and themes beyond higher education.[31]

Nevertheless, the skeptics believe that with more writers becoming academics, writers (and academic writers) are losing sight of the "real world" and its concerns. Gore Vidal summed up this skeptical position as well as anyone when he wrote that

> as most of our novelists now teach school, they tend to tell us what it is like to be a schoolteacher, and since schoolteachers have been taught to teach others to write only about what they know, they tell us what they know about, too, which is next to nothing about the way the rest of the population of the Republic lives . . . What tends to be left out of these works is the world. World gone, no voluntary readers. No voluntary readers, no literature—only creative writing courses and English studies, activities marginal (to put it tactfully) to civilization.[32]

Indeed, as someone who has read his fair share of them, I can say with confidence that there are plenty of navel-gazing academic novels. But the critical tradition I have laid out thus far gives us plenty of reasons for why this is a significant genre that deals with issues beyond academia, and that the university itself is relevant beyond a small group of specialized professionals or college students. On the contrary, the university has proven to be one of the most important institutions in American life, one where ideas, policies, and scientific breakthroughs are made. Or, to borrow a rebuttal from Lodge, "There's a tendency for people to sneer at the genre as if it's played out, while actually they take a good deal of interest in reading it. The fact is that universities change and societies change, and therefore there are always new fictional possibilities."³³

This brings me to my own "strangely neglected topic" à la Lucky Jim Dixon. There is no better place to see those changes that Lodge describes than in black academic fiction, where there is a variety of institutional experience represented and where there is a narrative of historical change from novels mostly about black colleges in the early twentieth century to novels about black students and professors at predominantly white universities (also at black colleges) in the twenty-first century. There is also no better place to contest Gore Vidal's claim that the world is "left out" of the academic novel when one reads the novels by a group of scholars who are marginal to the academy, whose existence in the academy is inherently politicized, and whose work often deals with the encounter between the academic life and the "real world."

That said, critics of the academic novel deserve some blame for failing to take black academic fiction seriously, thereby limiting their scope of understanding about the university and its politics. Reading the critical literature on the genre one would hardly know that black people ever went to college or that their presence on campus was contested, or that their marginalization represents a major challenge to the core ideals of the university, let alone that black intellectuals might have their own thoughts about these things. Some of these critics mention a few stray titles here and there or discuss a few minority characters in academic fiction, but few go into any detail about black-themed academic novels and their importance in the genre, with some exceptions: Womack's *Postwar Academic Fiction* contains an informative chapter on multiculturalism in Ishmael Reed's *Japanese by Spring*. And John Kramer's annotated bibliographies list college novels from a diverse range of black academic novelists, from "literary fiction" to commercial genres, including authors such as Connie Briscoe, Omar Tyree, Chester Himes, Cyrus Colter, and Pamela Thomas-Graham. But critics of academic fiction have mostly ignored this literature depicting the lives of students and professors whose place in the university could not be comfortably assumed and whose work is imbued with a criticism of the institution and its history, and in doing so they have impoverished their analysis of the genre and myopically limited their understanding of higher education.

Literacy, Higher Education, and the Black Literary Tradition

Understanding the significance of the black academic novel requires not only a revision of academic-fiction criticism but also an engagement with black literary theory and its emphasis on the importance of literacy and education in the production of black literature. In *Figures in Black: Words, Signs, and the "Racial" Self*, Henry Louis Gates Jr. identifies an intricate relationship between literary criticism and black literary production. He states that "few literary traditions have begun or been sustained by such a complex ironic relation to their criticism: allegations of an absence led directly to a presence, a literature often inextricably bound in a dialogue with its potentially harshest critics."[34] From Thomas Jefferson's dismissal of Phillis Wheatley's poetry in *Notes on the State of Virginia* to Hegel's suggestion that Africa is not a part of world history, black literature was burdened with the need to prove black humanity against the weight of Western thought. As Gates puts it, "Unlike almost every other literary tradition, the Afro-American literary tradition was generated as a response to eighteenth- and nineteenth-century allegations that persons of African descent did not, and could not, create literature." And therefore, "the African living in Europe or in the New World seems to have felt compelled to create a literature both to demonstrate implicitly that blacks did indeed possess the intellectual ability to create a written art and to indict the several social and economic institutions that delimited the humanity of all black people in Western cultures."[35]

This history is the source of what Gates calls black literature's ironic relationship to Western literary theory. "For the ex-slave," Gates writes, "to become subjects, as it were, black ex-slaves had to demonstrate their language-using capacity before they could become social and historical entities. In short, slaves could inscribe their selves only in language."[36] Thus from the beginning, black writing and black education were bound up with the destiny of the race. The earliest black writers were tasked with proving the intellectual competence of an entire race. The role of the black intellectual was codified as that of a racial representative, and the work of black writers would continue to be racialized in specific ways. The twentieth-century novel, and the apparatus of fellowships and awards around it, continues this burden of "proving" black intelligence, and this burden of proof maintains an uncomfortable presence in black artistic production even as black artists resisted and challenged it.

The black academic novel is part of a long tradition of "education as liberation" in black writing. Even after emancipation and throughout the twentieth century black writers drew on slave narratives and produced stories of education as liberation, including in memoirs such as Richard Wright's *Black Boy* and *The Autobiography of Malcolm X* and in fiction works such as Alice Walker's *The Color Purple*, Sapphire's *Push*, and Octavia Butler's *Parable of the Sower* and *Parable of the Talents*. Though the works that I am reading in this study deal with a level of education far above that of basic literacy, they all carry within them some version of this idea of knowledge as a tool of liberation and freedom, and all these narratives are situated in this history of black education as a project of emancipation, uplift, and progress (even as some of these works problematize discourses of progress).

Every black academic novel has within it a response to two fundamental concepts in the politics of the black intellectual: responsibility and representation. That is, all black academic novelists are forced to confront, in one way or another, the expectation that the black intellectual does or does not have a responsibility to the black community to apply his or her knowledge and talents to the social and political problems facing the African American people. This idea was most powerfully articulated by W. E. B. Du Bois in his notion of "the talented tenth," in which he stated that "the Negro Race, like all races, is going to be saved by its exceptional men."[37] The dire conditions of black life in America—defined by slavery, subjugation, social inequality, and poverty—pushed the black intellectual into a representative role as spokesperson on behalf of other members of the race, a role that Du Bois himself took on as one of the most educated black Americans in his time.

Black academic novelists dramatize the way in which the individual black intellectual must confront expectations of representation, and they map out the different strategies available to the individual, but none are able to sidestep the question entirely. This is a reality that Percival Everett alludes to in the character of Thelonious "Monk" Ellison in *Erasure*. Ellison's novels as a literary fiction writer were not meant to be direct commentaries on the black experience, and yet he finds his racial identity is inseparable from his literary production. Eventually he takes out his frustrations in the form of the satirical novel that is at the center of *Erasure*.

Gene Jarrett's *Representing the Race: A New Political History of African American Literature* further examines this close relationship between black literary history and a burden of racial representation. Jarrett writes as follows of the double meaning of black racial representation: "First, it signifies the aesthetic portrayal of African Americans, and in some cases the African Diaspora more broadly, in literature. Second, it signifies this group's political delegation of its collective authority to an individual person or another group."[38] The political condition of blacks as noncitizens and the restrictions on black literacy placed the earliest black writers in the position of representatives pleading the case for black humanity, and it's a role that black intellectuals have been writing with and against ever since. Or as Gates put it in *Thirteen Ways of Looking at a Black Man*, "The grand theme of your career may be that the burden of representation is an illusion—a paradigm, par excellence, of ideological *mauvaise foi*—but that will only heighten your chagrin when you realize that it follows you everywhere like your own shadow. It isn't a thing of your making, and it won't succumb to your powers of unmaking—not yet, anyway."[39] What Gates describes here is exactly the attitude of Monk Ellison in Everett's *Erasure*. Monk subscribes to the social construction of race and wants to think of race as an illusion and a trope, but he finds that this burden of representation follows him around, and he is unable to shake it. Several black academic novels contain different versions of this same type of resistance. The genre allows the writer to "signify" on racial politics (to use another Gates term from his follow-up study *The Signifying Monkey*) by undercutting them with satire, interrogating them philosophically, and moving beyond their basic proscriptions to show black intellectuals engaged in political, creative, and intellectual pursuits beyond the race question altogether.

This criticism of racial representation is famously the focus of Ralph Ellison's *Invisible Man*. One lesson to take from Ellison's title character is that his resistance to the pressure of being a racial representative was not about shirking his responsibility but instead about finding a sense of agency, a sense of intellectual freedom. Ralph Ellison's critique of Richard Wright's *Native Son* in his essay "The World and the Jug" was about the disconnect between the novelist Richard Wright and the character Bigger Thomas, which led Ellison to say that "Wright could imagine Bigger, but Bigger could not possibly imagine Richard Wright. Wright saw to that."[40] The black academic novel has served as a space for black writers to create characters commensurate with their own lives as capacious intellectuals, to do what Du Bois asked in *The Crisis* and "tell the truth about their own class," to create characters who could be based on fellow students and professors, to even craft black characters based upon literary characters from other academic novels and to create characters who have a sense of interiority, who refuse to allow racism to determine every aspect of their lives and intellectual interests.

Gates's approach to black literary criticism, focusing on the meaning of black literacy and the theoretical importance of writing as a skill and a technology, clears a path for me toward a theory of the black academic novel. *Figures in Black* is also an exploration of the development of formal literary criticism on black literature up to that point, reviewing the 1970s and the work of critics such as Addison Gayle, Stephen Henderson, and Houston Baker. In short, *Figures in Black* was an attempt to create a formal black literary criticism that did not rely on racial essentialism and did not insist that only black critics could read and interpret a black text. In effect it was a rejection of what Gates called the race and superstructure model of black literary analysis. In this paradigm, consciousness is predetermined by color and culture. The problem with this model, as Gates sees it, is that blackness is treated as an entity rather than a metaphor or sign. Blackness is something that just *is* rather than something writers *do*. Perhaps the most quoted and controversial sentence from the book is the following: "Blackness is not a material object, an absolute, or an event, but a trope."[41] Therefore, the critical tools needed to evaluate black literature must be tools that any critic can use regardless of background. Another contested implication of Gates's formulation is that "blackness" can be found in texts of nonblack writers as well. I think of Gates's theoretical challenge when I look to the small but significant cluster of white writers who have written academic novels centered on black characters, including T. S. Stribling, Worth Tuttle Hedden, Bucklin Moon, and Philip Roth.

Stribling's 1922 novel *Birthright*, about a black Harvard man returning to teach in the South, becomes the basis for one of the earliest black academic films, directed by Oscar Micheaux. Worth Tuttle Hedden's *The Other Room* (1947) is an interracial drama about a white woman who teaches at a black college in New Orleans in the 1920s. Bucklin Moon's *Without Magnolias* (1949) is set on a black campus in Florida and features an ensemble cast of black characters, including a local family whose daughter works at the college and dates a young male professor, as well as the marital drama of a black college president and his wife. Philip Roth's drama of passing, *The Human Stain* (2000), is about the life of Coleman Silk, a light-skinned black man from New Jersey who attends Howard University but decides to pass while pursuing his graduate education in classics and lives the rest of his life as a white (Jewish) professor at a liberal arts college in upstate New York before getting snagged in a culture-wars debacle.

Admittedly, these examples present some challenges to my own attempt at limiting "black academic novel" to black writers, showing how such categories are inherently porous and contingent, and this is a thorny and treacherous theoretical problem that my little book will not solve. But I do note that even among the "black" writers that I have identified, there are variations. Some of their autobiographical information indicates they grew up in mixed-race families. Mat Johnson, for instance, followed up his academic novel *Pym* with an autobiographically inspired comic novel called *Loving Day* that explores interracial identity in a story line with allusions to the 1967 *Loving v. Virginia* interracial marriage case. Likewise, Emily Raboteau's *The Professor's Daughter* deals with an interracial academic family, as does Zadie Smith's *On Beauty*. Similar novels, like Nella Larsen's *Quicksand* and Chester Himes's *The Third Generation*, explore life on the color line with light-skinned characters who feel stuck in a liminal existence between blackness and whiteness. Other novels are by diasporic black writers born and living outside the United States who interrogate America's racial codes. Chimamanda Ngozi Adichie's *Americanah*, for example, is an African diasporic exploration of twenty-first century America's racial landscape in which she riffs on long-standing issues between "American Blacks" and "Non-American Blacks" through the story of an educated Nigerian woman who comes to the United States and experiences the 2008 election of Barack Obama. The following chapters show many other examples where black academic novels push against easy conceptions of race and nation as static boundaries.

Ultimately, I come back to the discourse of overeducation as the key to understanding not only the black academic novel but also the overall condition of the black intellectual. It's an idea rooted in the history of enslavement and its racist ideologies, and it persists in the language, culture, and institutional structures of higher education. In Christina Sharpe's *Monstrous Intimacies: Making Post-Slavery Subjects* (2009) and *In the Wake: On Blackness and Being* (2016), she articulates the condition of contemporary black literature as one shaped by a postslavery subjectivity in which the violence and racialized subjugation of chattel slavery, particularly carried out in intimate sexual and social relations between enslaver and enslaved, have continued to shape ideas about race into the present. As she writes, "I mean *Monstrous Intimacies* to intervene in and to position us to see and think anew what it means to be a (black) post-slavery subject positioned within everyday intimate brutalities who is said to have survived or to be surviving the past of slavery, that is not yet past, bearing something like freedom."[42] For black intellectuals, one of the ways that past remains present is in the questioning and challenging of black intelligence and ideas, and these are not just the challenges from a few random racists but also ideas that can be traced back to proslavery justifications. Other recent works such as Craig Steven Wilder's *Ebony and Ivy*, Ta-Nehisi Coates's *Between the World and Me*, and Michelle Alexander's *The New Jim Crow* have helped to encourage a reckoning with the ways in which regimes of control and containment that originated with enslavement have morphed into other forms (policing, incarceration, housing discrimination) that continue to pervade the lives of black people in these United States.

The narratives of black academic fiction express what it means to be a black intellectual in this postslavery context. They are about what it means to live with that past that is not yet past, and may never be past, and how that past still has its residue in the world where black intellectuals live and work, speak, teach, and produce knowledge. Even now, as I write this, universities are still under pressure to relitigate the case on black intelligence as conservative groups invite intellectual hacks like Dinesh D'Souza, Charles Murray, Andrew Sullivan, and other white-supremacist pundits/trolls to lecture on their campuses, where they insist that we must have an "honest debate" about how black people's pea-sized brains are the real cause of inequality.

White America has always maintained a fundamental incredulity and resentment toward black higher education. Students who attend historically black colleges are read as separatists and reverse racists ("What if white people had white colleges?" the bewildered ahistorical racist asks). Black students at majority-white institutions are seen as unworthy, unqualified interlopers who are there only to fulfill diversity quotas. This overeducation discourse has historically played a role in educational policy, from the vocational model of education, to current debates on for-profit colleges, to struggles over integration, to anti-affirmative-action cases, to culture-wars rhetoric, and to political campaigns condemning political correctness.

During a court hearing in the *Fisher v. University of Texas* case in which a white woman, Abigail Fisher, sued the University of Texas over its affirmative action admissions policy, Supreme Court Justice Antonin Scalia questioned whether black students belonged in elite colleges and pulled out this nice bit of backhanded concern trolling about black higher education:

> There are those who contend that it does not benefit African Americans to get them into the University of Texas, where they do not do well, as opposed to having them go to a less-advanced school, a

slower-track school where they do well. One of the briefs pointed out that most of the black scientists in this country don't come from schools like the University of Texas. They come from lesser schools where they do not feel that they're being pushed ahead in classes that are too fast for them.[43]

Here Scalia gives us a fairly representative white-supremacist take on black education, couched in the passive-aggressive language of "There are those who contend . . ." But this isn't just some random dude mouthing off on an internet message board. This statement was made by a member of one of the nation's most powerful institutions, founded in 1789, which did not have a black member until 1967 and has seen only two black justices, one Hispanic justice, and four women justices in its entire two-hundred-twenty-six-year history (at the time of that statement). Scalia's comments were not just the outlier attitude of one cantankerous racist but also reflect a long history of systemic inequality in educational institutions and educational policy. These institutions have been and continue to be shaped by a court populated with judges and lawyers trained at the nation's most elite educational institutions.

All the novels I cover in this book address, in one form or another, the discourses discussed here on black intelligence and educability. But even as they confront these racist ideas, what makes them dynamic, valuable, and even subversive documents is the fact that they also insist upon a complexity of black life and thought, a black interiority, that articulates what it feels like to experience these public race struggles from the inside out.

Chapter 2

✦

Educating and Uplifting the Race, 1876–1919

Reading through the literature on postbellum black education reveals a constant anxiety among white Americans about the consequences of black higher education. They are wary of how the college-educated black person might begin subscribing to a troublesome belief in "social equality." Higher education might lead blacks to think of themselves as virtually indistinguishable from white people and therefore feeling entitled to the same rights and privileges of citizenship. Educated black people would begin to feel empowered to share public spaces with white people. Particularly odious was the prospect of black men interacting with white women. White southerners expressed fear of "Negro Rule," and the events of Reconstruction, in which northern interlopers had placed black men into state houses across the South, allowing them to legislate over white people, confirmed the worst of those fears.

Black higher education began in this Reconstruction era (and continued to grow in the years after). It was coterminous with the extension of the franchise to black voters and the election of the nation's first black congressmen and government officials. In response to these historical developments, the late nineteenth and early twentieth centuries saw a backlash to black progress, a backlash that included the Supreme Court's 1896 *Plessy v. Ferguson* decision that legalized segregation and finalized a rollback of Reconstruction policies in the South. The post-Reconstruction era saw the Ku Klux Klan's reemergence and a series of antiblack riots in Wilmington, North Carolina (1898), Atlanta (1906), East St. Louis (1917), and Tulsa (1921). There was also a backlash expressed in popular culture, with white consumers devouring nostalgic images of the gallant white South and enjoying the derogatory depictions of black people as simple, inferior beings put on this earth by God for the service and amusement of white people.[1]

Finnie D. Coleman's biography of the black preacher, novelist, and activist Sutton Griggs positions the work of Thomas Dixon as an important white literary response to Reconstruction, and Dixon's novels exemplify the type of negative images of blackness that circulated in popular culture of this era, images that Sutton Griggs sought to counteract in his novels and other writings. Dixon's trilogy of novels *The Leopard's Spots* (1905), *The Clansman*

(1905), and *The Traitor* (1907) were popular best sellers that had a profound effect as prosegregation propaganda, most notably when *The Clansman* was adapted into filmmaker D. W. Griffith's landmark racist film *The Birth of a Nation* (1915). Both the book and the film illustrate the struggle over the black image in popular media and the power of degrading images of blackness to compel white audiences into action. Griffith's revisionist history of Reconstruction spoke directly to white fears that the country was headed toward disaster if it did not seize control of its black populations and restore the discipline and obedience that had been established under slavery and extended through Jim Crow. Dixon articulated the beliefs of many white Americans when he stated about Booker T. Washington that "no amount of education of any kind, industrial, classical or religious, can make a Negro a white man or bridge the chasm of centuries which separate him from the white man in the evolution of human nature."[2] As a writer, as a propagandist with the power to shape public opinions on race matters, Dixon's attitudes toward black education were part of a larger field of white-supremacist theories on black education and intelligence. Sutton Griggs responded to Dixon's work in his book *The Hindered Hand*, where he offered a counternarrative of black education and destiny, stating that "be it known unto you, oh Americans, that it is through his mind, his spirit, the exhalations of his soul, his dreams or lack of dreams, that the Negro is to leave his mark on American life."[3]

This historical background on black higher education and its white opposition is crucial context for interpreting the first black academic novels that appear on the scene at the beginning of the twentieth century. All the work in the period 1899 to 1919 (and in the following years) respond to these discourses on black intelligence and educational prospects, including the first two full-length black academic novels, Sutton Griggs's *Imperium in Imperio* (1899) and W. E. B. Du Bois's *The Quest of the Silver Fleece* (1911). Though this early period of black academic fiction does not contain much in the way of novels, the short stories and nonfiction narratives that it produced are also significant to the academic novels (and films) to come. This period includes Du Bois's first short stories, all of which reveal an interest in academic fiction. These nascent literary experiments provide some perspective on the relationship between his theories on black education and his literary ambitions. The period also includes some notable first-person autobiographical narratives by educators such as Anna Julia Cooper (*A Voice from the South*) and Booker T. Washington (*Up from Slavery*). These nonfiction works helped to prepare the way for the fictionalizations of black academic life found in the black academic novels that followed. In the case of *The Quest of the Silver Fleece*, the lack of a campus setting is a conscious historical detail that Du Bois uses to call attention to the limited opportunities for educational advancement among its black intellectual characters.

By the end of the nineteenth century Anna Julia Cooper had published *A Voice from the South* (1892), a work containing her thoughts and experiences as an advocate of college education for black women in an era dominated by vocal race men. Cooper's work belongs in the conversation with Du Bois and Washington, who have been exalted in the classical-versus-industrial argument about black education. At the age of sixty-seven Cooper received her Ph.D. from the University of Paris, Sorbonne, in 1924, making her the fourth African American woman to ever earn a doctorate. She was the principal of the M Street High School in Washington, D.C. (later the Paul Laurence Dunbar High School) and served for a decade as the president of Frelinghuysen University, a night school for adults. In "The Higher Education of Women," an essay featured in *A Voice from the South*, Cooper shared her vision that black women must be included in the uplift project of education and that she wanted to make "it a common and everyday affair for women to reason and think and express their thought."[4] We can see part of Cooper's influence in Du Bois's *The Quest of the Silver Fleece*, a novel with a female protagonist and in which Du Bois pays careful attention to domesticity, colorism, and the gendered expectations of education and leadership. Cooper famously challenged the race men of her time to take black women's concerns seriously when she wrote, "Only the BLACK WOMAN can say 'when and where I enter, in the quiet, undisputed dignity of my womanhood, without violence and without suing or special patronage, then and there the whole Negro race enters with me.'"[5]

In *Beyond Respectability: The Intellectual Thought of Race Women* (2017), Brittney Cooper analyzes the work of Anna Julia Cooper and other black women intellectuals such as Pauli Murray, Mary Church Terrell, and Toni Cade Bambara to argue for the concept of "embodied discourse" as a framework for thinking about black women's scholarship, art, and activism. She offers this as a supplement to the commonly used black feminist concepts of "culture of dissemblance" (Darlene Clark Hine) and "politics of respectability" (Evelyn Brooks Higginbotham), noting that these theories have served black women's scholarship well but also do not fully take into account the specifically raced and gendered way that black female bodies exist in the world and how black women thinkers have asserted their corporeality as an intrinsic part of their work. This is especially relevant in my study, where I am writing about how black bodies are experienced and reacted to in academic spaces. As Cooper writes, "*Embodied discourse* refers to a form of Black female textual activism wherein race women assertively demand the inclusion of their bodies and, in particular, working-class bodies and Black female bodies by placing them in the texts they write and speak."[6] Her concept of embodied discourse is specifically about black women, but it is a useful paradigm for thinking about how all black intellectuals exist in academic spaces, particularly when it comes to their variations of gender, body type, and color and the perceived sexual differences of black people, which are all concepts that various black academic novelists address in their work.

Booker T. Washington's 1901 autobiography *Up from Slavery* remains one of the most important and contentious books about black education, and scholars have made note of the literary devices that Washington used to make the book more appealing. As literary scholar William Andrews writes of the book, "What made *Up from Slavery* different, and virtually guaranteed its popularity among an extensive white readership, was Washington's skill in masking his personal and social agenda behind an apparently simple, almost folksy, brand of unassuming storytelling."[7] Washington as a historical figure would make appearances in later works of black academic fiction, most famously as a subtext to Ralph Ellison's *Invisible Man*, and in other forms, such as an inspiration to Ishmael Reed's Benjamin Puttbutt in *Japanese by Spring* or in the name of a secondary character in Spike Lee's *School Daze*. In general, Washington remains an avatar of a complex black political strategy of conservatism, respectability, and accommodation.

When it comes to the actual novels of this era, *Imperium in Imperio* and *The Quest of the Silver Fleece* cry out to be read by critics of black literature as academic novels and to be included in the critical literature on academic fiction. In these novels one finds much of the subject matter that would come to occupy the attention of later black academic novelists, including the history and ideology of black colleges; the discourse of overeducation; the place of black education in the broader labor economy; intraracial politics of class, color, and gender; and the importance of racial representation in the media, particularly in the need for black intellectuals to see possibilities of a blackademic life and the extent to which such images were either missing or degraded in the broader literature.

Enter the New Negro

Sutton Griggs (1872–1933) was a Baptist minister, author, and activist who was born in Chatfield, Texas. He attended the now-defunct Bishop College, then in Marshall, Texas. (Bishop College was founded in 1881, moved to Dallas in 1961 but folded in 1988. Its former campus was purchased and incorporated into another HBCU, Paul Quinn College.) Griggs continued his education at Richmond Theological Institute in Richmond, Virginia, where his father had once attended. He was ordained as a Baptist minister and become pastor of a church in Nashville, Tennessee, while also serving in many administrative capacities in black organizations, including as corresponding secretary for the National Baptist Convention.

Griggs's life is one of a consummate turn-of-the-century "race man," an educated black man who felt called to be a religious and intellectual leader of his people. *Imperium in Imperio: A Study of the Negro Race Problem* puts that "race man" image into literary form. Griggs's novel is already recognized among literary critics as a pioneering work of African American fiction. He is counted among the earliest black novelists, and one of the first to experience some measure of "commercial" success, mainly through selling his novel independently at black churches and convention meetings. Indeed, Griggs is likely the first black writer to aim most of his work at black audiences. The slave narratives were largely about garnering white sympathy for abolition, and in the postslavery era, the earliest black writers like Pauline Hopkins and Charles Chesnutt wrote largely for white audiences and pandered to their literary tastes and expectations. As an independent publisher and someone writing for a newly developed black readership that was produced by advances in late nineteenth-century black education, Griggs could write with the expectation of an audience of black readers in mind while also recognizing an opportunity to influence white readers who might encounter his work as well.

Imperium in Imperio contains a fantastic plot about an alternative black government that exists underground at a (fictional) small black college in Texas called Thomas Jefferson College. And when I say underground, I mean literally *underground*. In a scene near the end of the novel, the two main characters are dropped through a secret passageway into a subterranean chamber where a shadow government of black leaders meets beneath the college. Disenchanted with the lack of legal rights for African Americans under U.S. law, this cadre of black leaders had plans to seize land in Texas and form an independent black nation.

Griggs has often been referred to as an early black radical, and there was indeed something radical about publishing such a work of literature that imagines black political independence in a time when outspoken black leaders were often targets of violence. But Finnie D. Coleman's biography of Griggs provides an important corrective to that idea, showing that Griggs actually had more in common with Booker T. Washington than with the radical black leaders depicted in *Imperium in Imperio*. Nevertheless, he was also an admirer of Du Bois's (who was also aware of Griggs), and the novel offers a unique portrait of black education in post-Reconstruction America, one that would seem to confirm the fears that highly educated African Americans could in fact help organize the race into a resistance movement.[8] Though conservative in outlook, Griggs was not entirely an accommodationist, and he wrote eloquently about the dangers of white-supremacist ideology, particularly in the novel *The Hindered Hand*, in which he responds to Thomas Dixon and examines the various permutations of white-supremacist beliefs among different classes and regions of white Americans.

Imperium in Imperio begins as a coming-of-age story about two young men, Belton Piedmont and Bernard Belgrave. Belton, the dark-skinned young man from a poor farming family in Texas, eventually goes on to attend Stowe College in Nashville (named for author Harriet Beecher Stowe of the influential novel *Uncle Tom's Cabin*). Bernard is a light-skinned young man who is light enough to "pass for white" and was raised by his equally light-skinned single mother, who is secretly living off money from the child's wealthy white father (later revealed to be a very prominent white politician). These characters represent the interracial intimacies of plantation life and the routine sexual violence that enslaved women endured at the hands of their enslavers and the complicated genealogical relationships that intertwined the lives of slaves and masters in the postemancipation South. Because of her ties to his father, Bernard's mother is able to give him a comfortable life and the best education, eventually sending him to Harvard University, where he studies law. Therefore, from its inception, class and color are centered in the black academic novel in the form of these two characters, and these concepts would reverberate throughout many subsequent black academic novels.

The narrative begins with Belton Piedmont's mother, Hannah, speaking to her young son as she prepares him for school. In the following passage Griggs distills the widespread education gospel that defined black life in the postemancipation era.

> "Cum er long hunny an' let yer mammy fix yer 'spectabul, so yer ken go to skule. Yer mammy is 'tarmined ter gib yer all de book larning dar is ter be had eben ef she has ter lib on bred an' herrin's, an' die en de a'ms house."

And in the very next line Griggs situates Hannah's commentary in the political struggle of the era.

> These words came from the lips of a poor, ignorant negro woman, and yet the determined course of action which they reveal vitally affected the destiny of a nation and saved the sun of the Nineteenth Century, proud and glorious, from passing through, near its setting, the blackest and thickest and ugliest clouds of all its journey; saved it from ending the most brilliant of brilliant careers by setting, with a shudder of horror, in a sea of human blood.⁹

That passing of the end of the nineteenth century that Griggs refers to here is a period that the historian Rayford Logan dubbed the nadir of black life in America, a period of unspeakable violence and political repression in the wake of Reconstruction. In Hannah's speech Griggs uses the phonetic language of black "dialect" as a class marker (one of the few instances of dialect in the novel), articulating the hopes and aspirations of poor, uneducated blacks who wanted their children and future generations to have educational opportunities that were not available to them. And here we can see from the first pages of the novel the idea of "education as liberation," an idea deployed and interrogated throughout the black academic novel.

But these aspirations were not immediately realized. Black schools often struggled on limited resources, and in this case Griggs paints a disturbing portrait of a white teacher and his violent condescension toward his black students. Hannah is concerned and considers removing young Belton, but the local black preacher (in another passage of dialect in the text) encourages

Hannah to keep him in school. His reasoning indicates an internalization of white-supremacist ideas about black people and the need for discipline.

> Let me gib yer my advis, Sistah Hannah. De greatest ting in de wul is edification. Ef our race ken git dat we ken git ebery t'ing else. Dat is de key. Git de key an' yer kin go in de house to go whare you please. As for his beatin' de brat to make him larn, and won't dat be a blessed t'ing? Se dis scar on side my head? Old marse Sampson knocked me down wid a single-tree tryin' to make me stop larning, and God is so fixed it dat White folks is knocking es down ef we don't larn. Ef yer take Belton out of school yer'll be fighting 'genst de providence of God.[10]

Here Griggs speaks to a prevalent conception of the institution of slavery as a kind of "school" for blacks, as a regime of discipline. The idea is noteworthy because it recurs in the mouths of white characters in Du Bois's fiction as well, and the attitude is also represented among white skeptics of black education, who are concerned that schooling will lead to insubordination and a loss of the work ethic cultivated under enslavement. The parson's words also indicate slavery as a kind of divine Providence, a necessary evil that black folks had to endure to gain the opportunities that were becoming available to them now. As distasteful as these ideas may seem now, Griggs is representing the ways in which African Americans made meaning out of the miseries of their existence and attributed some divine purpose to the suffering and abuse of servitude and racial subjugation.

Griggs continues the critique of the teacher, writing, "Despite the lack of all knowledge of his moral character and previous life, he was pronounced as much too good a man to fritter away his time on 'niggers.' Such was the character of the man into whose hands was committed the destiny of the colored children of Winchester."[11] With this sarcastic dig at white educators Griggs makes the case for the necessity of black teachers in black schools and creatively illustrates the problem that led Du Bois to define his concept of "the talented tenth," that African Americans needed institutions of higher education to train teachers and professors (and other professionals such as doctors, lawyers, and business leaders), otherwise the task of black education would be left up to white teachers, including the unsavory type that Griggs depicts here.

Belton eventually graduates from high school and makes his way to Nashville to attend Stowe University, and it is there that he experiences an epiphany during an assembly, where for the first time he sees a black professor. It is clearly meant to be an important moment in Belton's life, and it is a moment that also signifies so much of what the black academic novel is about and its meaning as a vehicle for representing black higher education. The black professor in the scene is introduced as a new and heretofore unforeseen possibility. "To Belton's surprise he saw a colored man, sitting on the right side of and next to the president." The very presence of a black person onstage next to the white teachers, not as a servant but as a peer, was a stunning sight for Belton. "He let his eyes scan the faces of all the white teachers, male and female, but would end up with a stare at the colored man sitting there." Belton had known that there was a colored teacher at the school but "had no idea that he would be thus honored with a seat with the rest of the teachers." And during the prayer at the assembly Griggs writes that "though he, as a rule, shut his eyes when prayer was being offered, he kept them open that morning, and peeked through his fingers at that thrilling sight,—a colored man on equal terms with the white college professors."[12]

In this passage Griggs provides a stark portrayal of how the de facto segregation of the South did not stop at the gates of the black campuses. In fact, Atlanta University, where Du Bois taught and which he depicts in *The Black Flame*, was specifically known as a troublesome institution by white politicians in Georgia because the school had chosen to integrate its dining facilities, a topic that Du Bois addresses in his depiction of the college and its politics. Here in *Imperium in Imperio* Griggs uses the representation of a black professor, and the possibilities of that professor living in an integrated context, as a way to introduce the first inkling of social equality into Belton's mind.

Later Belton tries to sneak outside the building where a faculty meeting was being held so that he could get another look at the professor. "Knowing that the colored teacher was vice-president of the faculty, he saw that he would preside. Belton determined to see that meeting of the faculty if it cost him no end of trouble. He could not afford, under any circumstances, to fail to see that colored man preside over those white men and women."[13] But in his attempt to eavesdrop on the meeting he is nearly discovered by another professor who walks in, and Belton flees into a nearby chicken coop. Here Griggs is deliberately playing with a derogatory image common to the minstrel shows of his time, that of the Negro chicken thief, which is what the faculty determines is the result of the commotion as they laugh it off and resume the meeting. And in the subsequent passage Griggs drives the point home in eloquent, if melodramatic, fashion: "Thus again a patriot is mistaken for a chicken thief; and in the South to-day a race that dreams freedom, equality, and empire, far more than is imagined, is put down as a race of chicken thieves."[14]

The students get together and decide that this black professor should not have to eat separately, as was the custom in all other spaces in the South, and that he should be allowed to dine with his white coworkers. This small measure of integration becomes a cause taken up by the students. It is remarkable that this early novel has a story line of student activism, showing the students banding together to demand a significant political change to the campus culture. They deliver a letter to the president with the demand, which the president dismissively addresses in an assembly. The students quietly refuse to leave the assembly, and at Belton's signal lift their hands to show each hand bearing a small sign saying, "Equality or Death." The teachers were taken aback and quickly huddled and agreed to make the change and allow the black professor to eat with them. "The students broke forth into cheering, and flaunted a black flag on which was painted in white letters; 'Victory.' They rose and marched out of doors two by two, singing John Brown's Body lies mouldering in the grave, and we go marching on."[15] And with that victory the seeds were planted for Belton's militancy, though they would not sprout until later in the story. But in this narrative Griggs is showing the possibilities of confidence that the educational environment could instill in these students, as if to say yes to all those white supremacists, yes, this is exactly what black education will lead to, and you better get ready for it!

And to cap off that episode of protest, Griggs remarkably uses a term that would soon become popular, referring to a "new Negro" that had emerged out of the protest, writing that "the cringing, fawning, sniffling, cowardly Negro which slavery left, had disappeared, amid a new Negro, self-respecting, fearless, and determined [that] the assertion of his rights was at hand."[16] Literary scholar Hugh Gloster, an early critic of Griggs's work (and later president of Morehouse College) had years ago identified Griggs's novel as the first literary work in which the term "New Negro" is used in this context, and Coleman's biography confirms that this is likely the case.[17] Griggs uses the term later in the novel in the Resolutions drafted by the Imperium. The document states that the Imperium must "endeavor to impress the Anglo-Saxon that he has a New Negro on his hands and must surrender what belongs to him."[18] With these two clear references, Griggs anticipates the figure of the New Negro who would emerge twenty-five years later when Harvard graduate and Howard University philosophy professor Alain Locke edits the famous *Survey Graphic* issue on "The New Negro," signaling a new movement of thought, art, and politics centered in the New York neighborhood of Harlem and reaching around the globe. That movement was fueled by the very phenomenon that Griggs describes here, the experiences of young black people growing up beyond the shackles of slavery, many of them now living in cities, who are more college educated than ever before, filled with new ideas of social equality, with a new political militancy for civil rights, and new visions of artistic freedom. But their college education could be fraught with problems in a society entrenched in white supremacy, and *Imperium in Imperio* also depicts a phenomenon often referenced in black literature, that of the overeducated African American who has difficulty finding employment or works as a laborer despite having a college education, a trope featured prominently in Ralph Ellison's *Invisible Man*, where the narrator, in New York, is repeatedly referred to by his coworkers and neighbors as a "college boy" and finds himself in a liminal space as someone with too much education to do manual jobs yet also locked out of professions where he might utilize his education.

Belton graduates from Stowe, moves to Virginia, where he works for a while as a schoolteacher, and gets married. He also starts a side project of publishing a small newspaper in the community. However, his decision to run a controversial article about black voter disfranchisement ends up getting him fired, and he has to search for another job. The passage about that episode is worth quoting and evaluating at length.

> Belton began to cast around for another occupation, but, in whatever direction he looked, he saw no hope. He possessed a first class college education, but that was all. He knew no trade nor was he equipped to enter any of the professions. It is true that there were positions around by the thousands which he could fill, but his color debarred him. He would have made an excellent drummer, salesman, clerk, cashier, government official (county, city, state, or national), telegraph operator, conductor, or any thing of such a nature. But the color of his skin shut the doors so tight that he could not even peep in.
>
> The white people would not employ him in these positions, and the colored people did not have any enterprises in which they could employ him. It is true that such positions as street laborer, hod-carrier, cart driver, factory hand, railroad hand, were open to him; but such menial tasks were uncongenial to a man of his education and polish. And, again, society positively forbade him doing such labor.
>
> If a man of education among the colored people did such manual labor, he was looked upon as an eternal disgrace to the race. He was looked upon as throwing his education away and lowering its value in the eyes of the children who were to come after him.[19]

The line "he knew no trade" seems like a confirmation of Booker T. Washington's warnings about humanistic education and the need for vocational training and makes Belton's anxiety of overeducation seem justified. That "white people would not employ him in these positions" is owing to the idea that education marks him as someone potentially uppity and disobedient and overqualified for service jobs. Griggs addresses a sincere concern among black people about employability after college, as the educated black worker could end up stuck in a kind of professional purgatory, too educated for the labor that whites wanted him to do but not able to find employment as a black professional in the black community, where there was no infrastructure to support his skills ("the colored people did not have any enterprises in which they could employ him"). And in the sentences that follow, Griggs makes a direct connection between this question of black higher education and labor.

> This set Belton to studying the labor situation and the race question from this point of view. He found scores of young men just in his predicament. The schools were all supplied with teachers. All other doors were effectually barred. Society's stern edict forbade these young men resorting to lower forms of labor. And instead of the matter growing

better, it was growing worse, year by year. Colleges were rushing class after class forth with just his kind of education, and there was no employment for them.[20]

Griggs's prescient analysis of the relationship between race, labor, and education anticipates similar concerns that Du Bois takes up in *The Quest of the Silver Fleece* with his depiction of the cotton economy in the South and how it represented a challenge to establishing black schools, since southern politicians were concerned that educated blacks would compromise the labor needed to sustain profits in the cotton economy, whether by refusing to work or by encouraging black laborers to demand higher wages, rebel, or organize. As much as black educators were invested in the idea of an educated black populace, they had real concerns about their employment, even though educators like Du Bois understood that there were other potential social benefits of higher education that made it a politically worthwhile endeavor.

Furthermore, this is an instance where black academic narratives belong in contemporary conversations about higher education and labor. In the works by Griggs and Du Bois at the dawn of the twentieth century (and later in works by Nella Larsen, Ralph Ellison, and Chester Himes) black intellectuals were thinking about issues that not only affected black workers but also would become prevalent for the educational policy of the nation as a whole. From this depiction of education and labor in Griggs's novel, one can easily project out toward much larger questions. If one cannot find employment after receiving a college education, then what is the purpose of college? Was college ever meant to be a vehicle for increased earning potential? Should college be a place for the pursuit of knowledge or mere professional training, or both? Is there some greater collective value to college that justifies it as a public investment beyond individual employment? Again, how might our approach to critical university studies be different if we made these narratives, and these concerns on the part of black intellectuals, central to our theorizations of what the university is, what it has been, and what it could be?

Imperium in Imperio is also remarkable for Griggs's attention to matters of gender and sexuality. There are two scenes in particular that call out for a queer of color critique. The first comes when Belton goes to New York disguised as a black woman. Through this fascinating story line Griggs shows Belton fighting off the sexual advances of white men and addresses the constant threats of rape that black women lived with as domestic workers. Although the gender transgression is played up for comedy and is meant to be a practical illustration of black women's oppression, there is also an element of homoeroticism in this scene and elsewhere in another scene where Belton is nearly lynched.

In one of the most fantastic sequences of the novel, Belton is cornered by a lynch mob, hanged, and shot but manages to survive the lynching. Before Belton is attacked, the character Dr. Zackland urges the mob to keep his body intact for scientific observation, a plot development that points to the prevalence of scientific racism and a history of black bodies as nonconsensual objects of scientific experimentation. Dr. Zackland clearly takes a perverse pleasure in Belton's body before and after the lynching. Grigg pays attention to the white male gaze in his descriptions of Zackland ogling Belton's (living) body, particularly with the vivid line "The doctor's eyes followed him cadaverously."[21] The homoeroticism in this scene constructs the white supremacist as a figure of perversion (while also bearing homophobic undertones), and it speaks to what scholars have theorized about the relationship between race and sexuality, that the language of racial difference is often articulated through beliefs and observations about bodily and sexual difference.[22]

The Dr. Zackland character may be partly influenced by the white-supremacist physician John H. Van Evrie and his infamous tract of antiblack propaganda, the 1867 book *White Supremacy and Negro Subordination, or Negroes a Subordinate Race and Slavery Its Normal Condition*, one of the earliest texts in American literature to explicitly use the phrase "white supremacy" and articulate its meaning in scientific terms. Van Evrie's book is mentioned directly in *Imperium*, and it is responsible for the tragic suicide of Bernard Belgrave's fiancée, Viola, who is black and agrees to marry Bernard but later kills herself because of her belief in white-supremacist myths about miscegenation, that the children of "mulattoes" were defective. In her suicide note she cites Van Evrie's *White Supremacy* on how racial intermixture was sapping the black race of its vitality. She writes of how she had sworn never to marry a mulatto man but had fallen in love with Bernard, and she instructs him to "study the question of the intermingling of the races" so that the issue may be settled and understood. In this development, Griggs melodramatically registers the cost of white-supremacist pseudoscience. The plot development is certainly sensational, but it is also an indicator of how Griggs is thinking about the consequences of faulty knowledge and misinformation about race and reproduction.

The real-life physician John Van Evrie is also documented in Craig Steven Wilder's *Ebony and Ivy*, and Wilder links him to the development of race science at elite white universities, noting how he translated and published racist scholarship from Europe to help disseminate it in the United States.[23] To read the history documented in *Ebony and Ivy* along with academic novels by Griggs, Du Bois, and others is to reckon with the role of white research universities as producers of proslavery propaganda (in the humanities and sciences) and as incubators for pseudoscientific knowledge on race and sexuality that would have a lasting effect on American culture and thought for generations to come.

Eventually Belton Piedmont and Bernard Belgrave reunite at Thomas Jefferson College in Waco, Texas, and it is there that we learn of this clandestine group known as the Imperium, which has tapped Bernard, now a Harvard-trained lawyer, to be the leader. Bernard falls down into the Imperium meeting where Belton is already involved. Bernard finds that Jefferson College is in reality the capital of a black shadow government. The story line speaks to the subversive potential of the black intellectual, and Griggs imagines the institution as a clandestine site of black resistance. The name of the college evokes Thomas Jefferson and his conflicted legacy as founder of the University of Virginia, as an Enlightenment man of letters, as America's first great philosopher-president, as an advocate for the importance of education in a participatory democracy, and as the owner of more than two hundred human beings as property. Query XIV in *Notes on the State of Virginia* articulates his scientifically racist thinking about black bodies and sexuality and the aptitude of blacks for hard labor. His thoughts on the black poet Phillis Wheatley's work are particularly revealing of his belief that her writing, and the writing of any black person, could be only an imitative parlor trick at best and could never achieve the heights of classical literature. The irony of this Imperium at Jefferson College is that according to the man for whom it is named, such a group was a scientific and metaphysical impossibility. The beliefs about black intelligence underscore the racist idea behind the "outside agitator" as an instigator for black discontent. From slave revolts, to the civil rights movement, to Black Lives Matter, the ideas about black intelligence are the source material for the trope that blacks are incapable of organizing themselves and therefore *must* have received help from other nefarious groups if there were any signs of organized disobedience. Griggs understood that by depicting the Imperium he was depicting the very danger of educated Negroes that white supremacists had been warning everyone about, and depicting the cognitive dissonance at the heart of white supremacy and its beliefs about black educability, beliefs that said the black person is intellectually inferior and incapable of higher forms of thinking, but also that black education was dangerous and needed to be contained.

The last several pages of the novel, in which Griggs explains the mission of the Imperium and the reasons why it was formed, include an incisive analysis of the legal, cultural, and economic condition of African Americans in the postemancipation era, stating that "for the Emancipation Proclamation, as we all know, came not so much as a message of love for the slave as a message of love for the Union; its primary object was to save the Union, its incident, to liberate the slave."[24] And part of what this Imperium narrative accomplishes is a further challenge to Booker T. Washington's ideas by enumerating the ways that a lack of civil rights restricts the possibility of black advancement without any protection under the law and without the right to participate in government. "In olden times, revolutions were effected by the sword and spear. In modern times the ballot has been used for that purpose. But the ballot has been snatched from our hands. The modern implement of revolutions has been denied us."[25] The Imperium also speaks to the hypocrisy of white political support for black education without a commitment to further economic and racial justice when it states that "[Whites] will contribute the public funds to educate the negro and then exert every possible influence to keep the negro from earning a livelihood by means of that education"[26]

The full text of the Imperium's "Resolution 3" shows the context in which Griggs uses the term "New Negro" and the radical political action associated with it:

> 3. *Resolved.* That we spend four years in endeavors to impress the Anglo-Saxon that he has a New Negro on his hands and must surrender what belongs to him. In case we fail by those means to secure our rights and privileges we shall, all at once, abandon our several homes in the various other states and emigrate in a body to the State of Texas, broad in domain, rich in soil and salubrious in climate. Having an unquestioned majority of votes we shall secure possession of the State government.[27]

For these reasons the Imperium decides that an independent black nation is the only solution. This passage and others like it show Griggs's novel to be an important document of black nationalist thought, an ideology that began to coalesce in the pre–Civil War era with the protest pamphlets of David Walker and the speeches of convention lecturers such as Maria W. Stewart and, most notably, in Martin Delany's *Blake, or the Huts of America*, the groundbreaking 1852 novel that advocated emigrationism and articulated the idea of black America as "a nation within a nation," a concept directly invoked in Griggs's title *Imperium in Imperio*.[28] Black nationalism would soon find one of its most visible and important iterations two decades later, during the New Negro Movement that Griggs prophesied, with Marcus Garvey's Universal Negro Improvement Association in the 1920s.

Griggs's idea of a black collectivism in the South would be taken up on different terms by W. E. B. Du Bois in *The Quest of the Silver Fleece*. Du Bois's vision of a black socialism is not presented in the clandestine revolutionary terms that Griggs imagined but as a program of collective economics that would help to create an infrastructure for black financial independence and prosperity, social equality and education, even if necessarily on Jim Crow's separatist terms.

A Fellow of Fisk and Harvard

> "But Mrs. Vanderpool," she protested, "is it right? Is it fair? Why should we spoil this black girl and put impossible ideas into her head? You can make her a perfect maid, but she can never be much more in America."
> —*The Quest of the Silver Fleece*

The black girl here is Zora, the heroine of Du Bois's *The Quest of the Silver Fleece*.[29] It must be said up front that there is no evidence that the name of the character has anything to do with Zora Neale Hurston, the black novelist, folklorist, and anthropologist born in 1891 in Alabama—though the synchronicity is striking. Du Bois composed this novel about an independently minded, educated black woman from Alabama while Hurston was living, and he would become aware of Hurston later, as a fellow member of the black intellectual elite in Harlem. The quote is from the white Alabama schoolteacher Miss Smith to her wealthy New York friend Mrs. Vanderpool, who wants to take Zora on as her domestic servant. The arrangement eventually allows Zora to travel to New York with Mrs. Vanderpool by train and see the country for the first time. It also allows Zora time to read and learn, and it indirectly alters Mrs. Vanderpool's ideas about the intellectual potential of black people.

The quote encapsulates a prevalent attitude among the white characters who populate Du Bois's *The Quest of the Silver Fleece*, people whom Du Bois himself undoubtedly observed in his own time. They weren't necessarily opposed to a black girl being educated, but what good could it possibly do her? ("It would only make him discontent and unhappy," said Frederick Douglass's slave master about *his* literacy). Once again, we see the "overeducation of the Negro" appearing in a work of academic fiction, this belief that any serious education for black people was actually overeducation, that basic literacy and manual-labor skills were all they needed to get by, and that anything more could be dangerous. Understanding this discourse is the key to understanding how *The Quest of the Silver Fleece* functions as an academic novel of the post-Reconstruction South, where slavery was still a fresh wound and cotton still king.

The Quest of the Silver Fleece is Du Bois's first novel, but he had been experimenting with academic fiction from the beginning of his literary career. I maintain that Du Bois's creative writing projects, finished and unfinished, along with his sociological and historical work on black higher education, constitute an underrated archive with which to theorize the academic novel. Why did someone who had written so extensively about black education in other forms decide to write novels about higher education? This is a scholar who had conducted the groundbreaking Atlanta University Studies, a series of sociological studies that Du Bois resourcefully directed with little money and a meager staff of a few black scholars. Of the sixteen Atlanta University Studies that he supervised, four of them dealt specifically with black education. They include *The College Bred Negro* (1900), the first systematic study ever completed about African Americans in higher education, along with *The Negro Common School* (1901), *The College-Bred Negro American* (1910), and *The Common School and the Negro American* (1911).[30] Du Bois's sociological work on the black neighborhoods of Atlanta and Philadelphia laid the foundation for the discipline of sociology itself, as Aldon D. Morris argues in his 2015 study *The Scholar Denied: W. E. B. Du Bois and the Birth of Modern Sociology*. Du Bois had proven himself to be a gifted essayist and polemicist, reaching the pinnacle of literary accomplishment with *The Souls of Black Folk* in 1903. And along with all those writings Du Bois also found time to nurture his artistic side, feeling strongly enough about the art of the novel that he composed one that was eventually published in 1911. He would go on to publish five novels in all across his lengthy lifetime, and he drafted at least one more, a proposed work about black religion and the AME Church. What meaning did Du Bois find in the genre of the novel? What could the novel express that his other work could not? I believe that to think through some potential answers to these questions is to work toward an understanding of the academic novel's function and relevance in literary history.

Du Bois published his first work of fiction, "Tom Brown at Fisk," as a serialized story in three parts in the *Fisk Herald* between December 1887 and March 1888, when he was an undergraduate there. The title "Tom Brown at Fisk" is taken from Thomas Hughes's popular student novel *Tom Brown's Schooldays* (1857) and its less-popular but still influential sequel, *Tom Brown at Oxford* (1861). In *The English University Novel* (1957), an early study of academic fiction, Mortimer Proctor discusses the significance of *Tom Brown at Oxford* as an iconic work of university fiction. In one particularly interesting passage Proctor writes of the influence of Christian socialist reformer Frederick Denison Maurice on Hughes's work and thought, stating that "it was Maurice who, working in the slums of London, made Hughes aware of the hard world of poverty and suffering, and aroused in him the political and social consciousness that led him into the active practice of what he called 'the noble side of democracy.'"[31] The quote certainly resonates with Du Bois's own literary approach to academic fiction, depicting the tough lives of the formerly enslaved and rural poor who were being given their first opportunities at education after emancipation. It also resonates with the sociological work of *The Philadelphia Negro* (1899), in which Du Bois brought a social-scientific analysis to the urban problems of Philadelphia. So perhaps Du Bois saw in Thomas Hughes's writing a model for his own ideas about the relationship between literature, higher education, and social policy. It is striking that in the midst of all the sociological and historical writing that he did in his life, and all the political activism that he was involved in, Du Bois saw creative writing as an important vehicle for his ideas and chose the form of academic fiction in particular as the means by which to share these ideas. Du Bois would explore his ideas about black art and creativity directly in his late-career trilogy *The Black Flame*.

The earliest evidence of Du Bois's efforts to compose a novel, and another key piece in my claim for Du Bois as an academic novelist, is a two-page sketch of 1892 for a novel titled "A Fellow of Harvard." The proposed main character of the story is a Midwestern white farm boy who dreams of going to Harvard, eventually manages to gain entry there, goes on a fellowship to Europe, where he becomes indoctrinated as a socialist, and eventually returns to America, where he finds a position teaching at a southern black college.

Plot of a Novel

A Fellow of Harvard

The hero is a western farmboy of N. E. ancestry—somewhat eccentric from childhood. His delight in school (in St. Paul) was to pore over a Harvard Catalog and structure himself a fellow of Harvard. He wins the prize in his school which sends him a year to college. His committee prejudiced against Harvard wish him to go to x-coll. He tries to enter Harvard but passes an indiff. examination & rec'd no aid. He enters x, and after first year is supported by a church & urged to enter the ministry. He is disgusted by the narrowness at x—leaves before graduation and writes a capital brochure which secures him aid at Harvard where he enters as a Junior. His Junior year is spent in struggles for scholarships, his senior in questionings as to the meaning of life & what course he should follow. He misses aid for Senior year but secures prize & works. He secures no class day honors but his commencement secures him a fellowship. At the goal of his ambition he stands dazed and becomes a dabbler and only half does his seminary work, which however shows such promise he receives a European fellowship. He only half understands Europe—studies not at all, & becomes an avowed socialist. Returning therefore to America, the unreadiness of his thesis will not permit him to take his doctors degree. He seeks in vain for a position & at last finds one at a Southern Negro school where his eccentricities get him trouble with the blacks & his radicalism with the whites. His thesis now published is a brilliant success & secures him a position in the college of x—where his ideals clash with the mammonism & materialism of his surroundings. He neglects his duties & writes his masterpiece. At the same time that politics secure his dismissal his work is published. It falls flat amid much ridicule. He already monomaniac becomes hopelessly insane and dies "a fellow of Harvard"

Berlin
7 Dec '92

The sketch's ending, with the main character running afoul of the administration and falling into insanity, is reminiscent of the tragic narrative of Thomas Hardy's classic Oxford novel *Jude the Obscure*, which would appear four years later, in 1896. Even this outline of "A Fellow of Harvard" reflects Janice Rossen's argument in *The University in Modern Fiction* that in the academic novel the university is often depicted as a place of power, inclusion, and exclusion. Du Bois, perceptive as ever, and from the marrow of his experiences as the first black Ph.D. student at Harvard, certainly understood that universities were not neutral spaces of knowledge acquisition and production but were places specifically tasked with reproducing structures of hierarchy and exclusion that ran along lines of race and class.

The Souls of Black Folk contains more evidence of his interest in the genre of academic fiction. Two chapters in particular contribute to an understanding of Du Bois's engagement with the academic novel. The first, "Of the Coming of John," is an academic short story in which Du Bois depicts an allegory of two Johns, one black, one white, and the different directions that their lives take. The story deeply resonated with my own educational experiences when I first read it in an honors literature class in college. The part that struck me the most was the depiction of black John and the way that education unexpectedly drove a wedge between him and his people, something that I felt beginning to happen to me as well. In a remarkable conversation, his little sister asks John about his education.

> "John," she said, "does it make everyone unhappy when they study and learn lots of things?" He paused and smiled. "I am afraid it does," he said.
> "And John, are you glad you studied?"
> "Yes," came the answer, slowly but positively.
> She watched the flickering lights upon the sea, and said thoughtfully, "I wish I was unhappy,—and—and," putting both arms about his neck, "I think I am, a little, John."[32]

The story depicts the way that for the intellectual from a poor, rural, or working-class background, education can be a source of social alienation. This phenomenon appears in several works of academic fiction, including John Williams's melancholy academic novel *Stoner*, where the English professor William Stoner, who grew up on his family's farm in Missouri, drifts away from his agrarian background and into academic life, and the 1983 *Pygmalion*-inspired film *Educating Rita*, in which a middle-aged, working-class white woman gets turned on to the life of the mind and eventually finds it difficult to relate to her family and friends.

"Of the Meaning of Progress," an autobiographical narrative of his teaching days in rural Tennessee while at Fisk, is a key text in the evolution of Du Bois's racial consciousness. As Arnold Rampersad puts it, "At Fisk and elsewhere in Nashville he had been introduced to the children of the black middle-class or to other blacks who had adapted to an urban situation. Around his impoverished country schoolhouse Du Bois met for the first time the black peasant masses, who lived totally removed from the impact of formal education."[33] This experience gave Du Bois an understanding of just how repressive white supremacy could be in the former slave states, and *The Souls of Black Folk* is a record of his spiritual awakening. The book is a testament of his insights into the brutality of enslavement and Jim Crow, the desperation of rural black poverty, and the unique gifts of black culture, which found their most profound expression in what he famously dubbed the sorrow songs, a musical form he did not grow up with and that he first heard while living in the South.

The setting and the people of rural Tennessee would also lend Du Bois much of the material for *The Quest of the Silver Fleece*. The tragic narrative of poverty and a lack of educational opportunities that concludes with Josie's death in "Of the Meaning of Progress" is given a more hopeful trajectory in *The Quest of the Silver Fleece*, with characters who strive for higher educational opportunities despite the lack of resources and with an educated heroine who takes on the Jim Crow plantation system. It is a story of black education that ties the uplift narrative of educational destiny to the political economy of the cotton trade and to the need for political rights that would allow African Americans control over their own labor, and the fierce opposition and obstacles they faced in doing so.

In his 2016 article "'Behold the Land': W. E. B. Du Bois, Cotton Futures, and the Afterlife of the Plantation in the US South," Jarvis McInnis begins his analysis of *The Quest of the Silver Fleece* by noting how previous scholars have focused on the matter of genre in their interpretations of the novel, particularly through the "interplay of romance, realism, and naturalism."[34] While I, too, am guilty of approaching *Quest* through genre by drawing out Du Bois's emphasis on higher education and reading it as an academic novel, I also remain attentive to the labor and economics in the novel, and McInnis's article illuminates Du Bois's exploration of the "afterlife of the plantation" and the role of the cotton economy in the lives of his black southern characters. In fact, these two aspects of the novel are related, since Du Bois situates the challenge of building black higher education in the context of labor, the South's plantation economy, and its Jim Crow legal structures. In *Quest* Du Bois repeatedly addresses the fact that resistance to black higher education was often driven by white fears about what education would do to the black worker.

The Quest of the Silver Fleece charts Zora's evolution in her ideas about books and education. Early in the novel Zora is skeptical about education, recognizing that education has not made the white people who rule over them any more moral. By the end of the novel Zora comes to embrace the power of books, and Du Bois depicts her intellectual and political growth.

The novel begins with young Bles traveling through the woods on his way to school. It is on this journey that he meets his romantic interest, Zora, who lives in the swamp, and Du Bois associates the swamp with their hopes and dreams, an undeveloped place where they would devise a scheme to make money from cotton on their own land, away from the plantations where much of the Tooms County, Alabama, black population worked. Bles meets Zora while traveling from his home state of Georgia to the Tooms County school run by the white teacher Miss Smith. Zora is initially skeptical of Bles's educational aspirations. But Bles argues with her that "even if white folks don't know everything, they know different things from us, and we ought to know what they know."[35]

Miss Smith is also the principal of the black school, and she is trying to convince her wealthy white friends to help fund her educational mission. Mary Taylor is a white Wellesley graduate who reluctantly comes South to Miss Smith's school to teach there at the behest of her brother John Taylor, a Wall Street speculator who paid her way through college and now wants her to run interference for his economic interests in the South, particularly to make connections with the Cresswell family, the largest plantation owner in Tooms County. Through this story line of these two wealthy white families from the North and South, Du Bois ties the cotton economy of the South to corporate interests of the North, and the novel represents a kind of triangular relationship between Alabama, Wall Street, and Washington, D.C.

Zora is a remarkable character as one of the earliest dark-skinned heroines in American literature. As Nellie McKay puts it, *The Quest of the Silver Fleece* is "the first novel in the black American literary canon in which a woman, black in color, stands at the center, not in a stereotypical role, but as an autonomous, positive character in a position of leadership."[36] Du Bois's depiction of young Zora is that of a free-spirited country girl, witty and full of raw intelligence and rightfully suspicious of formal education. Describing her at the beginning of chapter 5, he writes, "Zora, child of the swamp, was a heathen hoyden of twelve wayward, untrained years. Slight, straight, strong, full-blooded, she had dreamed her life away in wilful wandering through her dark and sombre kingdom until she was one with it in all its moods; mischievous, secretive, brooding; full of great and awful visions, steeped body and soul in wood-lore."[37] In one scene at the school Miss Taylor calls out to Zora, who pretends that she does not hear her. Miss Taylor then attempts to lecture Zora on the virtues of honesty, but Zora flips the script on her and in her sharp rebuttal to Miss Taylor questions her patronizing attitude and her obvious discomfort with the black children. "Is it wrong," asked Zora, "to make believe you likes people when you don't, when you'se afeared of them and thinks they may rub off and dirty you?"[38]

Colonel Cresswell meanwhile is suspicious of this whole Negro education enterprise, and he says so outright: "Damn it! This thing is going too far. We can't keep a maid or plough-boy in the place because of this devilish school. It's going to ruin the whole labor system."[39] The goal of the planters, and the northern speculators, is to keep the plantation economy that existed before the Civil War humming along and profitable, and black education was only valuable to the extent that it helped to achieve that goal and fortified the existing racial hierarchy. And Creswell was particularly suspicious of Bles for this reason, because he represents what might happen if this education went too far: "Mr. Creswell knew the Negro by sight and disliked him. He belonged in his mind to that younger class of half-educated blacks who were impudent and disrespectful toward their superiors, not even touching his hat when he met a white man." Cresswell thinks that "if this went on, the day would surely come when Negroes felt no respect or fear whatever for whites? And then—my God!"[40]

In one scene, a local white minister, Dr. Boldish, visits Miss Smith's school and speaks to the students, and what he says to them is indicative of the discourse of overeducation in the novel: "Remember that slavery of your people was not necessarily a crime. It was a school of work and love. It gave you noble friends, like Mr. Cresswell here."[41] There's a perverse validity in what he says. Slavery was a kind of school, and the regimes of discipline in enslavement were a kind of education designed to condition the enslaved to her place outside whiteness and humanity. Formal education had the potential to erode those carefully maintained boundaries, and no one saw that more clearly than the southern white leaders, who made it their business to keep watch over what was being taught in black schools.

The chapter "The Rape of the Fleece" is essential to understanding Du Bois's political philosophy and his criticism of Booker T. Washington's accommodationism. Zora takes the cotton that she has worked so hard to cultivate and plans to sell it to Colonel Cresswell, but Cresswell insists that she owes back debts and takes the cotton from her without pay, stealing the fruit of her labor knowing that she has no legal recourse to take it back or get a fair price for it.[42] The plot development underscores the critical importance of legal rights for black people in the Jim Crow South, for without any legal standing this kind of theft of labor, wages, and property was routine and would remain so no matter how hard they worked. Similarly, other acts of violence were perpetrated against black citizens, and their assailants could never be held accountable in court systems run by white supremacists. But eventually Zora manages to outwit Colonel Cresswell in court, in a remarkable passage that depicts how pervasive were the legal and spiritual underpinnings of white supremacy.

With *The Quest of the Silver Fleece* Du Bois positions the educational narrative in a larger political economy. For Bles and Zora the cotton fields are essential to their livelihoods. The latter chapters of the novel feature a kind of speculative utopian experiment wherein Du Bois considers what conditions would have to exist for black self-determination in the South, a self-determination that would allow for the cultivation of a black intellectual class. It certainly could not exist under the current system of peonage, which was a continuation of the plantation system. As he puts it in the narrative, "No Negro starved on the Creswell place, neither did any accumulate property. Colonel Cresswell saw to both matters."[43] Du Bois challenges the perception of slavery as something that ended in 1865, showing how the plantation economy, with its racialized hierarchy and lack of legal recognition and its default plundering of black wealth and labor, persisted well beyond emancipation and continued to prevent black financial or political independence.

A key moment comes near the end of the novel after Bles returns home from his adventures in Washington, D.C., and after Zora returns from a stint traveling as the domestic servant for Mrs. Vanderpool. By this time Zora has taken control of the house of the aging Miss Smith. When Bles enters Zora's room and sees her books, Zora tells him, "This is my university." In Arnold Rampersad's study of Du Bois's creative writing he emphasizes the significance of the books that Du Bois lists: Plato, Gorky, Balzac, Spencer, Tennyson.[44] Embedded in this scene is that familiar Du Boisian notion of liberal education as a key ingredient in the development of black self-determination. But in a gesture to Washington's utilitarianism, Zora's book collection also includes an encyclopedia of agriculture. "This is my university" also marks the absent presence of higher education in the narrative. This is an academic novel of a thwarted education. Zora, Bles, and the other black characters are specifically missing the opportunity to pursue a higher education because of a lack of opportunity and institutions, which Du Bois shows is directly related to the economy of the South, which keeps them bound to the land.

Du Bois sounds a remarkably feminist note in the novel's melodramatic conclusion. When Bles returns and sees all that Zora has accomplished, he is forced to revise the way that he had once seen her: "His mental attitude toward Zora had always been one of guidance, guardianship, and instruction. He had been judging and weighing her from on high, looking down upon her with thoughts of uplift and development."[45] Zora initially rejected his marriage proposal upon his return, but in the end Zora reverses gender roles and proposes to Bles. Du Bois, playing off the genre expectations of the marriage plot and the happy ending, ensures that Zora ends up being the hero. She defies the patriarchal leadership of the black church, whose pastor questioned her plans to build up the swamp; she outwits Colonel Cresswell in court to get the money she was owed for the cotton she helped to cultivate; and on top of that she gets her man back in the end!

Du Bois creates one of the first dark-skinned heroines in African American literature and thereby addresses the prevalence of colorism as a component of antiblack racism, although his own attitudes toward color in his literature would remain complex. The issue of color speaks to the racialized embodiment of the black intellectual, and it's a topic that black academic novelists return to repeatedly to address the lived experiences of race as a bodily experience, not just an intellectual abstraction. Race is often read, and misread, according to skin color and body type, and in black literary history this topic receives more extensive treatment in works such as Wallace Thurman's *The Blacker the Berry* and James Weldon Johnson's *Autobiography of an Ex-Colored Man*. Colorism plays a prominent role in academic novels as well, a topic I evaluate further in my readings of Nella Larsen's *Quicksand* and Chester Himes's The *Third Generation*.

Du Bois's fiction provides the case for all academic fiction. Despite the nonfiction writing that he had already done, the academic novel was for him a way to contribute to the creation of a black literary canon. *The Quest of the*

Silver Fleece was his attempt to aestheticize the black educational experience, to give it a heroic trajectory, to solve the problem that he had laid out in "Of the Coming of John," of the melancholic condition of the black intellectual estranged between two worlds. The novels that follow *Imperium* and *The Quest of the Silver Fleece* document this struggle, with students matriculating through HBCUs and predominantly white institutions (PWIs) alike, navigating the land mines of bigotry, while confronting existential questions about the nature of academic institutions. All these novels insist upon complex portrayals of black life, refusing to be stories of respectability and hat-in-hand pleas for humanity. Having spent several years reading these novels—melodramas, tragedies, satires, with highbrow and lowbrow themes—I now see them as a means for black intellectuals to articulate their subjectivity as intellectuals, artists, producers of knowledge, to talk back against white supremacy, to share with other black intellectuals that the very idea of a blackademic life is possible, and that such a life need not follow a script of servility and subservience but one of confidence and self-determination.

At the beginning of *The Quest of the Silver Fleece* Du Bois articulates his own take on the aesthetics of the novel:

> He who would tell a tale must look toward three ideals: to tell it well, to tell it beautifully, and to tell the truth.
> The first is the Gift of God, the second is the Vision of Genius, but the third is the Reward of Honesty.

Ironically, scholars have questioned his abilities as an artist and whether his novels told the story beautifully. I come back to this idea of Du Bois's aesthetics and explore it further in my analysis of *The Black Flame*. For now, I will say that my approach to the black academic novel involves mining it for its thematic and political significance, but I always keep at the center of my analysis that it is a work of art produced by artists who aimed to tell their stories beautifully (by whatever aesthetic standards they chose), and I try to honor that artistic vision even as I plumb them for my own selfish purposes. I try to keep in mind that for these artists there are myriad strategies through which they can pursue their own aesthetic visions of black life.

In the years after *Imperium in Imperio* and *The Quest of the Silver Fleece*, the artistic ideals that Du Bois and Griggs expressed in their groundbreaking black academic novels would be taken up by a new cadre of young writers, who would go on to fulfill Sutton Griggs's prescient vision of the New Negro.

Chapter 3

✦

The New Negro, 1919–1954

The New Negro, whom Sutton Griggs saw on the horizon in the 1890s, emerged in the form of the New Negro Movement, also known as the Harlem Renaissance, a literary and cultural movement led mainly, but not exclusively, by college-educated black intellectuals. From its first announcement with a 1925 *Survey Graphic* issue on "The New Negro" edited by Alain Locke (a Harvard graduate, Howard University philosophy professor, and Rhodes Scholar) the politics and consequences of this movement have been debated endlessly. The works that came after this complex movement have expounded upon some of its central themes, including urbanization, education, black pride, black cultural production, uplift ideology, and the politics of gender and sexuality. The literature of the Harlem Renaissance proved to be an important venue for the literary depiction of black intellectuals and academics, and the movement's literary, cultural, and political influences would appear in many later works of academic fiction.

This period that I have isolated comprises the active years of the Harlem Renaissance, generally dated from around 1919 to 1936, and the two decades after, a period the literary critic Lawrence Jackson calls the indignant generation.[1] Jackson identifies the novelist and critic J. Saunders Redding, author of the academic novel *Stranger and Alone* (1950), as one of the representative figures in this generation of black writers, and Redding plays a prominent role in Jackson's literary historical study *The Indignant Generation: A Narrative History of African American Writers and Critics, 1934–1960*.[2] On the subject of higher education, Redding's work reveals the conflicted ideas among black intellectuals about the role of black colleges in the twentieth century, and he presents these ideas vividly among the students and professors of Arcadia College, the fictional institution at the center of *Stranger and Alone*.

The periodization of this chapter ends with the landmark 1954 *Brown v. Board of Education of Topeka*, a Supreme Court decision that paved the way for integration of public institutions and specifically opened up a new era of interracial schooling that would reshape black colleges and create the conditions for why they are now called historically black colleges and universities.

The post-*Brown* era would also transform PWIs, with new minority-student populations that brought change, and conflict, to campuses across the country.

Of the many Harlem Renaissance novels featuring black intellectuals, Nella Larsen's *Quicksand* may be the one that most qualifies as a college novel. In Wallace Thurman's *The Blacker the Berry* Emma Lou Morgan is a dark-skinned college graduate dealing with color prejudice. George Schuyler's *Black No More* includes a caricature of W. E. B. Du Bois as the pretentious professor Shakespeare Agamemnon Beard, and Schuyler skewers other members of Harlem's Negro elite. The physician and novelist Rudolf Fisher's *The Walls of Jericho* (1928) and *The Conjure-Man Dies* (1932) both feature college-educated black characters. Jessie Fauset's *Plum Bun* (1928) is another novel of class and color, and while it also features educated black characters, it doesn't quite engage with the topic of higher education directly as an academic novel.³

My analysis of this period is centered on four novels: Nella Larsen's *Quicksand* (1928), Ralph Ellison's *Invisible Man* (1952), J. Saunders Redding's *Stranger and Alone* (1950), and Chester Himes's *The Third Generation* (1954). But I also include some discussion of W. E. B. Du Bois's *Dark Princess* (1928) (though it is less an academic novel than his other four novels) and of the 1935 short story "Professor" by Langston Hughes. All these works are set in black colleges, and the three novels of the 1950s hark back to the earlier years of black college history. It is significant that the latest of these novels, Himes's *The Third Generation*, shows a character who grew up on black college campuses but eventually ends up attending a PWI, a signal of the changes that were to come in the post-1954 years of American higher education.

Neither White nor Black

Nella Larsen's novel about Helga Crane, a disaffected professor teaching at a southern black college, starts with the Langston Hughes poem "Cross":

> My old man died in a fine big house.
> My ma died in a shack.
> I wonder where I'm gonna die,
> Being neither white nor black?

The choice of poem frames this novel as one about racial belonging, alienation, and color consciousness. According to the literary critic Keguro Macharia the poem relates to the novel's concern with what he calls a black nativism, and by placing it in the epigraph Larsen positions the novel's protagonist as a queer figure whose identity is a challenge to essentialist notions of race. As Macharia writes, "Not only does the epigraph link race to place, but it also identifies a nativist logic of belonging that binds race to place," and from there he elaborates upon the character's transnational genealogy as a woman of African American and Danish heritage.[4]

Quicksand is indicative of a particular preoccupation with color in many black academic novels. This colorism is part of America's long adventure with race, sexuality, gender, and class. This recurring motif in blackademic novels speaks to the peculiar antiblackness of American racial culture and to the privileges afforded those black people of mixed racial ancestry, whose features are closer to mainstream white beauty ideals. Larsen's *Passing* is a canonical work in passing literature, and the passing novel is such a resilient genre because it not only addresses the color line in American law and culture but also plays with questions of truth, authenticity, choice, and deception.

Speaking of truth, before I dive into the novel's criticisms of race, class, and gender, there is a much more basic issue to address about *Quicksand*'s literary integrity. Erika Williams's article "A Lie of Omission: Plagiarism in Nella Larsen's *Quicksand*" introduces a quandary from the beginning that not only challenges my reading of *Quicksand* but also raises some questions that may be relevant to all the novels I'm reading here.[5] Williams makes a case that parts of *Quicksand* were plagiarized from other sources, particularly John Galsworthy's short story "The First and the Last." She focuses on the first paragraph of *Quicksand*. What she finds there and elsewhere in the text is that Larsen copied from Galsworthy's story by "replicating phrases verbatim and by barely altering phrases or sentences."[6] Certainly what Larsen does in the text could be interpreted as a conscious artistic technique of pastiche, allusion, or mimicry rather than plagiarism. Williams explores that fine line between what Larsen does and what all writers do when drawing inspiration from other texts (as all writers must do in one form or another, whether by unconscious or direct imitation), but she concludes that Larsen essentially copied from other sources without attribution, based upon the way she reproduces the diction from the original text. Famously, Larsen's stunted career has been attributed to the fallout after she was castigated for plagiarism in her short story "Sanctuary."[7]

The case raises important questions about the nature of composition and appropriation and the meaning of the "author," essentially the very questions that intensified in literary theory beginning in the 1970s with the infusion of postmodernism and poststructuralism into American literary studies. The insecurity that this introduces into my readings is that I can't say that I have done similar vetting for all the other authors covered here. Might these other authors have stolen texts in the same way and have not been called out the way that Larsen was? Furthermore, is this a practice that all literary scholars must do before discussing any author's intentions in the construction of a text?

However, even if we take Williams's observations into consideration and accept that *Quicksand* is a work with plagiarized parts, the constructed story line and characterization in the novel do represent a kind of intentional narrative about a unique character, Helga Crane, and her life in a black college and thus represent Larsen's vision of black college life and the lives of black intellectuals.

In her introduction to the Rutgers University Press edition of *Quicksand* (and *Passing*), Deborah McDowell positions *Quicksand* in a history of literary representations of black college life:

> Naxos, no doubt, is a composite of Larsen's experience at Tuskegee Institute in Alabama and Fisk University in Tennessee. In her novel *Meridian* (1976), which owes much to *Quicksand*, Alice Walker titles her Southern black college "Saxon," criticizing—as does Larsen of her fictional college—its attempt to erase all distinctiveness and to encourage conformity to an Anglo-Saxon "norm."[8]

The name Naxos, an anagram of "Saxon," calls attention to the racial politics of the historically black college. In the next chapter I explore how Alice Walker takes up that same topic, turning subtext into text by rearranging Saxon into its original form. Walker takes a more direct shot at the black college and its white-supremacist undercurrents in a novel exploring a black women's college during the civil rights movement (based on Walker's experiences at Spelman College).

In the opening pages of *Quicksand*, Larsen shows Helga in her own space, in a proverbial "room of her own," underscoring the importance for a woman intellectual to have such a space. But the room also marks Helga Crane as a queer figure, as someone marginal to the college community where she lives.

> She loved this tranquility, this quiet, following the fret and strain of the long hours spent among fellow members of a carelessly unkind and gossiping faculty, following the strenuous rigidity of conduct required in this huge educational community of which she was an insignificant part. This was for her rest, this intentional isolation for a short while in the evening, this little time in her own attractive room with her own books. To the rapping of other teachers, bearing fresh scandals, or seeking information, or other more concrete favors, or merely talk, at that hour Helga Crane never opened her door.[9]

Larsen includes a touchstone of the academic novel in her depiction of gossip and drama among faculty members. Helga's room is a place where she can escape from the claustrophobic social world of campus life. But for the black woman academic that space is more than an escape from petty gossip. It is a physical and metaphorical manifestation of interiority, the space in which the black intellectual's self-conception lives, that space that, according to the most widely accepted ideas in American culture about the minds of black people, does not exist. For Helga Crane, the space also represents her queerness.

Naxos is not a place that accepts her individuality, seen in the line that comes later when she says, "Teachers as well as students were subjected to the paring process, for it tolerated no innovations, no individualisms."[10]

A stark contrast to this cerebral interiority that Larsen establishes in the first pages comes from one of the white preachers who visits Naxos and heaps condescending praise upon the school's faculty and student body, positioning them over and against the shiftless Negroes outside the college:

> If all Negroes would only take a leaf out of the book of Naxos and conduct themselves in the manner of Naxos products, there would be no race problem, because Naxos Negroes knew what was expected of them. They had good sense and they had good taste. They knew enough to stay in their places and that, said the preacher, showed good taste.[11]

The preacher's words indicate the perniciousness of respectability politics, that they are never merely about good behavior, never just about benign matters of decorum, but are always linked to white supremacy's demands for black obedience, regardless of educational status or class standing. And then comes this key line from the white preacher: "No other race in so short a time had made so much progress, but he had urgently besought them to know when and where to stop"[12] Again, the specter of overeducation looms behind the black intellectual. The preacher reminds the students and faculty of a black college that there is a point at which a black person can have more education than she needs, and that passing this point will have negative consequences. Again and again one finds the black academic novelist documenting this kind of thinking to articulate the particular challenges that black intellectuals face under white supremacy and how the black intellectual constantly confronts the mixed messages of progress and caution.

Helga Crane bristles at the comment from one of her fellow faculty members, who says that students act "like savages from the backwoods," a comment Helga finds especially cruel since many of them are from the backwoods. It was the job of Naxos to smooth out those rough edges. In one striking scene she notices a large, dark-skinned girl wearing an orange dress and how the girl was criticized for wearing something so flamboyant when she should have been wearing something more muted in black or white. As Helga put it, "These people yapped loudly of race, of race consciousness, of race pride, and yet suppressed its most delightful manifestations, love of color, joy of rhythmic motion, naive, spontaneous laughter. Harmony, radiance, and simplicity, all the essentials of spiritual beauty in the race they had marked for destruction."[13] For Helga Crane, her colorful clothes were seen as "queer," decadent, and immodest.

Helga's lighter skin tone is one of her defining characteristics in the novel. The recurring mentions of skin color in blackademic novels speaks to the prevalence of colorism in black higher education. The black college holds a special place in the literature on passing since this institution constituted schools with histories of colorist hierarchy where light-skinned students and faculty often considered themselves better than their darker counterparts. From Larsen's *Quicksand*, to Du Bois's *The Black Flame*, to Spike Lee's *School Daze*, one finds in these depictions of black college life an ongoing criticism of colorism among college-educated blacks. Larsen's novel addresses the unique challenges of colorism for black *women*, who are expected to conform to Eurocentric beauty ideals. Southern black colleges were often populated with students who benefited from their proximity to whiteness, in some cases by being the offspring or descendants of wealthy white men who secretly funded their educations. It is believed that some colleges admitted students based on a "brown paper bag test," a practice in which students who were darker than a standard brown paper bag were not admitted. The evidence of this practice is mostly apocryphal and anecdotal, yet it remains an indelible part of black college lore.[14]

We are invited to take Helga Crane's criticisms of Naxos at face value, but as the story goes on we find that her alienation is just as much because of her youthful self-righteousness and that she is hardly free from her own racial hypocrisies. *Quicksand* is similar to *Invisible Man* in that it is a novel that starts with the black college experience and then moves on to failure and exile, and yet the college experience remains the frame of reference for everything that comes afterward in the character's life. *Quicksand* anticipates and predates Ellison's and Redding's ironic stance toward black college life and their criticisms of uplift ideology. In this case Helga Crane abruptly leaves the college, refusing to wait until the end of the term, and decides to go to Chicago.

The portrayal of her friend, the Harlem socialite Anne Gray, who is described as "pro black but contemptuous of black culture," represents the hypocrisies of the Negro bourgeoisie.[15] But really, Helga is weary of all the race talk and wishes to avoid it entirely. "Why, Helga wondered, with unreasoning exasperation, didn't they find something else to talk of? Why must the race problem always creep in?"[16] In this way Larsen writes a complex character willing to voice her criticism of black people to show someone who is not always at ease with compulsory racial identification. Such expressions of skepticism could easily be read as naïveté or, worse, as a kind of racial treason. As will be seen in the case of Lillian Taylor in Chester Himes's *The Third Generation*, her desire to be free from blackness is one that nearly ruins her family life. But Larsen registers her character's ambivalences knowing they need not foreclose a sense of racial solidarity, and in Helga there is no lack of understanding about the history of racial injustice. What Helga wants to escape is the burden of responsibility and representation, the burden of being a race woman.

When Helga's uncle Peter sends her five thousand dollars, allowing her to go to live with her aunt Katrina in Copenhagen, she is given a chance to escape the race question in America as she had desired. And her experience in Copenhagen corroborates Keguro Macharia's reading of Crane as queer, and that her gender, color, and education are all markers of her queerness in relation to an essentialist blackness. As Larsen writes, "She didn't, in spite of her racial marking, belong to these dark segregated people. She was different. She felt it. It wasn't merely a matter of color. It was something broader, deeper, that made folk kin."[17]

While in Copenhagen there is an interesting moment where Helga sees a traveling show with a couple of black performers. Helga bristles at the performance in this context. Confronted by this minstrel image surrounded by a white European audience Helga is ashamed of the performers.[18] That moment converges with another moment later when she gets into a conversation about child-rearing, and she says to her friend James Vale, "Why do Negroes have children?"[19] Helga's question speaks to an existential crisis about the worthiness of black life under white supremacy, and it arouses ruminations in her that are not unlike those expressed by Albert Camus on the philosophy of the absurd in "The Myth of Sisyphus," which considers the nature of suicide and whether life is worth living. In this case Larsen shows Helga contemplating the pessimism of having children who will be doomed to a life of misery. Her thoughts are brought on by the shame of blackness she experiences surrounded by white people in Copenhagen and her longing for the familiar blackness of Harlem.

Soon we come to find that Helga's discontent is as much a personality flaw as a racial problem. She is discontent no matter where she is and admits as much. "Yes, if I hadn't come away, I'd be stuck in Harlem working every day of my life chattering about the race problem."[20] But in Helga's alienation, Larsen continues constructing a sense of interiority and individuality, that her problems are as much personal as social and that the two need not be mutually exclusive.

Helga leaves Denmark and returns to Harlem. One rainy, windy night on the streets of Harlem she ducks into a church to escape the elements and ends up getting caught up in the ecstatic scene of a church service. Helga is a disinterested observer of religion, but she becomes wrapped up in the emotion of the preacher's performance and the excitement of the crowd. With this scene Larsen seems to ironically contemplate the role of religion in black communities. (McDowell also cites this passage for its sexual undertones, since Helga's religious experience is as much about the physical pleasure and release she feels by participating in the service as about spiritual enlightenment.) Despite this momentary encounter with the Holy Ghost, Helga's religious skepticism, specifically her skepticism about Christian theology and the black church, reappears in the last chapter when she identifies "the fatuous belief in the White man's God" as one of the key problems of the race.[21] She questions black people's fidelity to Eurocentric portraits of a blond-haired, blue-eyed Jesus and marks it as an important contributor to the colorism that she has struggled with, that indeed many people of color in a culture dominated by Christian white supremacy must struggle with. This commentary is particularly salient in this academic novel because it's an important recognition of the predominance of Christian theology in the history of black colleges and universities and a moment of reflection on the complicated legacies of faith and higher education.

Previous critics of the novel have tried to make sense of how *Quicksand* ends, and Deborah McDowell links its unsatisfying conclusion to other similar endings in black women's novels. For McDowell, the ending signals a difficulty that black women writers have with their heroines, that perhaps they had so few models to follow that they did not know how to conclude their stories. One of the main problems with *Quicksand* is how Larsen condenses so much time in the last chapters of the novel. We go from an eloquently observed and detailed narrative of Helga's life and travels into a rapid montage of the rest of her life back in the U.S. South. She is married and has children, but we know little about them or what the child-rearing experience was like for her, which seems a pressing question given her earlier statements questioning the wisdom of bringing black children into the world. A character whom we had gotten to know so intimately in the first chapters must certainly have thoughts and feelings on what it means to be a mother.

And yet reading this novel as academic fiction permits something appealing in this inconclusiveness. Larsen paints a portrait of a black woman whose blackademic life is interrupted. Her turn to domesticity seems unfulfilling, but this is the path she has chosen, and she must live it out. In her dissatisfaction is a bleak, but pointed, feminist critique of how women are constrained by gender normativity and the limitations on their professional development as scholars. If we take seriously Macharia's idea that Helga Crane was marked as queer, then she is able to find relief from this abnormality by assimilating into a more normative trajectory.

Quicksand's contribution to the black academic novel is in Larsen's vision of individuality, of a black woman trying to maintain her interiority in a world that expects her only to be a member of a race, and a flat representation of racial character, not a fully realized human being who might have her own hopes and desires beyond the narrow strictures of racial politics. That individuality is something that Ralph Ellison elaborates upon in *Invisible Man* when the narrator, after having moved to Harlem and joined the Brotherhood, has a moment where he says, "For the first time, lying there in the dark, I could glimpse the possibility of being more than a member of a race."[22] Larsen and Ellison suggest that racialization can be both a form of solidarity and a form of alienation, and the academic novel articulates that the condition of the black intellectual must be vigilant and strategic about how to protect her individuality and interiority under a white supremacy that denies black intelligence and humanity, under a patriarchy that denies women an intellectual life, while also dealing with the pressures of racial representation and a sense of responsibility toward the political aspirations of the race.

The Souls of W. E. B. Du Bois

There is less content specifically about higher education in Du Bois's *Dark Princess* (1928) than in his other novels, but it is notable for its protagonist, Matthew Townes, a medical student whose story of an unjustly thwarted education deserves inclusion in this discussion of black higher education and its literary representations.

Perhaps the most important contribution of *Dark Princess* to this conversation is its global vision organized around the interactions between the "darker races" of the world, in this case between the black American Matthew Townes and Princess Kautilya of Bwodpur, India, daughter of a maharajah. In *Dark Princess* W. E. B. Du Bois explores the global color line and imagines solidarity among black and brown people worldwide, an idea that would be taken up in more detail in *The Black Flame* as well as in a later academic novel of Afro-Asian politics, Ishmael Reed's *Japanese by Spring*.

Bill V. Mullen's book *Afro-Orientalism* (2004) describes a field of cultural and political thought that confronts the problem of Orientalism, a concept popularized by Edward Said in his highly influential text *Orientalism*. Mullen's work is linked to other critical studies in what has become a developed field within cultural studies organized under the concept of "Afro-Orientalism," a field that explores the linkages and tensions between black, Asian, and Arab communities in the United States and abroad. These works include Vijay Prashad's *The Karma of Brown Folk* (2001), Helen Heran Jun's *Race for Citizenship: Black Orientalism and Asian Uplift from Pre-Emancipation to Neoliberal America* (2011), Julia Lee's *Interracial Encounters: Reciprocal Representations in African and Asian American Literatures, 1896–1937* (2011), and Crystal Anderson's *Beyond "The Chinese Connection": Contemporary Afro-Asian Cultural Production* (2013). Anderson's book actually includes some analysis of Ishmael Reed's *Japanese by Spring*, and I come back to it in my analysis of Reed and the culture wars.

Postcolonial critic Homi Bhabha praises *Dark Princess* but also criticizes the novel for being "too indexical," a criticism that seems applicable to all of Du Bois's novels. About the novel's Indian aesthetic Bhabha writes, "Although I have been rather parsimonious with my praise for its literary qualities, *Dark Princess* certainly plugs into the Bollywood aesthetic which has become such a fashionable vernacular idiom for contemporary popular cinema. As a boy from Bombay (Mumbai) all that glitter and garrulousness certainly gives me a filmic frisson."[23]

In this novel Du Bois takes up an idea that he would continue to explore throughout the rest of career and in his later novels, that the black American, constructed by white supremacy and its legal system as property, turns to the global as a way of discovering and recovering their humanity. For Du Bois it was traveling to Germany that fired up his imagination of a possibility outside the U.S. racial hierarchy. Black literary history is filled with similar stories of black writers, artists, and intellectuals traveling abroad for a physical and mental escape from the yoke of American white supremacy. Black intellectuals traveled to cosmopolitan centers in Europe, where they could experience some mobility, but they also soon found that they were just confronting different permutations of the same racialized oppression. But it was those global experiences of travel that led many of them to a connection and identification with other dark people of the world. That connection is essential for moving from a minoritarian consciousness to one in which the black intellectual views herself and her people as part of a global majority, since most of the planet's inhabitants would fall on the colored side of the Jim Crow color line. That kind of cosmopolitanism becomes a part of the black American intellectual's counternarrative to white supremacy, and Du Bois articulates that cosmopolitan vision in *The Black Flame*.

Early on in the history of the black academic novel, Du Bois and Sutton Griggs were articulating this international vision, and their vision reverberates in all the black academic novels that followed, from Paule Marshall's postcolonial Caribbean, to Ishmael Reed's Afro-Orientalism, to Zadie Smith's Anglo-Caribbean-American interracial cosmopolitanism.

Rebecka Fisher's article "The Anatomy of a Symbol: Reading W. E. B. Du Bois's *Dark Princess: A Romance*" points to some of the ideas of aesthetics that Du Bois had begun to explore in critical essays such as "Criteria of Negro Art" and that he was putting into practice with such works as *Dark Princess*. Fisher writes that "art for Du Bois is quite central to a political program that has as its goal the liberation of black folk, for it responds to the need for black folk to represent themselves, to put into play aesthetic renderings of African American experience that are at once mimetic and phantastic."[24]

That need for representation is what drives the academic novel into existence, but such representations came up against a marketplace fueled by white tastes and desires and against the naysaying of white critics. A 1928 *New York Times* review of *Dark Princess* affirms everything that Du Bois complained about in his 1926 "Questionnaire" editorial. On the one hand Du Bois's novel was reviewed in the *New York Times*, which was a rare occurrence for black writers, and Du Bois was one of the few black intellectuals who could gain entry to such a rarified platform. On the other, however, in that article the (anonymous) reviewer writes in the concluding paragraph,

> There is, however, real meat in "Dark Princess," and such proof of the author's power that it seems a pity he is not using his talent to show the natural ability of the colored man or the nobility of his

character, as in "Porgy," rather than to dwell, oversensitively, on social injustices which are inevitable in any period of racial transition and development—of white or black.

This reviewer not only insinuates that the white author DuBose Heyward gave a more authentic portrait of the Negro than Du Bois but also accuses Du Bois of being "oversensitive" on justice issues. This review is a stark reminder of just how long such accusations have been hurled at black writers and what white readers often expected from black art and performance.[25]

Langston Hughes borrowed elements from the life of Du Bois for the character Professor T. Walton Brown in his academic short story "Professor."[26] The story is about a black male professor of sociology who is an intermediary between black institutions of higher education and the wealthy white philanthropists who support them. "Professor" depicts the conundrum of black scholars who had to pander to Jim Crow politics to fund their research and keep their schools afloat.

Bucklin Moon, the (white) author of the 1949 black college novel *Without Magnolias*, gives a rather perceptive description of "Professor" in his 1952 *New York Times* review of Langston Hughes's story collection *Laughing to Keep from Crying*:

> "Professor" is a highly successful story. It tells of the feelings of a Negro from the faculty of a small colored college in the South who is going to dinner at the home of a prominent Midwestern philanthropist where he will have to sing for his supper because of the job he needs and knows he will get only if he Uncle Toms a little.
>
> The story concludes: "As the car sped him back toward town, Dr. Brown sat under its soft fur rug among the deep cushions and thought how with six thousand dollars a year earned by dancing properly to the tune of Jim Crow education, he could carry his whole family to South America for a summer where they wouldn't need to feel like Negroes."

Moon deftly points out the ironic ending of Hughes's story, that his character is like many black intellectuals whom Hughes had known in Harlem and abroad, who escaped to spaces where they could taste a little bit of freedom beyond America's racial caste system, though many of them would find those spaces full of their own antagonisms and disappointments. Hughes's story shows the condition of black higher education that Redding and Ellison would explore more elaborately in their black college novels.

Hughes introduces the professor as he sits in the lobby of the Booker T. Washington Hotel in an unidentified Midwestern city. He is on a lecture tour to raise money for the black college where he teaches in the South. Brown, wearing a white silk scarf, suit, and black overcoat, is picked up by the white limo driver of Ralph P. Chandler, the wealthy philanthropist at whose house he was going for dinner. He felt "a little unsafe at being driven through the streets of this city on the edge of the South in an expensive car, by a white chauffeur."[27]

In one rapturous sentence, Hughes articulates Dr. Brown's position as a representative figure, as a race man, who is there to speak on behalf of his students and on behalf of the other black scholars who may come after him and have to do the same dance:

> "We would need . . ." said Dr. Brown, speaking as a mouthpiece for the Negro students of his section of the South, and speaking for himself as a once-ragged youth who had attended the college when its rating was lower than that of a Northern high school so that he had to study two years in Boston before he could enter a white college, when he had worked nights as redcap in the station and then as a waiter for seven years until he got his Ph.D., and then couldn't get a job in the North but had to go back down South to the work where he was now—but which might develop into a glorious opportunity at six thousand dollars a year to make surveys and put down figures that other scholars might study to get their Ph.D.'s and that would bring him in enough to just once take his family on a vacation to South America where they wouldn't feel that they were Negroes. "We would need, Mr. Chandler . . ."[28]

In that passage is the dilemma of the black college, a source of pride for black students and professors but also a concession to Jim Crow segregated education that they knew would remain inferior despite the money of the philanthropists—or rather, because of it. In that passage is the challenge that so many black professors and administrators still face, as we were reminded recently when the presidents of black colleges met with Donald Trump for an Oval Office photo opportunity that they had to attend to make sure their black colleges stayed on the good side of a hostile administration, even while knowing the meeting would yield no new funding and no real improvements to their campuses. That position of the black educator would be explored in detail in Du Bois's *The Black Flame* trilogy in scenes where Manuel Mansart is also required to go into white spaces as a representative to plead for money for his college.

Social Responsibility and Social Equality

When it comes to the "black academic novel" as a specific concept, Stephanie Brown's chapter "J. Saunders Redding and the African American Campus

Novel" in *The Postwar African American Novel: Protest and Discontent, 1945–1950* (2011) is one of few literary studies to identify the black academic novel as a literary category. Brown praises Redding's *Stranger and Alone* as an important depiction of black college life, identifies its criticisms of the curriculum and administration on a black college campus, and recognizes the intraracial conflict within the institution. Brown's study of postwar black fiction also admonishes scholars to pay attention to the world of black journals, newspapers, and magazines, where novels like *Stranger and Alone* were reviewed and engaged with by critics and where scholars like J. Saunders Redding, in his role as a critic, were producing a body of criticism on black literature.

Brown makes some important distinctions between the concerns of the academic novels of white writers and those by black writers, and her interpretation in the following passage resonates with my own theorization of the black academic novel:

> Whereas the mid-twentieth century academic novel and its many offspring in subsequent decades take as a given the notion that the college campus is a circumscribed environment whose hothouse ideas and politics wilt in the harsh light of the real world, *Stranger and Alone* takes the position that, for blacks, higher education *is* the real world. Demonstrating both the relevance of education to "real life" and the centrality of "academic" debate to political discourse, *Stranger and Alone* presents the reader with a generic revision that is simultaneously a political intervention, presciently revealing the ease with which the typical narrative of the postwar campus novel would make itself complicit in marginalizing the intellectual work of university communities.[29]

There are certain assumptions about belonging that cannot be assumed by the black intellectual in campus spaces. Even Janice Rossen's notion of inclusion/exclusion as an inherent quality of campus life doesn't quite get to the particular history of exclusion and subjugation that defines the blackademic's life in the university. While campus novels emphasize the space for eccentricity among the professoriat, with tropes such as the bungling absentminded professor or the alternative/bohemian professor, the sorts of issues that I speak of here, questions about one's innate intelligence and belonging in the university represented by discourses of overeducation, are specific challenges that all black intellectuals in the academy have to confront, not just the ones who choose to be dissidents.

Brown also makes a critical contribution here by specifically focusing on the black college, where students and professors may be unified in a mission of educating black people but where it would be mistaken to claim exist utopian spaces devoid of white supremacy.

At the same time Redding's novel explores the complexities of the position of historically black colleges in the decades preceding the civil rights movement: these campuses were hardly ivory towers. Historically black institutions found themselves prey to a host of problems largely irrelevant to the small liberal arts colleges and state universities that provide the settings for most campus fiction; many of these problems derived from practical issues of funding and accreditation as well as more abstract questions about their utility and purpose. Consequently these institutions were in no position to shelter their faculties and students.[30]

Brown dissects the intraracial politics in Redding's novel, showing that while the black college did serve as a space for educational opportunities for black students, it was also fraught with debates about class, color, and political ideology. Black colleges were designed to nurture and encourage black students, but it was impossible to isolate them from the ugliness of the white-supremacist society that made these institutions necessary, and the student bodies came with their own complications and intraracial group conflicts along lines of class, color, and gender. All the while, they were also concerned about white people's public perceptions of their institutions, and HBCU administrators had to manage the image of the college against those outside expectations. (Similar questions arise in academic novels set at white women's colleges. Dorothy Sayers's *Gaudy Night*, for instance, addresses the issue at a women's college at Oxford, where administrators discreetly hire detective alumna Harriet Vane to find the culprit behind a series of threatening pranks at the college, but they also want her to extinguish the situation quietly because they are fearful that if the word gets out, it could threaten the precarious project of women's education.)[31]

The organization of J. Saunders Redding's *Stranger and Alone* exemplifies Elaine Showalter's idea of "academic time," that "novels about professors are set in academic time, which is organized and compartmentalized according to various grids and calendars, vacations and rituals."[32] Academic time in the academic novel can be represented by the peculiar calendar year that starts in the fall and ends in the spring, the four-year timetable of undergraduate degree completion, the frustratingly indeterminate number of years to complete a Ph.D., and, in the professor's life, the years marked toward promotion and tenure. In *Stranger and Alone* the novel's first four chapters are organized into Shelton Howden's four years at Arcadia College.

A key moment of intertextuality to other college novels comes when we find that among Shelton Howden's "books that he heard about and which he planned to read someday" are the classic college novel *This Side of Paradise* by F. Scott Fitzgerald and *Birthright* by T. S. Stribling.[33] The presence of these titles in the text makes explicit Redding's genre intervention of composing a novel about black college life.

The white professor in the narrative, Dr. Posey, who arrogantly teaches black students white-supremacist history and race science, represents an unfortunate history of miseducation in historically black colleges, where students were assimilated into and reproduced white-supremacist intellectual paradigms. The normalcy with which Redding depicts Posey's authoritative opinions is a reminder of how hegemonic whiteness reproduced itself, even in these institutions. In debates about the curriculum for black students, President P. T. Wimbush echoes the Bookerite logic that it is a waste of time to teach black students history when they should be learning more practical, skills-based subjects. At the same time, the novel depicts a growing political militancy in black colleges. The professor Spurgeon Kelly, for example, is punished for refusing to meet the white-supremacist governor on his visit to the college. The gossip about Kelly being "a pervert" gestures to the use of homosexuality as a political smear in postwar America and its association with dissident political behavior.

Also, just as in Sutton Griggs's *Imperium in Imperio*, Chester Himes's *The Third Generation*, and Du Bois's *Dark Princess*, there is the figure of the overeducated black laborer, who is working on the railroads while holding a college degree, and this becomes Shelton Howden's experience as well after graduation.

Structurally, it is apparent why this isn't considered a great novel. It trails off in the end, and we never quite figure out what to make of Shelton Howden's marriage to Nan. He's vaguely unhappy, still in love with the vivacious Gerry, the free-spirited daughter of P. T. Wimbush, but the story line doesn't really go anywhere. However, there is something poignant in the suggestion of what's to come. Published in 1950, the novel anticipates what lies ahead with school desegregation, civil unrest, the fight for voting rights, and other changes in black political consciousness that would affect both black and white colleges.

In a moment that resonates with Stephanie's Brown's observation that *Stranger and Alone* influenced Ralph Ellison's *Invisible Man*, Redding has Shelton Howden think about the problem of racial representation and individuality. "[Howden] did not want to think about the race problem nor live on two levels nor make life more difficult by trying to analyze everything. All he wanted was to get what he could out of life. He didn't want to spatter his brains against some walls."[34] He goes on to write that "what he wanted was a victory in his private battle against life. There was trouble a-plenty outside, but it was a passing show which he could watch through a window of thick plate glass."[35] That quest for individuality would be even more forcefully articulated in *Invisible Man* as its narrator goes on his picaresque adventures into New York City and encounters various people and political groups with conflicting expectations for him as a race leader.

A contender for the most important scene in any black academic novel might be the "battle royal" in Ralph Ellison's *Invisible Man*. This scene, often cited and written about, is not only one of the most powerful allegories for black leadership in all American literature but also an emblematic moment for the literary representation of the blackademic in novelistic form. In the scene, the nameless protagonist, the Invisible Man, who is invited to give a version of his Booker T. Washington–inspired valedictory speech to a group of wealthy white community leaders, finds himself in a staged fight with several other black men. Then, after winning the fight, with bloodied mouth he gives his speech to the crowd of sarcastic, contemptuous white men, who mock him but also award him with a scholarship to the state's college for Negroes.

The entire battle royal scene is a tour de force of surrealistic staging, description, and metaphor, from the concept of having black men fight one another for white entertainment, to the presence of a voluptuous white woman as a stripper—a conspicuous presence whom the black men must pretend not to notice—to the absurdity of having the Invisible Man give a serious speech on education with his mouth bloodied from fighting.

The part of the scene where the Invisible Man repeatedly stumbles in pronouncing the word "responsibility" and suddenly substitutes it with the word "equality" is worth reviewing here at length for the way that it crystallizes the plight of the black intellectual.

> Whenever I uttered a word of three or more syllables a group of voices would yell for me to repeat it. I used the phrase "social responsibility" and they yelled:
> "What's that word you say boy?"
> "Social responsibility," I said.
> "What?"
> "Social . . ."
> "Louder"
> ". . . responsibility."
> "More!"
> "Respon—"
> "Repeat!"
> "—sibility."
> The room filled with the uproar of laughter until, no doubt distracted by having to gulp down my blood, I made a mistake and yelled a phrase I had often seen denounced in newspaper editorials, heard debated in private.
> "Social . . ."
> "What?" they yelled.
> ". . . equality—"
> The laugher hung smokelike in the sudden stillness. I opened my eyes, puzzled. Sounds of displeasure filled the room. The M.C. rushed forward. They shouted hostile phrases at me. But I did not understand.

A small dry mustached man in the front row blared out, "Say that slowly, son!"

"What, sir?"

"What you just said!"

"Social responsibility, sir," I said.

"You weren't being smart, were you boy?" he said, not unkindly.

"No, sir!"

"You sure that about 'equality' was a mistake?"

"Oh, yes, sir," I said. "I was swallowing blood."

"Well, you had better speak more slowly so we can understand. We mean to do right by you, but you've got to know your place at all times. All right, now, go on with your speech."

I was afraid. I wanted to leave but I wanted also to speak and I was afraid they'd snatch me down.

"Thank you, sir," I said, beginning where I had left off, and having them ignore me as before.

Yet when I finished there was thunderous applause.[36]

The narrator's words come, of course, directly from Booker T. Washington's "Atlanta Compromise" speech, in which Washington reassured his white segregationist audience that "the wisest among my race understand that the agitation of questions of social equality is the extremest folly, and that progress in the enjoyment of all the privileges that will come to us must be the result of severe and constant struggle, rather than of artificial forcing."[37]

The discourse of overeducation is present in this scene. It's there in the businessmen's mocking condescension directed at the narrator for using words greater than three syllables, which indicates their attitudes toward the black intellectual in general. And yet after their statement warning the Invisible Man against "social equality" and all the mocking, they give him a scholarship to the state college for Negroes. He now owes that scholarship to the very men who mocked his intelligence. In that scholarship lies the paradox of the black intellectual's education, that he is rewarded with an education for assuring white supremacists that he will abide by the laws and customs of Jim Crow and that he will not upset the racial hierarchies already in place.

Invisible Man marks a turning point toward a more daring and ironic depiction of black college life. Ellison is certainly not the first satirist or ironist of black academic life (indeed, Nella Larsen's *Quicksand* predates Ellison's own ironic view of the black college), but he had the advantage of looking back upon those crucial postslavery years of black education. It was actually in Ellison's review of J. Saunders Redding's 1950 novel *Stranger and Alone* that he articulated what I have come to understand as a fundamental precept of the black academic novel: "At least we're going to have a group of writers who are aware that their task is not that of pleading Negro humanity, but of examining and depicting the forms and rituals of that humanity."[38] The burdens of responsibility and representation never entirely dissipate: Ellison's praise for *Stranger and Alone* also speaks to the content of later novels such as *The Nigger Factory* and *Japanese by Spring*, where black writers have insisted on their right to explore the rituals of the academy and the complexities of black intellectual life beyond the supplications of pleading and proof of black intelligence, even though such racist ideas never entirely evaporate.

Invisible Man has been listed by other critics as an academic novel, including John Kramer, who includes it in his bibliography under "student-centered fiction." I must admit that my first inclination was to not consider it as an academic novel. At first glance it may seem that the novel merely begins in a college setting, and then the narrator moves on to his picaresque adventures in the city. However, reading *Invisible Man* as a college novel reveals the way that the narrator's college experience informs and shapes all that happens to him afterward, and the way that his identity as a college-educated black intellectual persists throughout the novel, even as he moves away from the campus.

The first scene at the institute at the beginning of chapter 5 is among the most evocative depictions of campus life in academic fiction. The scene's descriptions mark the campus as a distinctive space, as a community apart from the rest of the world, what the architectural historian Paul V. Turner described as an "academical village."[39] In *Invisible Man* that academical village is based on the real-life Tuskegee Institute (now Tuskegee University), founded in 1881 by Booker T. Washington. Tuskegee is such an architecturally unique campus because its buildings were constructed partly by its students. The very physical structure of the campus is a monument to its pedagogy as an institute of industrial education. The buildings are a record of its mission to give students practical labor skills, and as such it stands in stark contrast with the university built by the hands of nonacademic laborers where privileged students go to learn abstract knowledge.

Booker T. Washington's presence looms over the novel, as it does over the actual Tuskegee campus. Prior to college, Ellison's narrator has already assimilated Washington's ideas about education and personal responsibility, indicated in the battle royal speech. Though in the narrative of the novel Ellison disaggregates the myth of "the founder" from the direct mentions of Booker T. Washington, Ellison is making an inside reference to his readers that this "barefoot boy who in his fervor for education had trudged with his bundle of ragged clothing across two states" whom the blind preacher Homer Barbee spoke of in his sermon is actually Booker T. Washington himself, and much of Barbee's sermon is based upon Washington's life story in *Up from Slavery*.[40]

Ellison's language in his evocative descriptions of the campus are indicative of the aesthetic values of the black academic novel. *Invisible Man* has endured not only because of its political themes but also because of the beauty of Ellison's writing, the sensory details he uses to evoke the settings of the novel, whether in rural Alabama or urban New York City, and in his ear for the speech of his characters from different ethnic groups and social classes.

One important moment where the significance of language and class difference is apparent is in Ellison's description of the sermons that the narrator hears at the college assemblies, and how he contrasts these speeches from the "wild emotion of the crude preachers most of us knew in our home towns." The narrator says that he felt fortunate "to belong to this family sheltered from those lost in ignorance and darkness."[41] The language and performance style of the preachers come to represent the class aspirations of the students at the institute, as markers of a life that they were aspiring to move beyond through their educations at the college. At the institute the narrator is happy to have escaped from his rural southern background, but he later recognizes that he has also developed a sense of shame about where he is from, and in his search for individuality he has abandoned one of the most potent sources of identity that could give his life meaning, that of a black folk culture, typified by the black humor, language, music, and style that he knew. This narrative of a struggle between education and authenticity is an idea embedded in many black academic novels, and it's a struggle that finds one of its most profound and creative articulations in Percival Everett's Ellison-inspired novel *Erasure*.

The reference to hearing the notes of "Swing Low, Sweet Chariot" in Antonín Dvořák's New World Symphony (1893) represents an idea that would come to be a key Ellisonian formation, the idea that America is a mulatto nation and that its white citizens have yet to fully reckon with the role that its black population has played in the formation of a national identity and national cultural forms.[42] In Dvořák's quest to create a definitive American symphony he incorporated elements of Native American and African American music. Likewise Ellison believed that America is a mulatto culture, a mélange of different styles and languages.

In some ways this entire novel is about the Invisible Man's confrontation with uplift ideology. In this concept of "uplifting the race" is the idea that one has an obligation to be on one's best behavior for the good of one's people, and inherent in that uplift formulation is a kind of weak capitulation to racialist (and racist) logic. One remains fearful that one's actions will not be read as individual and that one's failures will be read as failures of the entire group. Ellison expresses that burden of responsibility and representation when his narrator ponders, "Any act that endangered the continuity of the dream was an act of treason," and so the Invisible Man, particularly after his expulsion from the Edenic existence of the institute because of his blunder of taking the white philanthropist Mr. Norton to the other side of town to see the farmer Trueblood and hear the scandalous story of incest with his daughter, has failed the college and his race by showing this white man something embarrassing about black people, something the man should never have seen.[43]

One of the first indications that the Invisible Man is breaking out of the uplift mold is in his humorous encounter with a Harlem street vendor selling yams. The food makes him homesick, but he is reluctant to indulge in the countrified cuisine. But then he catches himself: "What a group of people we were, I thought. Why, you could cause us the greatest humiliation simply by confronting us with something we liked. Not *all* of us, but so many." And at the end of this passage he states, "This is all very wild and childish, I thought, but to hell with being ashamed of what you liked. No more of that for me. I am what I am! . . ."[44]

The Invisible Man's encounter with the Brotherhood is instructive in what it reveals about the perils of color-blind liberalism. The thing about the Brotherhood is that they spoke of themselves as allies and insisted that their political program was about transcending race, but right away you get a sense of the unchecked racism in their ranks. When he goes to a party with them, one white woman questions his authentic blackness, wondering whether he was dark skinned enough to be their black representative ("But don't you think he should be a little blacker.")[45] Another member at the party asks him to sing a Negro spiritual for them.[46] He laughs it off with "He hit me in the face with a yard of chitterlings! . . . He threw hog maw," but they don't understand why he's laughing.[47] This scene shows the function of racial authenticity in the black academic novel as both an anxiety articulated by the educated black intellectual and a discourse thrust upon blacks by white notions of ideal blackness.

An important exchange happens when Brother Jack asks the narrator, "How would you like to be the next Booker T. Washington?" The Invisible Man fires back, insisting that "the Founder" was more important, but goes on to say, "To hell with this Booker T. Washington business. I would do the work but I would be no one except myself—whoever I was. I would pattern my life on that of the Founder. They might think I was acting like Booker T. Washington; let them. But what I thought of myself I would keep to myself." Brother Jack's explanation to him that the Brotherhood is based upon a scientific approach to politics—"We are all realists here, and materialists"—is an expression of their Marxian interpretation of history, that history is based upon economic determinism, the labor system, and class struggle, not upon spirituality, religious beliefs, superstitions, or emotions. This is why they later condemned his speech for being too emotional. Brother Jack's criticism is also part of the class-first formulation among white leftists that Ellison interrogates and challenges throughout the novel.[48]

The smashed figurine that he breaks at Mary's place, stuffs into a briefcase, then carries around with him but can't get rid of is a metaphor for the dogged persistence of race and the minstrel caricature. That "Jolly Nigger" bank is a legendary piece of racist memorabilia in American culture (along with other figurines and statues). A version of the bank appears in Spike Lee's blackface minstrelsy satire *Bamboozled* (2001). What Spike Lee argued with that film, and what other scholars of minstrelsy such as Eric Lott (*Love and Theft*) and Camille Forbes (*Introducing Bert Williams*) show, is that blackface performance was at the foundations of American popular culture on the stage and in film and is therefore an indelible part of American culture as a whole.[49]

Racialized chattel slavery brought to American culture a fascination with black bodies, black sexuality, and black performance. Lott's title *Love and Theft* refers to the erotic fascination with these bodies and their images and the way that white people enacted performances of blackness.

Lott pays attention to working-class white European immigrants who went to minstrel shows as entertainment, and these shows became a part of their assimilation into American culture. From the minstrel shows they adopted the idea that no matter how poor and disenfranchised they were they could always have black people to look down upon on the next rung below them. The minstrel shows were their indoctrination into white supremacy. Instead of seeing themselves as allies of black people, who were often in the same boat as they when it came to poverty and low-wage labor, they learned to laugh at and degrade black people while identifying with wealthy white folks, even as those same wealthy whites were often exploiting them too. And those images of blackness remain difficult to exorcise.

The black academic novel endeavors to counter those images with fuller and more complex visions of black life, with the true variety of black experience across class boundaries and in its many permutations, but the minstrel images cannot be avoided here. Nella Larsen confronts them through Helga Crane's trip to Denmark, where she sees minstrel performers. Ralph Ellison confronts them in *Invisible Man* with the figurine and in Tod Clifton's vexing Sambo doll street performance. And in the next chapter, I examine how Percival Everett confronts them in *Erasure*. Collectively the message seems to be that when it comes to these images in the popular imagination, the only way out is through, that they are such an indelible part of American culture that the black intellectual must find ways to engage and defuse them, but rarely does she have the option to ignore them entirely. Minstrelsy is the lie that America needs to tell itself to face the unspeakable violence and subjugation of enslavement. And given that history, the image of the black academic becomes one of cognitive dissonance because it contradicts cherished beliefs in black simplicity, obedience, and careless happiness.

And maybe one of the most important moments in *Invisible Man*, the place where Ellison's "thesis" for the novel is most apparent, comes in New York as the Invisible Man starts to pull away from the Brotherhood when he has a flashback to a classroom encounter at the institute. The narrator remembers a lecture in a literature class back at the institute given by a Professor Woodridge in which he refers to Stephen Dedalus from James Joyce's *A Portrait of the Artist as a Young Man*—a major source of inspiration for Ellison's mythic structure in *Invisible Man*.

> Stephen's problem, like ours, was not actually one of creating the uncreated conscience of his race, but of creating the uncreated features of his face. Our task is that of making ourselves individuals. The conscience of a race is the gift of its individuals who see, evaluate,

record . . . We create the race by creating ourselves and then to our great astonishment we will have created something far more important: We will have created a culture. Why waste time creating a conscience for something that doesn't exist? For, you see, blood and skin do not think!⁵⁰

When after this memory the narrator says, "For the first time, lying there in the dark, I could glimpse the possibility of being more than a member of a race," Ellison makes an association between the college lecture on literature and his character's transformation into the artist, the writer, the one who chronicles his experiences and the experiences of his people.⁵¹ After the narrator has fallen into the hole and begins writing out the story, he says, "So why do I write, torturing myself to put it down?"⁵² His goal has become that of one who records the "unrecorded history" that he refers to when he was telling the Brotherhood about the barbershops and beauty parlors of Harlem having an unrecorded history.

But the lives of black academics also represent a kind of unrecorded history. As a representative figure, the black intellectual speaks on behalf of the illiterate and disadvantaged of his group ("Who knows but that, on the lower frequencies, I speak for you?"), speaks for those who cannot record history for themselves. At the same time, the Invisible Man's record is also meant to be an honest, candid account of his own life, a way to register his feelings about what it meant to him to come from the South, to go to a black college, to migrate to the North, to live through betrayals, and to search for his own identity. What's invisible to Mr. Norton and the members of the Brotherhood is the interior life that the Invisible Man records, and he insists that this same interiority exists among his people as well.

Black intellectuals, whether inside or outside academia, are often illegible. There is a kind of survivor's guilt at the success of becoming a working intellectual in whatever capacity, something seen as a luxury among a people who are largely economically depressed. There's also the sense of being stuck in a narrative of exceptionality, of being exceptional to the rule, and there's a paradox in that exceptionality, that one is expected to be a representative of the group while also being marked an inauthentic member of that group because of one's exceptional status. So what the black academic novel represents is a recorded history of blackademic lives, of intellectuals who have grappled with this and related questions in their work and created expressions of what it means to live as black intellectuals under a white-supremacist society in which black education is both precious and precarious.

I end this chapter with Chester Himes's *The Third Generation* (1954), a novel that connects these "uplift" and "New Negro" historical periods that I have outlined here. In this heavily autobiographical novel, Himes reflects back on the uplift era of black education in the South in the story of a black family with a professor, his biracial wife, and their three sons, the youngest of which, Charles, is a stand-in for Chester Himes himself. "Cross," the Langston Hughes poem that Nella Larsen used as the epigraph to *Quicksand*, could just as well apply to the character of Lillian Taylor, the professor's wife in *The Third Generation*, as it could to any number of other characters who populate these academic novels. Lawrence P. Jackson's 2017 biography of Himes corroborates many of the real-life details included in the autobiographical novel, including the Himes family's connection to historically black colleges and their volatile itinerant life throughout the South and Midwest.[53]

Himes's description of the professor at the small black college is a powerful statement on the purpose of black education during these early years and the meaning of such schools for their rural black student populations:

> Professor Taylor liked it there. In spite of the indignities there was a certain inalienable dignity in the work itself, in bringing enlightenment to these eager young black people. It wasn't as if they could come there with the easy assurance of an upper Bostonian enrolling in Harvard. For what they learned, they and their mothers and fathers and sisters and brothers paid in privation, in calico in January, corn-pone diets and pellagra deaths. Professor Taylor was one of them, a little short, black, pigeon-toed, bowlegged, nappy-headed man; he'd come from the same background with the same traditions; he was just more fortunate.[54]

The reference to Professor Taylor's darkness is not incidental. *The Third Generation* is partially Chester Himes's take on the passing novel. Lillian is white enough that in some contexts she might have been able to pass, and so much of her hatred of her husband's darkness, much of her unease around black people, stems from the fact that she feels as if she *should* be able to live as white, not unlike the real-life Homer Plessy, who felt his white looks and ancestry should overrule the portion of blackness in his lineage that would force him into the Jim Crow car.

Professor Taylor accepts a teaching post in Pine Bluff, Arkansas (based on the present-day University of Arkansas at Pine Bluff), but when the family has to move to St. Louis, he is forced to leave the profession and go to work as a laborer doing odd jobs. Himes eloquently explains what being a college professor meant to a black man like William Taylor: "Professor Taylor had no ability at all for city life. At heart he was a missionary. He'd lived life in Southern Negro Colleges. There, a professor was somebody. He counted in the neighborhood. His family counted too. But in St. Louis he didn't count. He'd gotten a job waiting tables in a roadhouse out near Carondelet."[55]

The black college, like the black church, was a space wherein an educated black person could be in a leadership position and could find some measure of dignity and respect. It was a space where black men could assume a leadership role and be respected as men and not as "boys" who served white people.

And while black women often struggled against patriarchy, they too found space to be practicing intellectuals in black institutions. It is in the "counting" that the black academic novel finds its meaning. In black academic novels blackademics count in a way that they simply do not in the rest of the genre of the academic novel, where their representations are sparse to nonexistent and where if they do exist it is only as the backstory to some white professor's profound life lessons.

As observable in *Stranger and Alone* and *Invisible Man*, though the black college campus is not utopia, it could be a space of reprieve from the constant humiliations of Jim Crow. For the black professor, the black college is an opportunity to develop his intellectual gifts and take on a leadership role. The honorific title "Fess Taylor" meant much to Charles Taylor but meant little to nothing in the white world. In Langston Hughes's "Professor" he also draws out this spatial contrast showing the black professor T. Walton Brown traveling in spaces where his education and title accrue him no advantage. Now one *could* read this desire for the titles and prestige of academia through an elitist lens, that the educated black person expects to be treated with deference because of his educated status and presumes that others should be content with lesser treatment. Of course, no one, with or without formal education, should have to endure the insults that the average black person endured under Jim Crow. But in this context, it is less about a sense of entitlement than about the thwarted opportunity for social mobility and the restrictions against the black intellectual to live a life of meaning and purpose according to her talents. The cultivation of that intellectual talent is what Du Bois was after in his theorizations of "the talented tenth." He insisted that all workers deserved labor rights and dignity, but that the black race also needed to allow its intellectuals an opportunity to pursue their research and scholarship, to attain professional credentials, and participate in the activities that white intellectuals did, as medical and legal professionals, scholars, political leaders, and people who could shape research, scholarship, and policy.

After Charles is involved in a car crash, Professor Taylor's family is held liable, and Mrs. Taylor refuses to chip in, instead using her money to buy a new place. The conflict between Mrs. Taylor and her husband's family, who took them in, is driven by her racial hatred. Lillian Taylor feels like she shouldn't have to live a black life, refusing to reconcile herself with blackness. It is an ugly portrait that Himes paints but one meant to reckon with the full cost of white-supremacist ideology and its psychological effects. The effect on Lillian Taylor is best seen in the way she tries to connect her children to their white ancestry:

> "Has mother ever told you about your great-grandfather, Dr. Jessie Manning? He was in the United States Senate before the Civil War." There was the queer note of pride in her voice which he despised.
> "Yes, you've told me all about all of 'em," he said harshly.

> She was suddenly saddened by his attitude. Why couldn't he realize his great potentialities? Why couldn't he be proud of himself?[56]

For Lillian the only available pride that she could find, the only pride that mattered, was in proximity to whiteness.

Much of the trouble that Charles encounters later in the novel can be traced back to the harrowing accident where he falls down an open elevator shaft while working at his hotel job. Himes describes Charles's injuries with gruesome clarity:

> The findings showed that he had three fractured vertebrae at the base of his spine, a compound fracture of the left arm above the wrist, a fractured jaw and twenty-two chipped and broken teeth. The extent of the internal injuries was indeterminable, but there was no indication of internal hemorrhage. He'd landed partly on the elevator guard and partly on the concrete floor of the shaft. His chin, back, and left arm had struck simultaneously.[57]

Although Charles heals well enough to leave the hospital and return to an active life, he never really recovers from the accident, feels self-conscious about his injuries, and loses interest in college. "As a consequence, college never got him, never got down inside him; he never became a part of it. He matriculated and went to classes, but he never became a student. He missed entirely the purpose of college, the idea, the realization that it was a place of higher learning. He was always just outside"[58] Charles is attracted to some aspects of the campus environment but repulsed by others: "There were too many students, six thousand of them, of which only five hundred were colored. He felt out numbered again. And the exclusiveness which at first he'd found so appealing carried its own bitter sting of exclusion."[59]

Himes manages to combine elements of the professorromane (in the first chapters about Professor Taylor and the family) and the college novel (in chapters 23 and 24 as Charles himself makes an aborted attempt at being a college student after his accident). And in its college-novel elements at a majority-white college (based on The Ohio State University, where Himes attended) it provides a stark contrast with the black college campuses that he grew up on:

> Negro students were barred from all the fraternities and sororities whose houses bordered the university grounds, nor were they invited to join any of the student clubs and honorary societies of the university itself. Nor could they patronize any of the privately owned restaurants, cafés and theatres of the neighborhood, which seemed so essential to a sense of ease. From the very first he knew he didn't really belong, and that he never would.[60]

The latter part of the novel hews close to its naturalistic mode as Charles intentionally smashes up the car that his mother was going to take away from him. When he takes up with whores and lives on the rough side of town with a pimp named Dave, the Taylors go looking for him, and when Dave slaps Mrs. Taylor, William steps in to defend her and is stabbed to death. It is only after the incident is over that Charles realizes that his parents were trying to reconcile after their divorce, and that they had gone there looking for him together, which makes him even more guilty in the end.

With this bleak, heavy ending, Himes clearly intends this to be a dark naturalistic novel about a character struggling with massive social forces beyond his control. *The Third Generation* challenges the uplift ideology of earlier periods and signals the discontent to come in the post–civil rights era as many young black Americans began to question the educational aspirations of their parents and whether the Education Gospel was enough to save them from the degradation of Jim Crow. By the 1960s some of them began to fashion new, defiant cultural identities and develop a new brand of militancy that would transform college campuses in the years to come.

Chapter 4

✦

Integration and Nationalism, 1954–1980

In the past several years there has been a flurry of scholarship reevaluating the history and politics of student activism in the 1960s and 1970s. It includes books such as *From Black Power to Black Studies: How a Radical Social Movement Became an Academic Discipline* (2007), by Fabio Rojas; *The Black Campus Movement: Black Students and the Racial Reconstitution of Higher Education, 1965–1972* (2012), by Ibram X. Kendi; and *The Black Revolution on Campus* (2012), by Martha Biondi. These studies chronicle the student protests that transformed American universities after the 1960s, creating changes that included the infusion of more black students and faculty on the campuses of PWIs as well as the development of black studies programs in both HBCUs and PWIs.

But here I'd like to take a cue from Roderick Ferguson's *The Reorder of Things: The University and Its Pedagogies of Minority Difference* (2012) and consider these student movements not just as historical markers but also as "pivots in the history of power's relationship to difference."[1] These movements created opportunities for inclusion but also raised more challenging questions about what Ferguson refers to as the biopolitics of institutionalization. What does it mean to have institutionalized black studies programs with degrees and curricula regulated by the board of a university that is inherently linked to the state and to the corporations that fund the university? What are the ways in which minority difference has been co-opted by universities through diversity initiatives that ensure tokenism but actively resist a politics of liberation?

These historical studies of student protest have arrived at a moment of resurgent campus activism. In 2015 a student revolt started by black women activists at the University of Missouri's flagship campus in Columbia, organized under the name Concerned Student 1950 and inspired by the Black Lives Matter movement, made national headlines when it was joined by the college's football team, part of the highly competitive, football-rabid Southeastern Conference. The football team refused to practice or play until the president, Tim Wolfe, resigned, and their protest threatened to lead to the cancellation of a game with Brigham Young University on November 14, 2015, that would have cost the university one million dollars (which also raised more conversations about "amateurism" and the revenue from big-time college sports). The college's president and chancellor eventually resigned under pressure from the students' demands.

The University of Missouri protest rang familiar to me because I had been reading Gil Scott-Heron's 1972 black college novel *The Nigger Factory*. In it a militant student group led by members of the school's football team organize into a black nationalist organization. The novel is set on an HBCU campus and thus has a different dynamic in its conflict between students and administrators. Furthermore, the real-life Missouri protest was initiated by black women activists, whereas *The Nigger Factory* has a rather patriarchal view of black protest with the efforts led mainly by black men.

Here I would like to explore Scott-Heron's novel with and against the womanist critique embedded in Alice Walker's 1976 student-protest novel *Meridian*. Both *The Nigger Factory* and *Meridian* resonate with the HBCU novels that came before them—particularly *Quicksand*, *Invisible Man*, and *Stranger and Alone*—in that all of them show the black artist and intellectual positioned against their conservative black institutions. They all criticize the historically black college as a place where students are indoctrinated into respectability politics and an allegiance to whiteness. Both novels reveal the fundamental tension that Roderick Ferguson describes in his work—that the institutionalization of knowledge brings with it many contradictions and challenges for black persons, to whom these institutions have been historically hostile and fundamentally antiblack. Both Walker and Scott-Heron insist that the regime of antiblackness in higher education includes the HBCUs, and through their novels they both interrogate what it means for black people to be educated in these institutions nominally for black people but wrapped up in the ideology of white supremacy.

This period between the two eras of the student protests of the 1970s and those of the 2010s marks a historical shift from black students and professors being relegated to the campuses of black colleges to an era in which black academics were accepted onto white college campuses. Kept in mind, of course, is the fact that HBCUs continue to exist, and in these same years many African Americans, including this author, made conscious decisions to study and teach at HBCUs. Although this chapter focuses on the integration era, the literature of 1954 to 1980 exists mostly in the world of black colleges, but the concerns of the creative works in this period also set the stage for what followed in the remainder of twentieth-century higher education.

The period I isolate in this chapter also includes Paule Marshall's 1969 novel *The Chosen Place, the Timeless People*, a novel that addresses developments in global black politics in the 1960s, including ideas of Pan-Africanism and anticolonialism. With its inventive story line about a team of white anthropologists doing field research in an impoverished section of a British Caribbean island, Marshall subversively examines the relationship between power, institutionality, and social-scientific knowledge production. And at the level of genre, Marshall's novel also reveals why "campus novel" is an inadequate designation, since her novel shows white American academics working outside the campus setting and outside the borders of the United States. In this international context Marshall presents a narrative about the American university's power and reach beyond the grove of academe and its complicity with capitalist interests abroad.

However, I begin my discussion of this period of integration and nationalism with a series of books that, at first glance, might seem to belong to the previous generation of novels. The story line of W. E. B. Du Bois's *The Black Flame* trilogy begins in the post-Reconstruction era and covers the same early years of black education depicted in the novels by Griggs, Larsen, Ellison, Redding, Himes, and others. However, the novels of *The Black Flame* were published post-1954, the last coming just two years before Du Bois died in Ghana on August 27, 1963, the day before the March on Washington for Jobs and Freedom. Whereas Du Bois did not live to see that seminal event (he was living in Ghana after his complete split with the United States), the narrative of the trilogy runs through the 1950s, and the influence of this burgeoning civil rights movement can be seen in Du Bois's taking stock of the political progress of black America and interrogating the narrative of "progress" at every step.

The Artist Denied

The fact that I can even include Du Bois in a conversation about post-*Brown* novels is just another example of the astounding length and breadth of his career. *The Black Flame*, a trilogy of novels of 1957, 1959, and 1961, is a window into Du Bois's perceptions of post–World War II America and where it would be headed after McCarthyism, after the civil rights movement, and in the age of integration, postcolonialism, and expansions of higher education to marginalized populations. In Brent Edwards's introduction to the Oxford edition of the second novel in the trilogy, *Mansart Builds a School*, he describes the novel as "perhaps Du Bois' most thorough attempt to elaborate—through the fiction of interpretation—on higher education of African Americans." Edwards also notes that the book portrays the world of land-grant black colleges funded by the second Morrill Act of 1890 and explores the impact these colleges would have on American higher education.[2] Of course, the development of those black colleges was not a separate but equal situation. Often these schools were constrained by the white-supremacist politicians who controlled their funding and development and wanted to ensure that these schools were educating black students to be respectful of white supremacy's racial hierarchy.

June Cara Christian provides one of the most extensive interpretations of

The Black Flame in *Understanding the "Black Flame" and Multigenerational Educational Trauma: Toward a Theory of the Dehumanization of Black Students*. In it she applies critical race methodology to the novels, emphasizing the importance of "counternarrative." Her description of counterstories as part of critical race theory are applicable beyond Du Bois to other black academic fiction, such as the work of legal scholar Derrick Bell, whose "chronicles" (as he called them) in works such as *Faces at the Bottom of the Well* and *And We Are Not Saved* leap across the boundaries between legal scholarship and academic fiction. As Christian writes,

> Counterstorytelling and counter-narrative, as a part of CRT [critical race theory] and critical race methodology in education, have five basic elements: (1) understanding the intercentricity of race and racism with other forms of subordination; (2) challenging the dominant ideology; (3) a commitment to social justice; (4) locating the centrality of experiential knowledge; and (5) presenting a transdisciplinary perspective.[3]

As I maintain throughout this study, the black academic novel operates as a counternarrative to ideas about black educability and to the racist structures of academic institutions. Individual novelists may differ in their strategies and perspectives regarding race and racism, but all of them necessarily confront these white-supremacist ideas. Black academic novels, as experiential knowledge about the university and as creative writing, contest the hegemony of antiblackness, celebrate black creativity, and affirm the place of black people in institutions of higher education.

Manuel Mansart's early life is closely linked with Emanuel African Methodist Episcopal Church in Charleston, South Carolina, a place that has now become part of the contemporary national conversation on racial violence. In *The Ordeal of Mansart*, we learn Manuel is born near Mother Emanuel, and his father, Tom Mansart, a Reconstruction politician, is lynched by a white-supremacist mob outside the church, near its front steps. It is now impossible to write about *The Black Flame* without mentioning one of the most heinous incidents of gun violence in American history (among the many, many, many mass shootings in America's bloody twenty-first century thus far).

On the evening of June 17, 2015, a twenty-one-year-old white supremacist, who had been radicalized by the toxic stew of racism on white-supremacist websites such as Stormfront, drove from his home in Shelby, North Carolina, to downtown Charleston, South Carolina. He walked into Emanuel AME Church to join the Wednesday night prayer meeting, a sacred tradition of midweek Bible study and worship in black churches. The members of the historically black church welcomed him in, talked with him, and prayed with him for nearly an hour. And then he rose and began shooting them one by one.

The nine people killed in this unspeakable act of terrorism included the minister and state senator Rev. Clementa Pinckney, 41; Cynthia Hurd, 54; Suzie Jackson, 87; Ethel Lance, 70; Rev. DePayne Middleton-Doctor, 49; Tywanza Sanders, 26; Rev. Daniel Simmons, 74; Rev. Sharonda Coleman-Singleton, 45; and Myra Thompson, 59. The website HBCU Story noted the prevalence of HBCU graduates among the victims. Pinckney, Sanders, and Simmons graduated from the AME-affiliated Allen University (named for AME founder Richard Allen), Coleman-Singleton from South Carolina State University, Hurd from Clark Atlanta University, and Thompson from Livingstone College and Benedict College.[4]

Reading Du Bois's trilogy in the wake of the Charleston massacre I was reminded of the historical links between the black church and the black college, two of the most important institutions for cultivating black talent and organizing black political power. This historic relationship is one of the reasons Du Bois sketched out a novelistic treatment of the black church in his unfinished manuscript "Bethesda A.M.E."[5] In *The Ordeal of Mansart*, Du Bois names his main character Manuel as an allusion to the biblical prophet Emmanuel and to the history of Emanuel AME Church. The name evokes the prophetic-heroic role that Manuel Mansart plays in an epic narrative of black life in the American South (and beyond) that stretches from 1876 to 1954. The church, and what it represents, is an important element in the story that Du Bois tells in *The Black Flame* about white supremacy and the struggle for black education in the post-Reconstruction years in a state that was the first to secede from the Union in 1861. The very existence of Mother Emanuel, a bastion of independent, educated, free black people since 1816, has always been seen as an affront to white supremacy. And the white supremacist's disdain for overeducated Negroes is an idea that Du Bois registers again and again in his novels about black education.

The historians who compiled the #CharlestonSyllabus project—Keisha Blain, Chad Williams, and Kidada Williams—have reminded us that this tragedy fits into a long history of white-supremacist violence and a long history of black defiance in the face of that violence.[6] And now, in the wake of the 2016 election, many people have likened this current political moment to other periods of backlash after black progress, such as the violent post-Reconstruction era that Rayford Logan dubbed the nadir of African American life.[7] The civil rights movement was riddled with assassinations along the way, and the 1965 Voting Rights Act gave birth to the Republican "southern strategy." It is likely that future historians will see the 2016 election as yet another example of the historical "whitelash" against black progress. The first black president of the United States was a measured, intelligent black law professor who spoke eloquently of the project of multiracial democracy (even if his policies fell short of his lofty rhetoric). His two-term presidency was followed up by white America's embrace of a profane, semiliterate clown of a businessman with ties to global white-supremacist groups who ran under a fascist "America First" slogan, stocked his cabinet and staff with devout white nationalists, implemented vicious anti-immigrant policies, and whose popularity was driven by the very same racist underground from which the Charleston shooter emerged (along with other recent white-nationalist terrorists).[8]

Over the course of *The Black Flame*, Du Bois documents the specifics of how that historical backlash took place, from the Ku Klux Klan's post-Reconstruction emergence to the series of antiblack riots in Wilmington (1898), Atlanta (1906), East St. Louis (1917), and Tulsa (1921). With detailed chapters in *The Ordeal of Mansart* on the Atlanta Riot (14) and its aftermath (15), Du Bois includes in this narrative the copious record of antiblack violence in the early twentieth century, and he is intent upon showing how that violence shaped the choices black intellectuals made about their scholarship and activism.

"It was October 1876 . . ." begins the first volume of the trilogy, *The Ordeal of Mansart*. This opening marks this as a story that begins at the end of Reconstruction, and Tom Mansart (Manuel's father) is a black Reconstruction politician. He is on his way to a meeting at the home of the wealthy South Carolina planter Colonel Breckenridge, and the way that Breckenridge describes the black man approaching his home, as "probably one of those half-educated darkies who were misleading and befuddling the bewildered Negroes," represents the feelings of many white southerners about such new, uppity black leaders.[9] Colonel Breckenridge is outraged that men who were formerly enslaved were now sitting in the same chambers in which John C. Calhoun, Edward Rutledge, and Charles Pinckney sat. And yes, it is striking that the name of the South Carolina political patriarch Charles Pinckney and the white Pinckney family are referenced in *The Black Flame*, and that one of the Charleston shooting victims was a black South Carolina state representative, Clementa Pinckney, who bore that same distinctive last name.

After his meeting with Colonel Breckenridge a riot instigated by the Ku Klux Klan breaks out, and Tom Mansart ends up cornered by a dilemma. He must decide whether to send Mrs. Breckenridge off by herself or go with her and try to protect her. "If he deserted her she would turn against him and his plans and her husband would certainly be his enemy. She might even be killed deliberately—even here in the city,—and her murder placed at his door. On the other hand, it was dangerous to drive openly into the very center of the city tonight with a planter's wife, and into the very midst of a gathering of the Klan."[10] He decides his best strategy is to help Mrs. Breckenridge escape. She faints in the buggy as they approach the downtown area, and Tom Mansart is dragged from the buggy and lynched in front of the church. At the same time that he is murdered, Tom's mother is in a nearby house with his wife, who is in labor with their first child. After he is born the boy's grandmother carries him into Emanuel AME Church, anoints him with his father's blood, and declares his name shall be Manuel.

The Black Flame's epic narrative is set against the backdrop of twentieth-century world history. The character of Manuel Mansart is not entirely autobiographical (a character suggestive of Du Bois makes a cameo appearance later in the novel), but he is an avatar for the ambitious black educational agenda that Du Bois fought for over the course of his career. As Manuel Mansart states at the end of the first volume of the trilogy when he recognizes and accepts his destiny as a race man and an intellectual leader, "I am that Black Flame in which my grandmother believed and on whose blood-stained body she swore. I am the Black Flame, but I burn for cleaning, not destroying. Therefore I burn slow."[11]

In a bitingly ironic passage in the beginning of *The Ordeal of Mansart* Du Bois imitates the thought of the southern aristocrats in the novel and their interpretations of black education, providing another example of how overeducation discourses appear in the literature and echoing the thoughts of Mississippi governor James Vardaman about the dangers of overeducated Negroes.

> Negroes must think of themselves always as workers and never as thinkers or owners; nor as men in the sense that whites were men. Shot across this obvious fact came a system of Negro schools, lugged in by the white Northern carpet-baggers, who ignorantly insisted that Negroes were men. They should have seen, said the Southerners, that their own popular education in the North was leading only to crime, poverty and a travesty on democracy. This might work out in time, since laborers were, after all, white. But it was worse than stupid to think the African could be educated. It was criminal misleading of a simple people born to be servants of men. The first effort, then, of the South for reconstruction of agriculture and normal life, was to stop the ruin of the working class. This was the well-nigh universal public opinion of those who had hitherto always expressed the opinion of the South.[12]

That oppressive "opinion of the South," representing the white-supremacist South that controlled the politics and resources and held power over black lives, is the context in which Manual Mansart must live and operate. In this narrative, Du Bois shows how Mansart's life intersects with the lives of the powerful southern white men who control the statehouses, corporations, and schoolhouses. Du Bois also shows the violence that often ensued when black leadership stepped out of line, was deemed too militant, or otherwise failed to show the proper deference to white-supremacist rule.

Critics of Du Bois's fiction, including Arnold Rampersad, Keith Byerman, and Claudia Tate, have frequently commented on the deficiencies in Du Bois's literary style, a topic to which I return shortly in a discussion of his aesthetics and politics. Du Bois inventively combines elements of historical fiction and the academic novel in this narrative of a young black man who grows up to become a college president and world-traveled intellectual. But the narrative is also bogged down by historical detail, and it is reasonable to suspect that some of the long blocks of historical exposition in the books are because of Du Bois's leaning more on his historical writing than his literary imagination. With such an expansive narrative, my interpretation of the novel and its cast of characters has to be selective; there are, however, several extended studies of *The Black Flame* that go into more detail.

A minor character who merits mention in this discussion is the black historian Sebastian Doyle, covered in chapter 10 of *The Ordeal of Mansart*, "The Vision of Sebastian Doyle." In his description of Doyle, Du Bois saliently articulates the plight of the black intellectual: "Doyle had not only studied the Negro problem, he embodied the Negro problem. It was bone of his bone and flesh of his flesh. It made his world and filled his thought."[13] Academia often exalts the image of the ideal scholar as a disinterested, objective observer of the world, but here Du Bois argues that for the black intellectual, who must operate in a profession and in institutions where he is not supposed to exist, there can be no such objectivity, and, furthermore, there never was such objectivity for white scholars in a white-supremacist academy. And the character of Sebastian Doyle echoes a concept that Du Bois writes about earlier, in the preface to *The Souls of Black Folk*, where he writes, "Need I add that I who speak here am bone of the bone and flesh of the flesh of them that live within the veil?"[14] This is a moment where Du Bois rejects his own exceptionality and declares himself to be a racial representative. He embraces racial representation as something that is not a burden on his individuality but, rather, an important strategy to connect his intellectual labor to the population of oppressed people whom he writes about and with whom he is associated.

The fictionalized version of "Pitchfork" Ben Tillman is vociferous in his hatred of Sebastian Doyle, an activist who believed in the power of the black vote and who, with the white populist Tom Watson, became involved in efforts to secure the voting rights of black citizens in South Carolina. About Tillman, Du Bois writes,

> Especially he was incensed at the phenomenon which Doyle, the Negro companion of Watson, represented. If he hated Negroes in general, his hate of educated Negroes was emphasized by fear. They wanted to be white; they talked white. Once they got a chance they would be white, lord it over poor whites and marry their sisters. It must never happen. This Doyle must be lynched.[15]

Du Bois, in the historian's mode, includes an extensive discussion of how the white supremacist Tillman rejected the interracial populism of Tom Watson and "became leader of the movement toward legal and permanent color caste in the United States."[16] Even among the liberal supporters of black education in the South there were still concerns about what kind of education it would be and what it might do to upset the racial order. In one passage about such educational efforts, Du Bois writes,

Conferences on Negro education began to be held by liberal Southerners, in Capon Springs, a Virginia vacation resort. Of course, no Negroes could attend; this was a white man's resort. The Negro must be educated, but his education at present must be limited to elementary subjects and industry, and it must be preceded by and predicated upon the earlier and better education of poor white children.[17]

But the Doyle character is also indicative of the frustratingly truncated nature of Du Bois's novelistic writing. There isn't much more about him in this narrative. There's a large cast of characters, some of whom are introduced and fall away. And even when it comes to Manuel Mansart, the novel's central character, there are parts in the narrative when he gets pushed offstage for pages on end while Du Bois pontificates on different episodes in history.

Mansart's move to a small Georgia town is an opportunity for Du Bois to apply his sociological analysis of a rural southern community based on race, land, education, sex, religion, and gossip. "Next to money and status in Jerusalem was sex: the thought, the planning, the dreaming of sex."[18] In a passage about life in rural Georgia, Du Bois makes a provocative turn toward the subject of race and sexuality and, with a rather sardonic tone, writes about the racial taboos in the South. "Every white man of any pretension was expected to have a white wife and at least one colored concubine. Each colored man could have a colored wife but he might be asked to share her with a white man. On the other hand, he must not dare even think of touching a white woman even accidentally."[19] That intimacy, the proximity of black and white bodies together in public spaces, was always a sexually charged matter. The tensions explode into violence later in the next volume, *Mansart Builds a School*, in the story of Mansart's son, Bruce, who is assaulted by a policeman after an encounter between two groups of students following a big football game in Atlanta. And that intimacy is also behind a rather problematic scene where an out-of-control Bruce intends to rape Zoe Coypel, the daughter of the prominent school administrator Arnold Coypel, and kills the policeman who assaulted him. The conceptualizations of sexuality and race are even more explicitly explored in the academic novels to follow, including the pornographic fantasies of Samuel Delany's queer characters in *The Mad Man* and their desires to violate the taboos of interracial sexuality.

When it comes to the academic novel, *Mansart Builds a School* is the most relevant single volume of this trilogy in its devotion to the history and politics of black higher education. From 1920 to 1946 Manuel Mansart serves as president of Georgia A & M State College for Negroes in Macon, and in chapter 11, "The New Education," Du Bois directly addresses the economics and politics of black higher education. *Mansart Builds a School* begins where *Ordeal* left off, with Mansart as superintendent of black schools in Atlanta. A bit of metafictional play comes when the northern black intellectual James Burghardt, who earned his Ph.D. at Yale, arrives at Atlanta University. The character is a device that allows Du Bois to conduct some self-reflexive criticism, to evaluate the reception of his ideas among other black intellectuals who criticized and challenged him throughout his career.[20]

The gender politics of the novel are complicated to say the least. Little is said about Mansart's wife, Susan, who gets only a glancing mention in the beginning and comes up again only in her righteous anger about her sons having to fight in World War I for a country that will not respect their rights. A notable moment of misogyny comes from Manual Mansart's own son, Douglass Mansart, who, upon meeting the sociologist Jean Du Bignon, "was rather repelled. He did not believe it was the business of girls to go to college or to become, as he put it, over-educated."[21] (Yes, there's that word again.) Du Bois also, once again, addresses the topic of colorism, writing that "when Jean Du Bignon actually arrived, there was added to Douglass' distaste for over-educated women, his further recoil from white colored folks." The language here is suggestive of Patricia Hill Collins's notion of a "matrix of domination," with Jean Du Bignon experiencing race, gender, and color discrimination simultaneously.[22] In fact, there's a whole section about Du Bignon and her fellow Louisiana native Sarah Breedlove, aka Madame CJ Walker. Du Bois includes a section ruminating on the ironies of Madame Walker's life as a proud black businesswoman whose beauty products were sold with appeals to lighter skin and straighter hair. Furthermore, touching on what Nella Larsen previously examined in *Quicksand*, Du Bois recognizes the prevalence of colorism from a different angle, in which people of mixed-race ancestry were not preferred for being closer to whiteness but were detested for their racial ambiguity. Du Bois also recognizes that the challenges for even educated white women are related to the South's rigid gender roles when he writes, "There is little worse in the South than the plight of a young white woman of social position without prospect of a suitable marriage. Education and career for self-support might do for Northerners, but the concept trickled into the South only with the new century, and then slowly."[23] Though Du Bois sounded an early feminist note in his earlier novel *The Quest of the Silver Fleece* (1911) with the dynamic character Zora, and though he wrote Jean Du Bignon as an assertive black intellectual in *The Black Flame*, there is also room for a critique of gender in the trilogy, as Celena Simpson provides in her critical article on the portrayals of women in the narrative.[24] In the next volume, *Worlds of Color*, "The Dismissal of Jean Du Bignon" shows Jean getting caught up in a red-baiting campaign, and the narrative clearly reflects the pain and frustration of Du Bois's last years as he ran afoul of America's anticommunist hysteria. The chapter mentions some of the touchstones of that hysteria, including the case of Julius and Ethel Rosenberg, the Harlem communist and city council member Benjamin Davis, and the case of black labor organizer Angelo Herndon.

The story of Manuel's son, Bruce, highlighted in chapter 11, "The Beautiful Brown Boy," is a melodramatic episode in which the young man's life goes off the rails. He is a star quarterback for the college's football team but shows little interest in his academics. His fall is precipitated by an incident of police brutality after the big football game versus Atlanta University when a group of black college students end up crossing paths with a group of white students from the game of Georgia Tech against the University of Georgia held on the same day in Atlanta. The depiction of Bruce essentially turns him into a heavy-handed caricature of the black male as rapist beast as he threatens Zoe Coypel and bludgeons to death the police officer who assaulted him during the incident in Atlanta. His life spirals out of control into a life of robbery and gambling in Kansas City that ends with him committing another murder and then executed by hanging.

In the part about Bruce as a football star, Du Bois seems aware of the significance of the black athlete as an important political figure in twentieth-century America. The chapter begins with Manuel Mansart as a college administrator contemplating the significance of athletics. He considers it a distraction from the university's mission but eventually concedes that it's an aspect of college life that he cannot avoid and must deal with. Reading that story line is one of many times that I have questioned my decision to exclude a more robust analysis of college athletics here, and I admit that it is one of those thorny theoretical problems that I've decided to sidestep, particularly since the black athlete is a figure that appears in other black college novels, including *The Nigger Factory*, and in films like John Singleton's *Higher Learning*. As I complete this work, the country is embroiled in debates over National Football League (NFL) quarterback Colin Kaepernick, who was exiled from the league for his kneeling in protest against police brutality during the playing of the national anthem. His protests sparked a national movement of athletes kneeling during the national anthem and drew out racist attacks from Donald Trump and other white-supremacist politicians, who saw an opportunity to use the caricature of the "ungrateful rich black athlete" as a weapon in the culture war. At the same time, there are ongoing conversations about the labor of college athletes who have helped build college sports into a multibillion-dollar enterprise while the National Collegiate Athletic Association insists on maintaining "amateurism" for college athletes despite the escalating profits. That so many highly visible athletes are black is a factor in the public attitudes about them as laborers and protesters.[25] This topic of college sports is one that intersects with my analysis of the black intellectual, and I can see the potential in a project that fully incorporates analysis of black athletes into a study of academic representations. However, there is also a glut of sports information, and college athletics already receives so much attention that I am willing to bypass it here, save for a few notable exceptions. I keep my attention on the plight of black students and faculty outside the sports world in hopes of illuminating the lives of academics in spaces on campus where they may be less visible to the general public.

Mansart Builds a School ends with a passage in which Mansart reflects on all that has come before, on his life's calling as an educator. It shows him walking on the college campus, affirming the significance of the physical space of the campus as a setting for the hopes and dreams of the race:

> [Mansart] wandered sleepless about his college grounds, as so often he had been wont to do in the early days of its beginning when evil lurked. He saw the same stars that shone on Washington, and the mist which started toward them. He believed that beyond the mist burned the Black Flame. How could it be black if it flamed? How could it burn without heat and wild destruction? Yet all this it did, and the dark blaze of its urge as it rolled and roared out of the South bound his heart and world, into one whole of Power and Peace, of Freedom and Law, of Force and Love. But not yet, not for a long, long time yet; and his tears blurred the mist that hid the stars.[26]

This image at the end of the second book, placing the black college in an international and cosmic perspective, sets up the third book of the trilogy, *Worlds of Color*, which depicts Mansart's evolving internationalism and his global vision of the black intellectual who lives in a Jim Crow society at home but sees the potentials for coalition with nonwhite populations around the globe, in Latin America, Africa, the Middle East, and Asia. For Mansart, his later tour of Europe and Asia helps him to broaden his intellectual horizons and to consider the interaction of capital, labor, and education and to explore the relations between the white-supremacist European nations and the United States and a broader "world of color" that includes Asia and Africa.[27]

The capitalist critique in *Worlds of Color* is an indicator of Du Bois's late-career engagement with Marxism. While in London, Mansart attends a dinner party at which his wealthy white English hosts express their curiosity about his thoughts on black labor. Mansart insists that value is created by laborers themselves and that what the wealthy do is not "work" at all. As Mansart states to one of the women, "Milady, you never picked cotton. You see, I was a child of workers. I was raised to work for what I wanted. You, if I may say so without offense—do not work."[28] This discussion between Mansart and his hosts on colonialism, property, and the law bears resonances with Paule Marshall's depiction of the colonial relations of the British Caribbean in *The Chosen Place, the Timeless People*. Indeed, one of the most important interventions that the black academic novel makes against the conventions of the genre is to situate academic institutions and academic knowledge production in the context of racial capitalism instead of depicting the campus as a cloistered world unto itself.

This chapter also shows Du Bois interrogating his idea of "the talented tenth" as a natural vanguard and aristocracy, giving Mansart a powerful statement on the condition of the black intellectual, not just as another academic, scholar, or administrator but as one who is inextricably linked to the history of black subjugation and thereby bearing a responsibility and a burden of representation to uphold (again keeping in mind that black intellectuals can have differing strategies for how they, individually, chose to deal with this responsibility and representation):

> You can't realize, Sir John, by what narrow chance I had the opportunity just to live, much less to grow healthy, go to school and college and get this work. I was born, sir, in my father's blood as he was shot to bits by a mob. My mother worked her hands to the bone to keep me in school. I cringed and crawled to keep my job as a school teacher and to head this college. And while I was doing this, thousands of black boys and girls had no chance, no opportunity and sank to hunger and crime and shameful death because God forgot them.[29]

This is another example of the black intellectual's refusal to be seduced by his own exceptionality and an affirmation of the statement Du Bois makes at the beginning of *Black Reconstruction*, that the black person develops as any other person develops given the same resources and opportunities, and that many of the boys and girls Mansart left behind had never been given the opportunity to do what he had done.

In "The Color of Europe" Manuel Mansart goes to France and Germany, in scenes that were likely informed by Du Bois's time studying there in the late 1800s. Of course, this would become a very different Germany by the 1920s, and Du Bois includes some commentary on the rise of Nazism and Hitler: "The greatest single invention of World War I was propaganda—the systematic distortion of the truth for the purpose of making large numbers of people believe anything authority wished them to believe. It grew into an art, not a science"[30] This chapter echoes Du Bois's critical view of Europe in the *Darkwater* essay "The Souls of White Folk" on the self-destructiveness of white supremacy and how the chickens of colonialism had come home to roost in Europe.

In "The Color of Asia" Manuel Mansart writes home a long letter about China, again one of those instances where Du Bois's biography coincides with the experiences that he gives to his character. And in chapter 6, "Color in the West Indies," Du Bois makes a statement on colonialism that sets the stage for what Paule Marshall covers in her postcolonial Caribbean academic novel: "It seemed curiously clear now to Jean what had happened since. Great Britain had transformed her investments in the West Indies, and in the name of emancipation exchanged West Indian plantations for new investment and expanded capitalism in African and Asian colonies. Thence came the industrial revolution and the new imperialism born of the blood of Negro slaves."[31] Mansart sends Jean to the West Indies, largely as the result of the influence of a Caribbean intellectual he had met in Europe: "A Negro named James gave me his book to read and it is revolutionary. We must include the West Indies in our survey." The reference is to the Trinidadian intellectual C. L. R. James, another one of the cameo appearances made here by historical figures and an example of Du Bois's global political vision and the anticolonialism that linked black intellectuals across the diaspora.

What the narrative shows is a gradual expansion of Manuel Mansart's world. Born into the bitter segregation of South Carolina he looks outward to a great world where the darker races are not inferior and are not a minority but are numerous, diverse, and stretch far across the globe. The latter chapters of *Worlds of Color* show the world-historical scope of the novel as Manuel Mansart's life and thought begin to expand beyond the narrowness of the domestic Negro Question in America. So much of his energy had been bound up in that struggle, but he comes to realize that his own particular situation is part of a much bigger geopolitical sphere, one that not only broadened his horizons but also complicated his role as a race man.

> Somehow it seemed to him that his students as individuals, and the seething dark millions back of them were melting away from his touch, were getting further and further from his influence. Once they were all his people. He had had his arms about them and was protecting and guiding them. This was no longer true. Other things, the world itself, had intruded, and come between him and the Negro people. He had been sucked up into greater and wider causes—Peace, Socialism, the meaning of all life. He wanted now to rid himself of diversion and get back to the Negro problem, to concentrate all his energy and hope there. And yet, if he and his folk were part of this wider world, how could he or they ever really separate?[32]

What Du Bois and other black academic novelists repeatedly address in their work is that the black academic is one who is specifically identified and hailed as constitutionally, biologically, and metaphysically incapable of being a scholar. The necessities of racial capitalism under slavery and in its afterlife mandated that blacks be constructed as property, as the raw material for wealth extraction, and not as fully formed human beings capable of equal citizenship or intellectual development. And the academy played an important role in the perpetuation of such ideas. From *Notes on the State of Virginia* to *The Bell Curve*, white supremacy has marshaled all its forces of pseudoscience, revisionist history, and racist theology to negate black intelligence and a black presence in history, even as it condescendingly admonishes black people to use education and respectability as a means of upward mobility. *The Black Flame* is such a remarkable and underappreciated literary accomplishment because it shows Du Bois using the malleable form of the novel to include historical and sociological commentary on these ideas and creating a counternarrative of black intellectual history. Collectively, *The Black Flame* serves as a document of Du Bois's commitment to the creation of black art, an attempt to fulfill his admonition in "Criteria of Negro Art" that black art is inherently propaganda and ever must be. Du Bois used the trilogy as a vehicle to explore his belief that black education, specifically black *higher* education, was an important component of the struggle against white supremacy. *The Black Flame*, like all black academic novels, constitutes a powerful counternarrative against white-supremacist overeducation discourses in higher education.

But a deeper interrogation into *The Black Flame* as a novel and Du Bois's approach to literature reveals some conflicted ideas about art and its role in a project of racial uplift. In his introductory "Note" to *The Quest of the Silver Fleece* Du Bois articulates his take on the aesthetics of the novel:

> He who would tell a tale must look toward three ideals: to tell it well, to tell it beautifully, and to tell the truth.
> The first is the Gift of God, the second is the Vision of Genius, but the third is the Reward of Honesty.

Du Bois's postscript to *The Ordeal of Mansart* echoes this idea some fifty years later. "This is the eternal paradox of history. There is but one way to meet this clouding of facts and that is by use of imagination where documented material and personal experience are lacking."[33] Du Bois as a historical writer understands the importance of beauty and art in the telling of history, that history is not merely an accumulation of facts but also includes the aesthetics of storytelling, the elegant condensation of historical events into mythology and poetry.

Mikhail M. Bakhtin's conception of the novel as dialogic helps to make sense of what Du Bois does in this trilogy, showing the novel to be an art form that can accommodate different types of speech and voices, including the voices of the author, narrator, and other characters in the novel, as well as those from extraliterary texts. In David Lodge's book *After Bakhtin*, the academic novelist and literary critic writes about the polyphonic quality of novelistic discourse, stating that "one of the essential peculiarities of prose fiction is the possibility it allows of using different types of discourse, with their distinct expressiveness intact, on the plane of a single work, without reduction to a single common denominator."[34] The novel is a resilient form in the way it incorporates different discursive modes, and the academic novel in particular is one in which different writerly forms, including academic papers and essays and the documents from the business side of the academic profession (letters, CVs, memos, tenure files), can be incorporated into the narrative. As a practicing academic, Du Bois takes these liberties in his novels, filling them with historical and sociological analysis and conversations between characters that allow him to explore theories of race and political economy.

To some readers this is precisely the "failure" of Du Bois's fiction writing. By many aesthetic standards *The Black Flame* is a convoluted narrative. There are places where the novels lapse into tedium and confusion because of the large cast of characters and dense historical details. Although there are certainly literary precedents for Du Bois's grand historical novels, such as the works of Leo Tolstoy, the critical literature on the trilogy seems to suggest its readers are attracted to the novels more from didactic, scholarly fascination than literary pleasure. The novelist and critic John Gardner, in *The Art of Fiction*, writes of the novelist's ability to produce the "vivid and continuous dream." That is, what makes the novel work as a fictional form is when the skilled novelist conjures images in the reader's mind of people and places that seem realistic even though the reader knows they are invented.[35] Furthermore, Gardner maintains, what constitutes "bad" writing in the novel are poor sentences, thin characterizations, or awkward plotting, all of which can have the effect of interrupting that vivid, continuous dream (leaving aside the experimental writer, who may intentionally resist such narrative conventions in the novel).

So there is room to question the aesthetic qualities of *The Black Flame*, but what Du Bois manages to do in these works is to demonstrate that the novel is a form capable of accommodating disparate discursive modes to serve the purposes of a particular concept. For Du Bois that purpose was to compose a monumental narrative of world history through the eyes of a black intellectual in America. Whereas a historical work such as *Black Reconstruction* might contain passages of lyricism and subjective insight, it would be considered unethical for the historian to invent characters and episodes in a historical work, just as this form of the scholarly monograph that I have composed here would be unacceptable if I did not exercise some fidelity to the facts of the lives of the writers I consider and the content that they produced in their novels.

"High Harlem," the fifth chapter of *Mansart Builds a School*, is a particularly representative section of this trilogy when it comes to both the aesthetic qualities of Du Bois's fiction writing and his politics of gender and respectability. I have found it to be a microcosm of everything that is thrilling and frustrating about Du Bois's novelistic writing. In the preceding chapters Du Bois shows Mansart keeping up with issues of *The Crisis* and thinking about what the political activities of the NAACP might mean for him and the black people of the South. In this chapter, Du Bois shows Mansart pondering the creative output of the Harlem Renaissance, including excerpts of black poetry placed in the text. In a long passage that reinforces his famous editorial "Criteria of Negro Art," Du Bois writes,

> This Harlem Renaissance was an abnormal development with abnormal results. It was not a nation bursting into self-expression and applauding those who told its story and feelings best, but rather a group oppressed and despised within a larger group, whose chance for expression depended in large part on what the dominant group wanted to hear and were willing to support. This, then, was but a

part of the true, uninhibited message, and there was consequently offered prizes to those willing to distort truth and play court fool to American culture. Even this situation produced a bit of Negro literature but nothing complete. For a real literature demands truth and real feelings and not submission to what others want to hear, especially when most of these "others" hate the ground on which these black artists walk, and pay well for any caricature which tickles their own false and cheap ego.[36]

In this passage Du Bois goes back to the territory of his editorial in *The Crisis*, thinking about the marketing of black art and how images of educated blacks will be received in the market environment that exists, and in the middle of a novel about a black professor and his struggles to build up a black college, Du Bois speaks to the significance of representations in popular culture, articulating how black art functions in a market as a part of profit-driven culture industries and how these culture industries often cater to the white audience's appetite for specific kinds of black images that affirm their preexisting beliefs about blackness. However, speaking again to the aesthetics of the novel, the narrative drifts away from the story of Mansart, and by the end of "High Harlem" Mansart has been pushed to the edge of the stage while the narrative addresses Harlem real estate, the internal workings of *The Crisis* magazine, the first two meetings of the Pan-African Congress, and the NAACP's relationship to labor.

Du Bois's criticism of the Harlem Renaissance particularly homed in on the more sexually explicit material and the images of black sexuality. One can get a taste of his prudish attitude toward sexuality in his 1928 review of Claude McKay's *Home to Harlem*, in which Du Bois said of McKay, "He has used every art and emphasis to paint drunkenness, fighting, lascivious sexual promiscuity and utter absence of restraint in as bold and as bright colors as he can."[37] He further suggests that McKay has set out "to cater for that prurient demand on the part of white folk for a portrayal of Negroes of utter licentiousness which conventional civilization holds white folk back from enjoying—if enjoyment it can be called." Du Bois leveled similar criticism against the white gay artist Carl Van Vechten (particularly over his scandalous novel *Nigger Heaven*), as well as against Langston Hughes and others.[38] The flip side of his "Questionnaire" admonishing black artists to create representations of educated blacks is that it also reveals how Du Bois was entrenched in a politics of respectability in which the black elite were ashamed of the habits and sexuality of the black lower classes and resentful of queer artists who dared to dramatize, satirize, or otherwise call attention to things that the black elite considered unsavory and undesirable about the lives of the poor and marginalized.

In his study of Du Bois's creative writing, *Seizing the Word*, Keith Byerman identifies a deeper issue in Du Bois's criticism of Claude McKay's decadence.

He suggests that Du Bois actually harbored a "fundamental distrust of aesthetics" and that "his literary assumptions leave no room for the complexity and ambiguity that is usually associated with great art."[39] It was those qualities of the aesthetic and the ambiguous that made a novel like Ralph Ellison's *Invisible Man* such an artistic accomplishment. Du Bois never created such a moral quandary in his fiction as Ellison does with the narrator's retreat into his hole full of lights at the end of *Invisible Man*, an image that still instigates arguments among critics about its meaning. Was this escapism? Is the hole a metaphor for the creative space that the artist needs? Is it a symbol of Ellison's fundamentally conservative approach to the political with a character who retreats into the Kingdom of Culture? Du Bois's Victorian values would not allow for a lurid figure like Trueblood, the sharecropper who regales a white philanthropist with his pornographic story of incest in which he impregnated both his wife and daughter. Ellison created such a vivid and vexing character precisely to spite uptight black intellectuals like Du Bois who would rather not see such indignities in black literature. Perhaps the damning flaw in Du Bois's novels is that, as Byerman puts it, "Du Bois repeatedly seeks ways to bring beauty in literature under the control of truth and goodness."[40]

Inasmuch as I read black academic novels for their political implications, the best of these works aspire to the condition of art, and through the aesthetics of the novel their authors seek the sublime in the black academic life, even when that aesthetic may be at odds with certain political orthodoxies.

All these academic novels confront a history in which black intelligence and educability are persistently interrogated by white supremacists, whose racist ideas about black people were firmly entrenched in American universities from the beginning and remain so. These novels are counternarratives to white-supremacist thought, and they insist upon complex portrayals of black intellectual life, depicting black people as practicing academics and intellectuals while also refusing to be stories of respectability and hat-in-hand pleas for humanity. All these novels—melodramas, tragedies, satires, with highbrow and lowbrow themes—are a means for black intellectuals to articulate their subjectivity as intellectuals, artists, and producers of knowledge and not mere objects of scholarly inquiry. That said, there are real pressures for black artists to create positive images of black people and real reasons to be wary of how their commitment to complexity might mean that their ironic negativity and satirical caricatures can be misinterpreted and misused against them. I attempt to explore this tricky terrain in this book's conclusion, "Blackademics On Screen."

Time and the Making of African Americans

W. E. B. Du Bois's 1899 sociological study *The Philadelphia Negro* was an extraordinary project in which he aimed to use social-scientific data to address the problems afflicting a black community in one American city. However, that very study has since been criticized for the author's construction of black family disorder, and the criticism has been extended to the disciplines of social science, which have often been used to verify black pathologies or to construct nonwhite people as alien, other, and objects to be studied rather than as people who may themselves be producers of knowledge.[41]

A key indicator of Paule Marshall's criticism of social-scientific knowledge production comes in an interview in which she discusses the postcolonial background of *The Chosen Place, the Timeless People*: "I was in Barbados in the fifties overhauling *Brown Girl, Brownstones* when a group of anthropologists who were having their first fieldwork experience came to town. Observing their interaction with the indigenous population both interested and troubled me."[42] *The Chosen Place, the Timeless People* examines the discourses of time in anthropology and challenges the conception of the academic as an innocent, objective observer, an idea that the team of anthropologists in her novel are naive enough to believe but that their research subjects, the people of Bournehills on Bourne Island, rightfully refuse to accept, having seen other academics come to their land before as agents of colonialism and capital.

Marshall's novel addresses the way that academic discourse constructs narratives of progress that justify racial and social hierarchies and denigrate nonwhite, non-Western cultures, but it also, read along with other academic novels, exposes the ways that black American intellectuals sometimes participate in such progress narratives against other diasporic black peoples, particularly in Africa and the Caribbean.

Paule Marshall's first foray into academic fiction was in the story "Brooklyn," featured in her story collection *Soul Clap Hands and Sing* (1961). Marshall described the story as one that came about "thanks to my trials and tribulations with a professor at Brooklyn College."[43] However, instead of being set at the bucolic CUNY campus in Flatbush, "Brooklyn" is set in the confines of a building in downtown Brooklyn, one that bears a striking resemblance to the campus where I now teach.

In the story, the main character is known only by the name that her older, Jewish male professor calls her, "Miss Williams." She is taking a French class with the disgruntled professor who lost his job in a McCarthyist purge at his former school and who fell into teaching at the small college. The professor latches on to her and tries to seduce the talented young student, who is on a summer break from teaching high school in the South and working toward a master's degree in French. The story is set in a time before the term "sexual harassment" became part of the popular lexicon, but this is precisely what Marshall depicts in the story. The end of the story plays out as a bit of revenge fantasy as the student accepts an invitation to take the train up to the professor's upstate home and go swimming in the lake behind his house, which he wished her to do for his lurid pleasure. Later she gets dressed, then tells him off about how his lecherous advances have affected her and angrily leaves him before taking her train ride back to the city. "Brooklyn" is striking in that it touches upon many important topics in higher education that were prevalent in its time and have reverberated since then, including integration, women's rights, McCarthyism, sexual harassment, and black-Jewish relations.[44]

Although *The Chosen Place, the Timeless People* is not a black academic novel with the archetypal black professor, Marshall presents us with a trope that is just as important in the politics of the black intellectual, the black person as an *object* of academic study. The novel's intervention is that it shows black people speaking back to the white social scientists who study them. The most important black intellectual in the novel is its main character, Merle Kinbona, who, it is later revealed, had studied West Indian history at a university in London. She has come back to Bournehills and is the town's resident radical intellectual. Her former boyfriend, Lyle Hutson, also studied in London but went in an opposite direction, becoming an agent for the British business interests investing in Bourne Island and its tourism industry. Another significant intellectual in the novel is Ferguson, who works as a foreman in the Cane Vale sugar factory, the most consistent employer in Bournehills. Ferguson is a diligent autodidact and a voracious reader of history books about the Bournehills slave revolt led by Cuffee Ned. The exploits of Cuffee Ned are acted out at carnival each year, and the celebration of the revolt is an important ceremony of remembrance and connection to the island's African roots as well as a reminder of its continued ties to regimes of enslavement.

The academic "space" is Bourne Island, a fictional British Caribbean island, which is home for its residents but to the white anthropologists is "the field," that place where social scientists go to live and work among a population of research subjects, an arrangement that is already loaded with stratification and othering. Funded by a lucrative American research institute, the anthropologists are there to research and learn about the people and economy of Bournehills, long considered the most unassimilable and impoverished section of the island. The research team is led by Saul Amron, a Jewish American anthropologist. He is accompanied by his wife, Harriet Amron, a moneyed heiress from Philadelphia, and research assistant Allen Fuso. Merle Kinbona, their host in Bournehills, is the spiritual center of the novel and serves as an intermediary between the people of Bournehills and this new contingent of outsiders.

Marshall tells a story that dramatizes the political importance of social science in the production of black diasporic identity. It is a novel about time and memory. The "timelessness" of Bourne Island and the people of Bournehills is a motif throughout the novel. A typical observation that recurs among both the researchers who come to the island and some of the people of Bourne Island itself is that "Bournehills is like some place out of the Dark Ages."[45] *The Chosen Place, the Timeless People* is striking in its intricate details of how social-scientific knowledge is produced. In the process, Marshall reveals one of the most potentially subversive aspects of the academic novel—that it examines the lives of producers of academic knowledge and, in this case, challenges the concept of the social scientist as an innocent intellectual observer. Bournehills is the poorest and least assimilable district on the island; it is a symbol of the past, a symbol of memory itself, and the source of its identity and its "problems" is that its people refuse to forget the legacy of enslavement.

The story line involving anthropologists calls attention to the vital importance of anthropology in shaping black American identity politics in the twentieth century, particularly as it relates to the African Diaspora. It was the work of anthropologists such as Franz Boas, Melville Herskovits, Bruno Malinowski, and Lorenzo Turner in the 1920s to the 1940s that led to the two most important foundational concepts in Afrocentric ideology, that of cultural relativism and African cultural survivals.[46] One can see the popularization of these concepts in the history of racial nomenclature in the United States, particularly the embrace of the term "African American" in the latter half of the twentieth century. But the anthropologist brings with him to the field conceptions of time that shape the way he sees himself as a researcher and the way he constructs the people whom he studies as people existing in another time.[47]

There has also been something of a "temporal" turn in black studies in recent years, with many scholars engaging with concepts of temporality as a physical phenomenon and as a way of conceptualizing black subjectivity. In *Physics of Blackness*, Michelle M. Wright presents a challenge to scholars in black studies to think of blackness as a "where" and "when" as opposed to a "what" or "whom." When it comes to conversations about the truth-value of race, Wright attempts to offer something beyond tired debates about biology versus social construction, essentialism versus antiessentialism. Instead, Wright insists that understanding how blackness functions requires an appreciation of the "phenomenology of Blackness—that is, when and where it is being imagined, defined, and performed and in what locations, both figurative and literal."[48] Wright problematizes "Middle Passage Blackness" as a paradigm in which the black person can enter history only as enslaved, can enter history only as an object. In this way, she joins other black intellectuals who have questioned white-supremacist temporalities that locate black people solely in relation to enslavement and construct black people as "slaves." Indeed, in recent years there has been a worthy push to reorient our language about slavery to refer to people as "enslaved," to resist the white-supremacist notion that "slave" is a natural condition for people of African descent.

The Chosen Place, the Timeless People is one of the best examples of why "campus novel" is an insufficient term and why novels that move beyond the campus setting can be just as illuminating about the politics of higher education as those that stay behind the campus walls. (Samuel R. Delany's *The Mad Man* is another example in this vein.) The academic novel of anthropology in particular has a built-in device for escaping the campus setting in its showing the researcher out in the field. Among black academic novels, Reginald

McKnight's *He Sleeps* uses a similar device of showing the social scientist in the field with a narrative of an African American professor of anthropology studying urban legends in Senegal, which allows McKnight to explore the connections and fissures between African and black American identities.[49]

Once again, Craig Wilder's *Ebony and Ivy* provides some valuable context in its exploration of the connections between the colonial American university and the West Indies. One chapter of the book, "The Very Name of a West Indian," draws its title from a comment by the Reverend John Witherspoon, president of the College of New Jersey (now Princeton University), in a letter sent to a potential patron in Barbados in which he says "the very name of a West Indian has come to imply in it great opulence."[50] It's an example of how Witherspoon and other college administrators in their roles as fund-raisers pandered to the elite colonial families in the West Indies to get them to send their children to American universities. Wilder traces the history of colonial American colleges that recruited the children of West Indian plantation owners as a means to raise money for their colleges, a phenomenon that increased the connections between American colleges and the sources of wealth being created by slave labor in the British West Indies.

Marshall's novel addresses this history of the university as a front for corporate interests, and Wilder's historical analysis in *Ebony and Ivy* helps us to see just how far back that story goes. In *The Chosen Place, the Timeless People*, the residents of Bourne Island are rightfully suspicious when Saul Amron and his team show up on the island. Saul attempts to reassure everyone that their interests there are purely intellectual, but the people of Bourne Island know full well that there is nothing neutral about a team of white American social scientists coming to their island.

The novel begins with a study in contrasts. Merle in her old beat-up car, one that Marshall suggests is a hand-me-down from one of the big-shot colonial leaders on the island, has to negotiate the muddy road as she heads to the airport to meet Saul and his team of researchers. Meanwhile, Saul and his team arrive on the island by airplane, flying high above the islands and seeing Bourne Island from above as one among a series of islands, former colonial properties. They descend to Earth to live among the people and learn more about Bournehills, a descent that represents a physical leveling of relations between them. However, the hierarchy and power relations between the white researchers and the people of Bournehills manifests in many other ways throughout the story.

After the team arrives and the introductions are made, there is a critical scene at the nightclub called Sugar's, a club aptly named for the commodity produced by the island and the deleterious health effects it has on the island's inhabitants ("sugar" being a colloquial euphemism for diabetes). Marshall also deploys "sugar" as a metaphor for the addiction of white Westerners to the bodies and sexuality of the black residents. Marshall shows Saul Amron observing all the people in the nightclub and paints a lascivious portrait of white tourists who come to the island to live out their erotic fantasies. "It's always a bit of a shock, don't you know, to realize that the thing that sweetens your tea comes from all this muck," the factory manager, Sir John, says to Saul in a later scene when they look at the rollers in the Cane Vale factory.[51] In that moment, and in this moment in Sugar's, Marshall succinctly captures how the lifestyles of British and American wealth are built upon the brutality of the slave trade and the peasant labor that still happens in the cane fields and upon the commodification of black bodies through sex tourism.

Another significant scene comes in the conversation between Merle and Saul after carnival. In this remarkable scene, Merle flips the script on Saul, forcing him to become the interview subject. The candid conversation between Saul and Merle is intense, cathartic, and erotic, full of intelligence and desire. It ends up creating even more problems when they decide to sleep together and later suffer the fallout from this fling.

The friendship between Merle and Saul's research assistant, Allen, is one that from the beginning is defined by a kind of queer solidarity. Both of them are outsiders, but the extent of their "queerness" is not revealed until later, Merle's in the form of her lesbian relationship with a wealthy white woman in London and Allen's in his grief for a former lover who had died in World War II and whose picture he carries with him. But later in the novel Merle encourages Allen to marry a woman, seemingly oblivious to his homosexuality or, somehow, in the social mores of that time, unable to consider the possibility of his making a life as a couple with another man, a possibility that Allen clearly entertains in his memories of his deceased lover.

Meanwhile, Saul Amron feels remorse about the death of his first wife and guilt that his life as a working anthropologist in the field compromised her health and contributed to her death: "For hadn't he, in his absorption in his work, subjected her year after year to the hardship of life in the field, when he knew her health had been nearly ruined by her youth spent in the camps."[52] As for the second wife, Harriet, her letter back to her friend Chessie allows the reader an entry point into Harriet's thoughts. Harriet is a privileged white woman who defied her WASP background to marry a Jewish professor and has never fully accepted her decision to cast her destiny with Saul.[53] Through Saul's marriages Marshall incorporates the lingering atrocity of the Holocaust and the persistent legacy of antisemitism among white Americans. The ritual of Cuffee Ned at carnival and its role in the narrative signifies that the people of Bournehills are a people who will not forget the past, who seem to operate by a different conception of time. Their resistance to "progress" is in that remembrance and in the rituals that they stubbornly refuse to let go of for the sake of modernity. At one point Saul speaks on the uses of history and the limitations of the work that he is doing as a social scientist to unravel the mystery of Bournehills. "You know I'm beginning to suspect what Bournehills needs is one of those old-fashioned soothsayers or diviners, somebody whose business is dealing in mysteries, not some poor half-assed anthropologist who's supposed to be concerned only with what's real."[54] Again, Saul's commentary shows an academic who has run up against the limitations of rationality and empirical research. There is something that Saul cannot grasp about the Bournehills people and their attachment to their myths. Marshall's novel is an amalgamation of her research on Barbados and her experiences on the island, and as a novelist she spins that history of the real island of Barbados into a lyrical and moving story about fictional people on a fictional island as a vehicle to explore what it means to live in the wake of atrocities like the Holocaust and the transatlantic slave trade. This novel is about what it means to try to understand such atrocities in historical and rational terms but also struggle to make sense of them in cosmic and spiritual terms. Why does such evil have to happen?

In this depiction of the people of Bournehills Marshall risks the reification of the stereotypical differences between a sensual Africanity and a cerebral white Western rationality. The novel's paradox of memory is that the people of Bournehills are accused of remembering too much, of holding on to the past through their rituals of the Cuffee Ned revolt, but it is Merle who desperately wants to have a memory that isn't there. She is tormented by the fact that when she was two years old, she saw a man shoot and kill her mother, but Merle cannot remember who the man was. She was too young to remember, and perhaps even if she could have, she had suppressed the traumatic memory. She blames herself for not being able to identify the murderer and is haunted by this fact.

Like Helga Crane in *Quicksand*, Merle's room of her own is also loaded with metaphorical significance. Having stayed in the guest part of the house, Saul finally sees her room near the end of the novel, and he associates the messiness and disorder of the room with her mental state. "It expressed her: the struggle for coherence, the hope and desire for reconciliation of her conflicting parts, the longing to truly know and accept herself—all the things he sensed in her, which not only brought on her rages but her frightening calms as well. He almost felt as his gaze wandered over the room that he was wandering through the chambers of her mind."[55]

Another academic character worth noting in this discussion is Lyle Hutson, the former radical who studied in London, who "had been a Bourne Island scholar and gone to England to study first to Oxford . . . then to London School of Economics, and finally the Inns of Court" but has now become a big-shot mediator for the corporate interests on the island.[56] Lyle and Merle ran in the same radical circles together in London and, briefly, were lovers. Since that time, Merle and Lyle had become playful rivals, throwing barbs at each other in familiar contempt. A bit of delicious melodrama comes late in the novel when Lyle snitches on Merle and Saul and tells Harriet about their affair. He says, "I was never one to tell tales out of school, Mrs. Amron, I was certain you knew."[57] But of course Lyle is exactly one to tell tales out of school, and the act fits with his characterization as a traitor to his people.

When Harriet passive-aggressively tries to pay Merle to leave by giving her money that would allow her a chance to go to see her estranged child, Harriet becomes to Merle yet another rich white woman trying to control her with her money and buy her affections, just like her former lover in London. This act becomes another signifier of white Western wealth, an act of emotional colonialism, and a scene of white women's complicity in the colonial enterprise. Despite all their intelligence, these characters find themselves unwittingly, unconsciously living out these colonial scripts.[58]

Marshall mentions Ralph Ellison's influence on her work, particularly through the essays of *Shadow and Act*, which she called her literary bible. As she states, "He is also committed to the notion of the worth and validity of our experience and the responsibility of the writer to celebrate that experience and not fall into the trap white sociologists have set for us in viewing our lives as totally negative. It is not one bleak history of degradation and despair."[59] The academic novel is about the escape from that kind of victimhood. The black academic novel explores the inherent risk in the image of a successful and accomplished black person, that such images will be used to dismiss the suffering of black people and to trivialize existing inequalities.

At the conclusion of the novel, Paule Marshall's closing line marks the years and locations in which she wrote the work: "Grenada, West Indies. New York. Yaddo. 1963–1968."

These years are historically associated in the United States as years of crisis. One thinks of the assassinations of Medgar Evers (1963), John F. Kennedy (1963), Malcolm X (1965), Martin Luther King Jr. (1968), and of all the civil unrest in the streets and on college campuses encompassed by those years. In the black diaspora, those years are also important years of postcoloniality as former European colonies in Africa and the Caribbean struggled to come to independence while still under the yoke of Western money and power, a dynamic that Marshall illustrates with such beauty and power in *The Chosen Place, the Timeless People*.

Everybody's Black College Protest Novel

Between 1965 and 1972, African American students at more than one thousand of America's colleges, including HBCUs and PWIs, organized and protested for black studies programs, black studies courses, black faculty, and higher black-student enrollments.[60] Gil Scott-Heron and Alice Walker, both activist-artists, documented this period of student activism in novelistic form, and their works portray the complex and sometimes contradictory strategies used by young people in this activism. Walker's *Meridian* is remarkable in its attention to feminist politics in the civil rights movement. That feminism is largely illegible in the masculine nationalism of Scott-Heron's *The Nigger Factory*. In *Meridian* one sees the formulation of Walker's conception of "womanism" as a movement that needed a separate framework from the concerns of bourgeois white feminists. Reading these two novels with and against each other is an opportunity to address the gender politics of mid-twentieth-century black activists and to explore the conversation that would continue through the 1990s and reappear in novels like *Japanese by Spring*, by Ishmael Reed, a novelist who, of note, has carried on a long feud with Alice Walker over the depictions of black men in her work.

To mention the name Gil Scott-Heron is to conjure that ruggedly soulful voice that gave us classic jams like "The Bottle" and bracing protest songs like "Winter in America" and the socially conscious humor of spoken-word tracks like "Whitey on the Moon." Often referred to as the father of rap or the godfather of hip-hop, Scott-Heron had a profound influence on rap and spoken-word artists, melding the musical styles of the blues with the militant poetics of the Black Arts Movement. Gil Scott-Heron is lesser known for the written word, but he began with aspirations of being a writer, publishing two novels, *The Vulture* and *The Nigger Factory*, and later a memoir, *The Last Holiday*. Scott-Heron was inspired to attend the historically black Lincoln University in Pennsylvania because it was the alma mater of one of his literary heroes, Langston Hughes.

The provocative title *The Nigger Factory* is the author's crude term for black colleges where students were indoctrinated into the bourgeois assimilationist politics of "the talented tenth." It begins by articulating the proud history of these institutions and defining what they have meant to black people but quickly turns to address the paradoxes inherent in the institutions and why a new generation of black students felt that the HBCUs must be critiqued and reformed.

> Black colleges and universities have been both a blessing and a curse on black people. The institutions have educated thousands of our people who would have never had the opportunity to get an education otherwise. They have supplied for many a new sense of dignity and integrity. They have never, however, made anybody equal. This is a reality for Black educators everywhere as students all over America demonstrate for change . . .
>
> Black students in the 1970s will not be satisfied with Bullshit Degrees or Nigger Educations. They are aware of the hypocrisy and indoctrination and are searching for other alternatives. With the help of those educators who are intelligent enough to recognize the need for drastic reconstruction there will be a new era of Black thought and Black thinkers who enter the working world from colleges aware of the real problems that will face them and not believing that a piece of paper will claim a niche for them in society-at-large. The education process will not whitewash them into thinking that their troubles are over. They will come out as Black people.[61]

With this caustic yet optimistic note, Scott-Heron links his novel to the prior generation of HBCU fiction that criticized the racial politics of the black college, playing up the irony that the same schools that offered educational opportunities for millions of blacks were also sites of indoctrination into white supremacy and servility—the so-called bullshit degrees and nigger educations that he refers to. The miseducation that Scott-Heron describes here manifested in the teaching of a Eurocentric curriculum, and reforming that curriculum to reflect the diversity of student bodies and the world itself was one of the common demands in the protest movements of this era. There was a sense of race pride existing in HBCUs, but as Nella Larsen articulates in *Quicksand*, and as other intellectuals and activists pointed out, that pride was too often about the black intellectual's proximity to whiteness.

That said, Scott-Heron's novel represents a distinct shift in this criticism that came about in the 1960s and 1970s, a shift that was brought on by Black Power and the black consciousness movement. As Scott-Heron writes later in the statement, "the center of our intellectual attention must be thrust away from Greek, Western thought toward Eastern and Third World thought. Our examples in the arts must be Black and not White. Our natural creativity must be cultivated."[62] Some of this thinking would be echoed years later in Spike Lee's *School Daze*, particularly in the apartheid-protesting campus radical named Dap (played by a young Laurence Fishburne).

Set in the fictional Virginia college Sutton University *The Nigger Factory* chronicles the exploits of a student group called MJUMBE—Members of Justice United for Meaningful Black Education. The organization is led by football player Ralph Baker, and most of the other MJUMBE members are football players as well. This story line is indicative of the novel's macho vision of black activism and was undoubtedly inspired by the discourse of masculinity in the movement itself, but as Walker's criticism shows, this understanding of the movement is incomplete without accounting for the role that women actually played.

The Nigger Factory also addresses the problem of money and the difficulty that HBCUs had in retaining black professors who were being lured away to teach at other institutions, which is another aspect of the novel's narrative of the integration era. Indeed, this integrationist period is one in which a talent drain occurs, pulling students, faculty, and student athletes away from HBCUs to predominantly white colleges with better facilities, funding, and resources. The story line about the football team is particularly prescient, as this era marked the first time many majority-white schools were integrating their athletic teams, enticing black athletes away from black colleges and welcoming them into programs with bigger budgets and television exposure.

At the beginning of a student strike, President Ogden Calhoun proposes the drastic move of shutting down Sutton University for the beginning of the semester and reopening after a readmission process that would eliminate all the student protestors from the school's enrollment. But the next chapter,

"The Final Word," gives some backstory on Ogden and Gloria Calhoun. We find that Ogden is a graduate of Howard University who went on to earn a Ph.D. in psychology in 1946, and that Ogden himself had run into trouble as a student activist for trying to instill a problack curriculum. He had since grown more conservative with old age and had now become the very kind of stuffy administrator that he once fought against as a student.

The novel ends with the National Guard on campus, a familiar story line in the history of student protest in the 1960s and 1970s. Ogden's wife, Gloria, disapproves of his decision to call the National Guard on the students. And in the violent ending, the gunfire from the rifle of a guardsman sets off a bomb that the students had planted. This explosive portrayal of the student protest movement pays homage to the students killed in protests at Kent State, Jackson State, Southern University, and South Carolina State University and depicts the institutional dynamic that contributed to this violence.

Scott-Heron's novel addresses the ambivalence of black college administrators toward their student activists' demands. And in that adversarial portrayal of students and administrators there is also a criticism of the fundamental conservatism of institutionality. One of the primary purposes of institutions of higher education is preservation: a preservation of continuity, protection of physical materials and infrastructure, and a continuity of the processes of knowledge production. As such, these institutions have a vested interest in maintaining and reproducing themselves. The violent responses to the student protest speak to the contradictory need for stable black institutions as places of higher education versus the dynamic demands of a student body pushing for change at a volatile time in the nation's history. The collaboration between black colleges and the police forces of the state that led to the student murders call attention to the precarious condition of the black college as an institution that on the one hand seeks to nurture and sustain black life and, on the other, is dependent upon the resources of a fundamentally antiblack state apparatus.

Alice Walker's 1976 novel *Meridian* begins on similar ground, with a student in opposition to her conservative black institution. The epigraph for the chapter titled "The Driven Snow" begins,

> We are as chaste and pure as
> the driven snow.
> We watch our manners, speech
> and dress just so;
> And in our hearts we carry out
> greatest fame
> That we are blessed to perpetuate
> the Saxon name!

In the name of the college and its song, Alice Walker emphasizes the images of whiteness behind the college mission. Unlike Scott-Heron, however, Walker imagines what this paradigm looks like for black women. That these two novels, both set in HBCUs dealing with the same era of protest, have such radically different images is reflective of the gender divide within black nationalist thought, but it also indicates a gendered dynamic that has long existed in black educational projects, the same dynamic that Anna Julia Cooper and her generation dealt with as educated women who challenged black male leadership. Walker inserts a counterdiscursive image to Saxon's white assimilationism by connecting the history of Saxon College to the history of enslavement through the image of a tree at the center of the campus, the Sojourner Tree. Meridian lives between black and white worlds, trying to reconcile herself to a reality in which black college women are encouraged to gain education but also instructed to wear white gloves and sing of white purity.

Meridian stands out for the way that it imagines the place of women in the civil rights movement and for its "town and gown" narrative in black academic fiction. Such scenes mark a certain class distinction between the Negro elites of the black college campus and the people in their surrounding communities. Spike Lee's Atlanta-based film *School Daze* also explores town-and-gown conflict when a group of young men from Mission College venture to a local chicken restaurant and end up being confronted by some local men (led by a character played by Morehouse alum Samuel Jackson), who tell them, "You Mission punks always look down on us." The "town" in *Meridian* is represented in the figure of a mentally disturbed woman on campus who is known as the Wild Child. Eventually the main character, Meridian Hill, rejects gown for town: "After the Wild Child's death she could not live on campus, although she continued to attend classes, and lived instead in the ghetto that surrounded it."[63] The decision marks a conscious effort by Meridian to be more engaged in the community, and her action is also a criticism of the HBCU as out of touch with the concerns of black people who have less education, wealth, and resources.

In one passage, Walker describes Meridian and her friend Anne-Marion as two outcasts on the respectable campus:

> Like Meridian, Anne-Marion was a deviate in the honors house: there because of her brilliance but only tolerated because it was clear she was one, too, on whom true Ladyhood would never be conferred. Most of the students—timid, imitative, bright enough but never daring, were being ushered nearer to Ladyhood every day. It was for this that their parents had sent them to Saxon College. They learned to make French food, English tea and German music without once having the urge to slip off the heavily guarded campus at five in the morning to photograph a strange face as the light hit it just the right way—as Meridian had—or to risk being raped in a rough neighborhood as they attempt to discover the economic causes of inner-city crime, as had Anne-Marion.[64]

This passage, and others, show Walker working out her ideas about "womanism," that the condition of black women requires a different name, different thinking, different strategies from white feminism. Her inclusion of "French food, English tea and German music" in that passage are meant to signify the inherent Eurocentrism behind the version of "Ladyhood" that Saxon wants its students to approximate. Confronting the problem of an expected assimilation into whiteness and dealing with the class differences between themselves as black college students and the African Americans in the city surrounding the campus required a more racially conscious framework than white feminism could offer. And in Meridian's relations to her white friend Lynne Rabinowitz we see the thing that Ellison and Paule Marshall were resisting, this white fascination with the "unrelieved suffering" of black people. "To Lynne, the black people of the South were Art. This she begged forgiveness for and tried to hide . . . If Mississippi is the worst place in America for black people, it stood to reason she thought, that the Art that was their lives would flourish there."[65] To Rabinowitz, Art is something that black people *are* rather than something they *do*, though Walker also makes the character self-aware of these contradictions in her thinking.

Meridian is a novel that bores deep into the soul of the civil rights movement, into the complications of integration and interracial cooperation, into interracial intimacies, even as a new militancy arose calling for black nationalism. Though she doesn't mention it directly, Stokely Carmichael's call for "black power" in Mississippi is an important historical marker and the fulcrum on which the movement turns from integration toward more nationalistic thinking. Walker also marks a significant day in the actual history of Spelman College, noting the April 1968 assassination of Martin Luther King Jr. and the Atlanta funeral, for which a visitation was held on the Spelman campus on April 8, 1968, a scene that produced the indelible Pulitzer Prize–winning photograph by Moneta Sleet Jr. of the black-veiled Coretta Scott King holding her five-year-old daughter Bernice.[66]

This image of the civil rights movement in Walker's novel signifies a new era of integrated schooling on the horizon. With the integration of higher education came increased opportunities for black students to matriculate on white college campuses. The coming years would introduce new tensions in higher education with the culture wars on campus and debates over institutionalized diversity initiatives, including policies of affirmative action. The novels that follow show a distinct move away from HBCU life toward more robust depictions of black intellectuals on majority-white campuses. The novels of Ishmael Reed, Percival Everett, and Samuel Delany explore the complications that the post–civil rights era would have for black students and faculty. The black academic would continue to be defined by the paradigms of responsibility and representation but would also need to confront the problems associated with the paradigm of "inclusion" on historically white campuses.

Chapter 5

✦

Culture Wars and Capitalism, 1980–Present

A War for the Soul of America, Andrew Hartman's 2015 study of the culture wars, takes its title from a speech by white-supremacist politician and pundit Pat Buchanan at the 1992 Republican National Convention. The speech has taken on new vitality now that Buchanan's ideas, which have always had an audience in the far-right wing of the Republican Party, have made their way directly into the White House with the 2016 election of Donald Trump, whose campaign was born in the conspiratorial fever swamps of websites like Breitbart, World Net Daily, and Infowars. After his shocking win in November 2016, Trump stocked his cabinet and staff full of white nationalists (Steven Bannon, Sebastian Gorka, Stephen Miller, and Jeff Sessions, among others) and began implementing a white nationalist agenda that includes measures such as a ban on Muslim immigration, Blue Lives Matter laws (targeting Black Lives Matter activists in the name of "protecting police"), overturning *Roe v. Wade*, and dismantling public education under the euphemism of "school choice." In fact, the appointment of charter school champion and billionaire heiress Betsy DeVos as U.S. secretary of education was almost a relief considering that Jerry Falwell Jr., an antigay, antichoice creationist who heads the evangelical Liberty University, had also met with Trump about the post. The election has also instigated new battles over campus speech, with white-supremacist trolls like Ann Coulter, Milo Yiannopoulos, and Richard Spencer booking speaking engagements through fringe conservative student groups at universities, then fanning the flames of victimhood whenever students, professors, administrators, and community members pushed back against these appearances.

Hartman's study is a synthesis of the culture wars that flared up in the 1980s and 1990s with political debates about ethnic studies, pornography, gay rights, feminism, and other topics, particularly as they played out in popular media, the arts, and on campus. However, the origins of the culture wars as a campus-based political phenomenon could be said to stretch back as far as William F. Buckley Jr.'s 1951 tome *God and Man at Yale*, with its accusations that an antireligious culture was fomenting on elite college campuses.

Hartman's book provides a useful schematic for thinking about the culture wars using the idea of "fracture" and how intellectuals from different camps in the culture wars thought about what had happened to America after the 1960s. As Hartman puts it, "Conservatives viewed American culture as something that, once whole, had been lost . . . Whereas the Left considered post-Sixties American culture a closer approximation of its ideal form."[1] In some ways it is necessary to reduce this argument to two "sides" to make sense of this era, but that very reductionist, polarized approach to politics is one of the terrible contributions of the culture wars.

Ishmael Reed deconstructs this very language of combat in his culture-wars academic novel *Japanese by Spring*. An evaluation of post-1980 black academic novels requires a confrontation with the language of the culture wars and the fundamental logic that some culture warriors have used, that a cohesive, unified America was fractured and balkanized by identity politics. In fact, I've already enumerated several ways in which the university should not be considered a unified, neutral institution, that it has served the interests of white supremacy, patriarchy, homophobia, and class inequality. Reed reconfigures the narrative of fracture by showing the ways that this formulation obscures historical inequalities and produces false equivalences.

This period of black academic novels that I isolate begins with the 1980 election of conservative Republican president Ronald Wilson Reagan. Reagan earned his conservative stripes as governor of California with his crackdown on student activism on college campuses, announcing him as a politician who would put down the unruly protests at the state's colleges (read Berkeley) and who would be a fierce champion of capitalist values and law and order in the White House. The Reagan administration would usher the United States through the fall of the Soviet Union, the defeat of communism, and a further expansion of global financial markets.[2]

College campuses have long carried the assumption of being spaces of open intellectual inquiry insulated from the venality of market values. This idea appears in the American academic novel as early as Willa Cather's 1925 *The Professor's House*, where she depicts professors voicing their concerns about the encroachment of industry into the campus science departments. These days the university has become more naked about its profit-making ambitions. By the 1980s there was probably less reticence about this idea of the corporate university than in Cather's time as market values became even more entrenched on college campuses with heavily managerialized administrations and corporate strategies for expansion. Some American universities have become multinational corporations with satellite campuses in other countries. Students are increasingly seen as vectors of consumerism for the merchandise and products created by university branding machines. However, there was still some reluctance to embrace the corporate university along the way, typified in a slew of books by wary professors and administrators bearing titles like *Shakespeare, Einstein, and the Bottom Line.*

Some of the touchstones of this era include the breakdown and reduction of tenured professorships, an increasing use of adjunct professors for instruction, the slashing of academic programs in the humanities, the digitization of archival materials and course content, and the growth of online distance education. Attendant with and related to all this corporatization has been the growth of highly profitable sports programs with massive TV contracts, apparel sales, corporate sponsorships of stadiums, and head-coaching salaries at some schools that reach into the millions.

This era of corporatization is concurrent with and related to the culture wars, this period of noisy debates about multiculturalism, postmodernism, gender, and sexuality in the college curriculum, though just how these cultural issues are related to political economy depends on the perspective. Some on the left see the new cultural studies as a product of the neoliberal university and its co-optation of identity politics as a cynical move, while some on the right see the university as a bastion of leftist professors brainwashing impressionable students with anticapitalist, anti-American, anti-Christian, and anti-white propaganda. It is at times a bewildering and contradictory field of debates, and my discussion here is not a comprehensive study of the culture wars by any means. But I address some of the vectors of debate to show how these issues are represented in the academic novels at the end of the twentieth century and the beginning of the twenty-first.

Black academic novels have flourished in this period. Roughly 70 percent of the novels in my bibliography were published after 1980. They represent a range of forms, settings, and political and aesthetic concerns. Other novels from this period include David Bradley's *The Chaneysville Incident* (1981), Reginald McKnight's *He Sleeps* (2002), Zadie Smith's *On Beauty* (2005), and the Ivy League mystery novels by Pamela Thomas-Graham *A Darker Shade of Crimson* (1999), *Blue Blood* (1999), and *Orange Crushed* (2005). They include the academic legal novels of law professor Stephen Carter with *Emperor of Ocean Park* (2002) and *New England White* (2007) and Mat Johnson's satirical novel of academia, race, and authenticity, *Pym* (2011).[3]

This era in the history of the black academic novel is also concurrent with representations of blackademic life on screen, such as the popular *Cosby Show* spinoff *A Different World* (1987–93); the Spike Lee film *School Daze* (1988); the Oprah Winfrey film *The Great Debaters* (2007), starring Denzel Washington as the poet and professor Melvin Tolson; and John Singleton's *Higher Learning* (1995), a film depicting a grab bag of campus issues from affirmative action to date rape to gun violence and more. In this chapter I focus on the black academic novel in the culture wars era, and in the conclusion I turn to a brief analysis of the blackademic on screen and its relationship to these literary representations of blackademic life.

The Afro-Eurasian Eclipse

Ishmael Reed's 1993 novel *Japanese by Spring* is the perfect entry point to examine the academic novel in the culture-wars era. All the novels I cover in this period depict the university embroiled in different aspects of the culture wars in greater or lesser form. Ishmael Reed's *Japanese by Spring* belongs alongside other culture-wars academic novels like John L'Hereux's *The Handmaid of Desire* (1996), Francine Prose's *The Blue Angel* (2000), Philip Roth's *The Human Stain* (2000), Saul Bellow's *Ravelstein* (2000), and Jonathan Franzen's *The Corrections* (2001), as well as David Mamet's controversial sexual harassment play *Oleanna*, which was adapted into a film.

W. E. B. Du Bois once described the concept of empire under white supremacy as "the domination of White Europe over black Africa and yellow Asia, through political power built on the economic control of labor, income and ideas."[4] Ishmael Reed's satirical academic novel *Japanese by Spring* is a literary examination of Western imperialism on these Du Boisian terms, with Reed probing white supremacy's relationship to the darker peoples of the world and the relationship of the nonwhite races to one another.

From the first sentences of *Japanese by Spring*, Reed displays the unique improvisational narrative style that he developed in earlier novels such as *The Free-Lance Pallbearers* (1967) and *Mumbo Jumbo* (1972), a style full of wit, puns, and allusions. The novel's opening paragraph introduces the main character, Professor Benjamin "Chappie" Puttbutt, and lays out the novel's main concerns about culture, education, and warfare:

> When Benjamin "Chappie" Puttbutt's mom and dad said Off to the Wars, they really meant it. George Eliott Puttbutt was a two-star Air Force general, cited and decorated for distinguishing himself in two of the three great yellow wars, the wars against Japan, Korea, and Vietnam, and Ruby Puttbutt's star was on the rise as a member of the United States Intelligence community. As a military brat Benjamin knew the techniques of survival and so, after reading that Japan would become a future world power, Puttbutt began to study Japanese while enrolled at the Air Force Academy during the middle sixties. It was the end of an upbringing characterized by regimen and discipline. George and Ruby Puttbutt's idea of education was similar to John Milton's. In his "Of Education," he recommends that "two hours before supper [students] . . . be called out to their military motions, under sky or convert according to the season, as was the Roman wont; first on foot, then, as their age permits, on horseback, to all the art of cavalry . . . in all the skill of embattling . . . fortifying, besieging, and battering, with all the helps of ancient and modern stratagems tactics and warlike maxims." That's not the only attitude they shared with Milton. With their continuous need for enemies,

their motto could have been taken from Milton's panegyric for Cromwell: "New Foes Arise." Their favorite blues singer was "Little Milton." Their favorite comedian Milton Berle.[5]

Here in Reed's opening salvo is a taste of what is to come in this culture-wars novel, with its emphasis on militarism and higher education, its Afro-Orientalist criticism of American imperialism, and its satirical political commentary. The discipline and strategy of military life would prove valuable to Puttbutt as a participant in academic battles, and Reed uses this narrative of warfare to criticize the term "culture war" and examine the ways that it is driven by actual U.S. wars of the twentieth century. One of the interventions that Ishmael Reed makes with this novel is to trouble the very language of "culture wars" by making his protagonist a black academic with an actual military background. In an interview about the novel Reed stated, "I got a clue from Frank Chin about the parallels between ancient tales from China and African-American folktales. That life is war, survival, and how one uses tactics and strategies, so I use that as a metaphor in the novel."[6]

Benjamin's father named him after two black military heroes, General Chappie James Jr. and General Benjamin O. Davis. "Chappie" attended the U.S. Air Force Academy but was kicked out for being involved in black activism.[7] Reed's narrative emphasizes the many U.S. wars of the twentieth century, particularly the wars waged in Japan, Korea, and Vietnam. In the novel Reed interrogates the use of the language of warfare by people on all sides of the debate, and though he does not spare leftist academia from satire, he clearly comes down on the side of the multicultural movement. He writes, "The diversity movement would win the Battle of the Books because it included artists. The other side was made up of education bureaucrats, critics and historians."[8] That statement is indicative of Reed's belief in the transformative power of art, a motif that he explores in *Mumbo Jumbo*, a novel in which the infectious "Jes Grew" (a metaphor for black culture itself) overtakes America precisely because Jes Grew's power comes from the realm of spirit and myth and not from the cold, rational world of politics and bureaucracy.

Japanese by Spring examines the different positions taken up by black intellectuals in the culture wars of the late 1980s and early 1990s and addresses some of the political implications of multicultural education. The literary critic Darryl Dickson-Carr writes in *African American Satire: The Sacredly Profane Novel* that Reed shows us "what a productive, transcendent multiculturalism should be, as opposed to what it has become in the face of American cynicism."[9] At its best *Japanese by Spring* is an example of what David Palumbo-Liu calls a critical multiculturalism, a multiculturalism that "explores the fissures, tensions, and sometimes contradictory demands of multiple cultures, rather than (only) celebrating the plurality of cultures by passing through them appreciatively."[10]

In the essay "Ishmael Reed's Female Troubles" Michele Wallace provides a salient gender critique of Reed's work, as well as one of the most apt descriptions of his literary aesthetic:

> Unencumbered by the uptight strategies of mimesis, this "cowboy in the boat of Ra" improvises plots that are perversely eventful parodies of the stodgy predictabilities of the Bildungsroman (*Free-Lance Pallbearers*, 1967), the Western (*Yellowback Radio Broke-Down*, 1969), the detective story (*Mumbo Jumbo*, 1972), the Greek tragedy (*The Last Days of Louisiana Red*, 1974), the slave narrative (*Flight to Canada*, 1976), the Gothic mystery (*The Terrible Twos*, 1982), and the epic (*Reckless Eyeballing*, 1986)[11]

Obviously, I would add the academic novel to her list of genres, and *Japanese by Spring* is essentially an extended improvisational riff on the academic novel. *Japanese by Spring* is to Kingsley Amis's *Lucky Jim* what Charlie Parker's bebop classic "Koko" is to the Ray Noble jazz standard "Cherokee." Parker took the familiar song, reimagined it, and redeployed it in his own creative vernacular, and Reed does the same with the academic novel in *Japanese by Spring*.

As Wallace goes on to argue, Reed does have some "female troubles," which have become an indelible part of the criticism on his work. The last novel Wallace refers to, *Reckless Eyeballing*, is one of Reed's most acidic works criticizing feminism. In it, he deploys a recurring motif depicting black feminists as tools of wealthy, powerful white feminists attacking straight black males. Reed's position is that despite their claims of being opposed to patriarchy, white feminists function as extensions of white male supremacy, a criticism one can find in black feminist thought, in any number of essays or interviews by Audre Lorde, for example. However, it's the turn to attack black women that is troubling, and Reed's jeremiads against feminism are well known in black literary circles. As Wallace states at the beginning of her essay, "Last winter Ishmael Reed calmly explained to me that there was a media-wide conspiracy to blame black men for male chauvinism; mainstream feminists, consolidating a reconciliation with white men, needed a scapegoat—black men were it."[12] While Wallace expresses a respect for his artistic contributions and values his work as a pioneer in the Black Arts Movement, she also challenges his adversarial approach to black women writers. Her insights about Reed's gender politics, underlain by a respect for his artistry, have informed my own reading of *Japanese by Spring*. His ongoing criticism of feminism is yet another layer in this novel's multilayered approach to the culture wars.

Japanese by Spring is set at the fictional Jack London College in Oakland, California. The state of California and its universities are vitally important in the history of the culture wars. Reed began teaching at the University of California, Berkeley, in 1967, and he and his wife, choreographer and director Carla Blank, moved to Oakland in 1979. In 1966, two students, Huey

Newton and Bobby Seale, who were enrolled at Merritt College, a community college in Oakland, founded the Black Panther Party for Self-Defense. In 1968 at San Francisco State University student strikes erupted with demands for changes in the administration, and these protests led to the founding of the nation's first ethnic studies and black studies programs. In the 1978 *Regents of the University of California v. Allan Bakke* case the Supreme Court upheld the constitutionality of affirmative-action policies.

In the genre of academic fiction this Bay Area setting and its academic history were satirized in David Lodge's academic novel *Changing Places* (1975) in the story of a British academic (Philip Swallow) and American academic (Morris Zapp) who take part in an exchange program to teach at each other's schools in 1969. In *Changing Places*, Berkeley is thinly disguised behind the name Euphoric State. Reed's *Japanese by Spring* is set in the Bay Area more than twenty years later, when some of the activists of the 1960s have become the proverbial "tenured radicals" and the battle between left and right continues over the curriculum of higher education.

Japanese by Spring follows the story of literature professor Benjamin "Chappie" Puttbutt III and his quest for tenure at Jack London College in Oakland. Puttbutt is a former black nationalist turned neoconservative and a vocal critic of black militancy on campus. His most famous book is *Blacks, America's Misfortune*, and it earns him an appointment in the ironically named Department of Humanity. Black conservatives are often praised as "mavericks" for going against mainstream black political thought. They are praised for being willing to publicly criticize black behavior and advocate self-help ideology over "dependency" on government assistance. In *Faces at the Bottom of the Well* legal scholar Derrick Bell wrote about the "Rules of Racial Standing," a set of tongue-in-cheek guidelines by which the black intellectual navigates through the political minefield. Bell made note of the special status given to the black intellectual who "publicly disparages or criticizes other blacks who are speaking or acting in ways that upset whites. Instantly such statements are granted 'enhanced standing' even when the speaker has no special expertise or experience in the subject he or she is criticizing."[13] Puttbutt truly understands this principle, and although he is a literature scholar, he finds himself a niche as a conservative political pundit when he publishes *Black, America's Misfortune*. Reed describes Puttbutt as "a member of the growing anti-affirmative action industry. A black pathology merchant." And that all one needs do to join this club of black conservative pundits is to

> throw together a three hundred page book with graphs and articles about illegitimacy, welfare dependency, single-family households, drugs and violence; paint the inner cities as the circles of hell in the American paradise ... and you could write your way to the top of the bestseller lists. Get on C-Span. It was the biggest literary hustle going and Puttbutt decided he was going to get his.[14]

Reed creates Puttbutt as a comic figure in the novel by portraying him as a shrewd opportunist who only half believes the things that he writes and says in the media.

Puttbutt starts taking Japanese lessons, not out of any sincere love for or interest in the language but as a strategic move to position himself for future political and economic gain. "As a military brat Benjamin knew the techniques of survival and so, after reading that Japan would become a future world power, Puttbutt began to study Japanese while enrolled at the Air Force Academy during the middle sixties."[15] In the United States of the 1980s, conspiracy theories were rampant that the Japanese were developing fast and plotting to eclipse American educational and economic supremacy (particularly as revenge for Hiroshima and Nagasaki). Consequently, Puttbutt decides to give the Japanese lessons another try. When he spots a listing for "Japanese by Spring" in a local newspaper he signs up with a private tutor named Dr. Yamato. In the spring of 1990 he starts taking the classes, "hoping that by spring of 1991 he would know enough to take advantage of the new global realities. He was talking that way now. Sounding like a student in political science. All about global realities. Geopolitics this. Realpolitik that. Weltanschauung this. He was sounding like an edition of *Foreign Affairs*."[16]

Japanese by Spring begins with an incident on the campus of Jack London College. A black student is attacked with a baseball bat by a group of white students and is being carried away by an ambulance. The instigator of this attack is Robert Bass Jr., a leader of the student conservative group calling itself the Amerikaner Student Society and the American Student Chapter of the Order of the Boer Nation. The title of the group is meant to gesture to the battles over apartheid in South Africa in the 1980s. (South Africa has a part in another important work of black academic fiction of the 1980s, Spike Lee's *School Daze*, which begins with a student protest at the historically black Mission College over the school's position on South African divestment.) Robert Bass Jr. is an unabashed white nationalist whose father, Robert Bass Sr., also happens to be one of the school's notable alumni and one of its biggest donors.

With TV crews on the scene to cover the incident, Puttbutt finds himself being interviewed by reporters. Puttbutt's response to the reporters works as a kind of satirical summary of the arguments often deployed by black conservatives when he says that "the black students bring this on themselves ... With their separatism, their inability to fit in, their denial of mainstream values, they get the white students angry" and, further, that "they should stop worrying these poor whites with their excessive demands," such as affirmative-action quotas.[17] The reporter reminds him that the attackers actually sent the black student to the hospital with a fractured skull, to which Puttbutt replies, "Was he wearing one of those Malcolm X caps?" (The reporter says yes.) "There. So you see. I was correct. He was confronting instead of negotiating ... this black separatism is tempting such reactions from the white students."[18]

The same white students were also behind a couple of other incidents, including the time when Puttbutt walked into one of his classes to find on the blackboard, "Dinner with Puttbutt. Bring your own watermelon."[19] (Reed revealed in a 2013 *Wall Street Journal* article that this was based on one of his own classroom experiences.)[20] In addition, the right-wing student newspaper, *Koons and Kikes*, published a cartoon caricature of Puttbutt sexually violating an ostrich. These incidents are explained away by the conservative think tank the Woodwork Foundation as harmless jostling that had in fact helped to spark an honest debate about race on the campus. It's worth pointing out here how prescient Reed's novel was in predicting some of the political developments of the 2010s, including the role of student newspapers in the development of right-wing rhetorical strategies. Übertroll Dinesh D'Souza got his start at the *Dartmouth Review* in the 1980s, where, among other things, he outed gay students on campus. D'Souza has gone on to become one of the most important propagandists for the Trump administration and chief architect of the "Democrats are the party of slavery, white supremacy, and the KKK" obfuscation that has gone from online trolling to a mainstream political position.

Despite these incidents, Puttbutt is on his way up. *Blacks, America's Misfortune* is a success, and he has also published some articles in literary criticism and is working his way toward tenure. As a career novelist and creative writer Ishmael Reed delivers a few barbs against academic literary critics in *Japanese by Spring*, an element of the novel reflective of this period in the 1980s when arguments about poststructuralism, French theory, and the prevalence of theoretical "jargon" in literary criticism began to flare up in academia. Janice Rossen's *The University in Modern Fiction* contains the chapter "Creativity: Novelists in Academe," in which she identifies a recurring trope of conflict between creative writers and critics in the academic novel. As she puts it, "Novelists are apt to feel that in writing about literary scholars they are attacking the enemy since critics read and judge their work—and this can infuse their novels with a tone of aggressiveness which academics in turn discern and respond to in their reading."[21] She also writes that "the university often works against the creative impulses of the novelist because literary scholarship is closely related to criticism, and its mere proximity threatens creativity at its source."[22] At several points in *Japanese by Spring* Reed depicts academic literary critics in a negative light, and he places his antihero on their side, showing Puttbutt as a crafty cynic willing to exploit the lucrative enterprise of criticism. "Now that the writer was considered as obsolete as the 1960s computer, [Puttbutt] could share in some of the profits of the growth industry of the eighties and nineties. Criticism. All you had to do was string together some quotes from Benjamin, Barthes, Foucault, and Lacan and you were in business."[23] In one scene in the novel, Puttbutt travels to an academic conference in Paris. While waiting at the airport for a limo that will take him to his hotel, he sees a group of black writers "standing in the rain, waiting for a bus . . . to their Left Bank hotel. They were lucky if they got a room with a bath. The critics, on the other hand, were to be housed at one of the fanciest hotels in Paris, located on the Right Bank near the Champs-Élysées."[24] Reed uses another allusion to Milton to illustrate what he interprets as an uneven power relationship between critics and creative artists: "Dr. Barbara Christian spoke of the Paradise Lost/Paradise Regained worlds of writers and critics. The high world of lit crit books, journals and conferences, the middle world of classrooms and graduate students, and the low world of bookstores, communities, and creative writers."[25]

Reed's depiction of criticism as a lucrative enterprise is an obvious exaggeration, but he does point to structures of academia wherein comfortable academic bureaucrats, with access to regular paychecks and institutional funding, produce scholarship on the work of artists who risk poverty in devotion to their craft and have sometimes suffered great personal and financial losses living without job security or health insurance. These academic critics write their books on these artists to leverage themselves toward tenure and promotion while remaining indifferent to the plight of the very artists they study. These unflattering portrayals of academia appear in several academic novels, and Reed's judgment here bears some points of contact with that Samuel R. Delany provides in *The Mad Man* with the cynical Irving Mossman, who wants to study the work of an iconoclastic intellectual as long as it doesn't involve any personal risks to his career and reputation.

Despite the assurances that he would be awarded tenure in either the African American studies, women's studies, or the Department of Humanity, Puttbutt ends up being denied tenure in all three. He is further humiliated when he learns that the administration has decided to hire and grant automatic tenure to April Jokujoku, a black feminist literary scholar. Earlier in the novel Puttbutt had scoffed at the fact that Jokujoku had only one article to her name, "something having to do with Clitoridectomy Imagery in the Works of Black Male Novelists."[26] She ends up being hired and appointed full professor in the departments of women's studies and African American studies at the outlandish sum of one hundred fifty thousand dollars per semester.

Reed's depiction of black women as privileged elites claiming oppression when they are in fact more advantaged than black men is oddly reminiscent of the same argument that conservative white men have made against affirmative action and other diversity initiatives. Again, Michele Wallace's analysis is germane here; she points out a contradiction inherent in Reed's arguments about black women as agents of white feminists. As she states, "The problem appears to be that Reed doesn't relish the idea of black women making public judgements about black men, although black men in the know, from the ubiquitous Dr. [Alvin] Poussaint (psych consultant for *The Cosby Show*) to Reed himself, insist on their right to define and describe black women."[27] Furthermore, there were already critical conversations among black feminists about their relationship to white feminism. Such questions led the writer Alice Walker to embrace the term "womanist" as a black alternative to white feminism, and as I pointed out in the previous chapter on *Meridian*, Walker was already working through this and related ideas in her fiction, albeit Reed considers that fiction inferior and castigates her for *The Color Purple*'s depiction of black male abusers.

After Puttbutt realizes he's been turned down for tenure he goes back to his house and pulls out his old Black Panther beret, and he takes down the picture of his hero, black conservative economist Thomas Sowell. He is about to take down the picture of Booker T. Washington as well but decides to leave it up because "Booker T. was complex."[28] The image of Washington here evokes his complicated political legacy. Washington's name has become synonymous with the proverbial sellout who panders to white racism in exchange for individual power. But he also founded Tuskegee University, one of the most important educational institutions in black America, and inspired the cultivation of other black schools and colleges in the South. The fact that Washington also inspired the militant black nationalist leader Marcus Garvey, who admired *Up from Slavery* and corresponded with Washington in the months before Washington's death in 1915, is just another part of that complex legacy, something that a former black nationalist like Puttbutt would certainly recognize.

The major surreal turn in the novel comes at the end of its second section, when Jack London College is purchased by a mysterious Japanese corporate faction. Soon the Japanese administration begins requiring all faculty and students to take an IQ test designed by a Japanese educational firm. Puttbutt looks at some of the questions on the exam:

> Who was the first novelist and name her book? Name the monk who introduced Zen Buddhism into Japan? What was the former name for Tokyo? For Kyoto? Name three Kabuki plays and their plots. So as to deflect the criticism that the test was Nihon-chu-o, they had included some questions about European thinkers. What famous philosopher said that Indian literature was more imaginative than Homeric literature?[29]

Obviously, the questions were designed to upend Western intellectual hegemony, and the Japanese administration also anticipated that there might be some complaints about the questions. Dr. Yamato goes on to explain about the last question on Homeric literature, stating that he included the question so that students wouldn't complain that the test wasn't multicultural. The administration also proposes some additional tutelage to help the American faculty along, and if that didn't work then maybe it was proof that Americans were of inferior intellect and should be put to work in service jobs, for which they are more suited. Last, Yamato proposes a change to the title of the Ethnic Studies Department: "'And another thing, Ethnic Studies will now be called Bangaku.' Bangaku. Puttbutt wrote the word down. He looked it up when he got home. It meant 'barbarian studies.'"[30]

By the end of the novel it is the conservative "Back to Basics" scholar Dr. Crabtree who becomes the most outspoken critic of the Japanese administration's efforts to turn the college into a monocultural institution, and he is reborn as a passionate advocate of multicultural education. In a faculty meeting he stands up, lashes out at the administration using Yoruba phrases (that he had learned after being forced to take classes in Yoruba required by the new Japanese administration's curriculum, at the behest of Puttbutt himself), and gives one of the novel's big speeches, stating in part, "We should be the ones to lead our students and our country to new intellectual frontiers. Instead we're like the archaic Dixiecrats of the Old South, but instead of yelling segregation forever, we're yelling Western culture forever."[31]

Another way to approach *Japanese by Spring* and, additionally, the academic novels of Du Bois, particularly *Dark Princess* and *The Black Flame*, is through an increasing body of critical work connecting research on the Asian and African diasporas. Bill V. Mullen's book *Afro-Orientalism* (2004) doesn't discuss Reed's novel directly, but Mullen lays out a critical framework that is relevant to Reed's ideas in *Japanese by Spring*. Afro-Orientalism, as Mullen describes it, is a distinct strand of cultural and political thought that contests the long-standing, dominant discourse of race and nation that has come to be identified as Orientalism, a concept popularized by Edward Said in his highly influential text *Orientalism*. Mullen borrows Said's terminology and framework and refashions them as a way of thinking not just about how "the West" views the "other" but also as a means by which different peoples categorized as "others" banded together in anti-imperialist and antiracist solidarity. Mullen evaluates various Afro-Asian criticisms of U.S. imperialism—including writings by Richard Wright, Detroit-based activists James and Grace Lee Boggs, and civil rights leader Robert F. Williams. Mullen sees Afro-Orientalism as a challenge to ethnic studies and postcolonial studies, particularly as scholars in these fields try to find new ways to approach race, diaspora, and hybridity. Nikhil Pal Singh's writing, including *Black Is a Country* (2005), is also a part of this critical field, and for Singh the black civil rights movement in the United States, which often gets reduced to the easily co-opted saints of Martin Luther King Jr. and Rosa Parks, was actually a global protest movement that linked intellectuals and activists in various locations. Singh writes, "From Martin Luther King's embrace of Gandhi's principles of nonviolence to the revolutionary nationalism of Malcolm X, Robert Williams, Harold Cruse and Huey Newton that looked toward Cuba, Africa, China and Vietnam, antiracism and anti-imperialism remained powerfully fused within the black political imagination."[32]

Crystal Anderson, in *Beyond "The Chinese Connection": Contemporary Afro-Asian Cultural Production*, expresses some skepticism about Reed's depiction of the Japanese characters in the novel, stating that "Reed's critique uses the Japanese as an object . . . He consistently casts the Japanese as Other in order to underscore the conflict between Blacks and whites."[33] The story line about Puttbutt's Japanese lessons and the detail with which Reed explains the process of learning Japanese grammar indicate a deep respect for Japanese culture, and his narrative is clearly informed by the history of racism against Asians in the United States, including the internment of Japanese citizens during World War II. But while the novel celebrates Japanese history and culture it also objectifies that history and culture, making it difficult at times to tell whether this is a novel that criticizes racism against the Japanese or reproduces it, particularly through its caricatures of Asians. Perhaps this is where the complexity of satire comes into play, as the use of humor to ridicule stereotypes can sometimes slip into that uncomfortable territory where it is difficult to tell whom the joke is on, and the artist can't control how the joke is used.

Although Reed takes his swipes at academic literary criticism, it seems the structure and content of *Japanese by Spring* are partly influenced by Bakhtinian theory of the novel, and this connects Reed's project to my earlier reading of Du Bois as a novelist and the dialogic quality of *The Black Flame*. Throughout his novel Reed mentions a fictional organization called Glossos United, a radical underground multicultural organization started in the 1970s. The name Glossos United is also a reference to Bakhtin's idea of "heteroglossia" and "hybridization." The organization seems to represent Ishmael Reed's ideal organization of resistance against what he calls the Anti-Glossos, the white Western monoculturalists. The name Glossos also invokes "glossolalia," the ecstatic religious practice of "speaking in tongues" commonly associated with Christians of the Pentecostal faith. Glossolalia is a powerful metaphor for the kind of multilingualism Reed advocates in his novel. Reed's incorporation of different languages in *Japanese by Spring* dramatizes his theories of multiculturalism while also gesturing to the heteroglossic nature of the novel itself as a literary form uniquely suited to accommodate a diversity of voices and cultures, in the hands of the right artists.

Real Compared to What?

In Percival Everett's *Erasure*, the novelist and English professor Thelonious "Monk" Ellison, author of several literary novels on a variety of subjects, finds himself under pressure from critics and his literary agent to write books that are more legibly black in their content. Ellison is annoyed by the critical and commercial success of a "street" novel called *We's Lives in Da Ghetto* written by an author named Juanita Mae Jenkins. He believes that the novel is of questionable literary value and that it is composed of offensive racist caricatures. Much to Ellison's chagrin, the book is a best seller, gets favorable reviews in literary magazines, and is even embraced by some of his colleagues and friends. Disgusted with the success of the novel, Ellison decides to pen a satirical novel titled *My Pafology* under the pen name Stagg R. Leigh. Though written as a farce, his novel unexpectedly gets picked up by a publisher, and Ellison is forced to decide if he should reveal himself as its author.

With *Erasure* Percival Everett utilizes the academic novel as a forum to explore concepts of racial authenticity in black literary and cultural history and to reexamine Ralph Ellison's theories on black literature and creativity. Everett's novel is best understood through an analysis of "the politics of authenticity" in black literature, and I consider here how this particular racial discourse came to be so pervasive in black literature and in other forms of black cultural production.

Erasure is a recursive, metafictional novel, with passages of literary and cultural theory embedded in the narrative, allowing Everett to comment on the form of the novel and interrogate the construction of the text itself. Like other academic novelists, Everett uses the malleability of the novel as a form to incorporate various forms and genres of writing that are particularly related to the academic profession. In his book *About Writing* the author and critic Samuel R. Delany writes that one of his revelations as a budding novelist was the realization that the novel is essentially "a structured arrangement of different modes of rhetoric."[34] Everett's *Erasure* is an illustration of that concept in its incorporation of various rhetorical forms, including letters, jokes, literary criticism, imaginary dialogues between historical figures, the curriculum vitae, the conference paper, and the book blurb.

Though most of his work gets filed under "literary fiction," Everett's writing has bounded across genres and themes. His first novel, *Suder* (1983), is the story of a black professional baseball player who is experiencing a batting slump and becomes obsessed with the music of jazz saxophonist Charlie Parker. Among his other novels are *Frenzy* (1997), a retelling of the Dionysus myth set in ancient Greece, and *God's Country* (1994), an American Western set in the 1870s. Throughout Everett's career he has been closely associated with the literary journal *Callaloo*, where several of his short pieces have been published. In fact, my introduction to Everett came in 1998 when he participated in a *Callaloo* conference at Morehouse College. I found his reading there strange and mystifying at the time, but its central image—a silent baby conversant in literary theory lobbing an interior monologue of insults at his parents—stayed with me for some reason. I later discovered that the novel he read from that day was the academic novel *Glyph*, published in 1999 and reissued in 2014 by Graywolf Press.

Everett has ventured into the academic novel on other occasions as well. His 2009 novel *I Am Not Sidney Poitier* features a young protagonist named Not Sidney Poitier who becomes a student at Morehouse College, where he meets a professor named Percival Everett who teaches a class on Nonsense. The novel contains a vigorous critique of respectability politics, including a scathing portrayal of Bill Cosby. Like other academic novels I cover here by W. E. B. Du Bois, Chester Himes, Nella Larsen, and others, *I'm Not Sidney Poitier* addresses the topic of color consciousness among the black elite in historically black colleges. In a parody of the classic Sidney Poitier film *Guess Who's Coming to Dinner*, Everett has the dark-skinned black protagonist going home with his light-skinned black girlfriend to meet her upper-class black family.

For a while, *Erasure* was the subject of Hollywood interest. Angela Bassett purchased the screen rights to the novel, it was listed in the Internet Movie Database (IMDb) as being in preproduction, and the project received write-ups at the black film website Shadow and Act. The last working title for the project was "Book of the Year" as late as 2013. But with the listing now deleted from IMDb and no mention of the film elsewhere, it is likely that the project has been permanently scrapped.[35]

Thelonious "Monk" Ellison's name, derived from the bebop jazz pianist, is a signifier of his status as a member of the black bourgeoisie. "Monk" is the nickname that most of his family and friends call him. His family surname, Ellison, is not only an allusion to the famed black novelist but also a device through which Everett reevaluates Ellison's ideas about black art, representation, and creativity. Ellison's classic essay "The World and the Jug" is an essential companion piece and subtext to *Erasure*. (Because I discuss the actual Ralph Ellison in this book, I attempt to avoid confusion by referring to the main character of *Erasure* as the characters do in the novel, by his nickname "Monk.")

From the very first page Monk's racial identity is front and center. "I have dark brown skin, curly hair, a broad nose, some of my ancestors were slaves and I have been detained by pasty white policemen in New Hampshire, Arizona and Georgia, so the society in which I live tells me I am black; that is my race."[36] This opening salvo immediately signals Monk's social-constructionist attitude toward racial identity, that it is as much a product of the sociopolitical context in which one lives as it is a product of the self. But it also reiterates Brittney Cooper's idea of "embodied discourse," even as a male character and from a male writer, and it underscores my contention that raced and gendered embodiment is a critical part of the blackademic novelist's political intervention.

The reference to the policemen is a gesture to the all-too-familiar phenomenon of "driving while black" and "stop and frisk" operations. The police reference also implies Louis Althusser's notion of "interpellation," the process of social and political marking and self-identification through which identities are produced. According to Althusser, the main purpose of ideology is in "*'constituting' concrete individuals as subjects*," and it is through interpellation that individuals are turned into subjects. Althusser's main example of this is the "Hey, you there!" hail from a police officer: "Experience shows that the practical telecommunication of hailing is such that they hardly ever miss their man: verbal call or whistle, the one hailed always recognizes that it is really him who is being hailed."[37] Althusser's police metaphor describes the way that racial identification functions. Monk indicates his skepticism about the truth-value of race when emphasizing "the society in which I live tells me I am black" instead of saying, "I am black." And yet he also feels that this same society that hails him as black also deems him to be inadequately black: "Some people in the society in which I live, described as being black, tell me I am not *black* enough. Some people whom the society calls white tell me the same thing."[38]

This introduction contextualizes Monk's perspective on race throughout the novel. To parse the logic of racial authenticity one must understand the social construction of race: that what we call race is not static throughout all time and space but is a concept that is specific to various locations and historical periods in which such categories of identity have social currency and are stabilized by legal structures. Social constructionism also implies that race is but one way in which human beings have organized themselves; ethnicity, gender, nationality, color, religion, and sexuality are others, and these are also provisional categories.

Erasure provides an opportunity to examine questions of racial authenticity and the "acting white" theory. One of the reasons I have emphasized "overeducation of the Negro" as a white-supremacist discourse on black education is to challenge this frivolous but pervasive idea of "acting white," an idea that has often been deployed by conservative thinkers as a way to explain gaps in educational achievement between black and white students. The acting white theory is a part of the black pathology logic that places the blame for social problems upon black culture and black behavior, as if black antipathy to education is the *only* impediment to achievement and equality.[39] If anything, I hope that this book joins the copious literature on the history and theory of black education that shows an extensive history of black Americans pursuing higher education. This literature reveals an evangelical faith in the education gospel, even to the point of blinding naïveté. As I have made pains to show here, the academic novels I discuss are counternarratives to a history of sustained, vigorous, and effective white-supremacist opposition to black higher education, including even the concern of some sympathetic white supporters of black higher education that educated black people stay within their social boundaries. In *Erasure*, Percival Everett delves into this territory of racial identity, higher education, and class.

Monk's family life is one deeply entrenched in "the talented tenth." His grandfather, father, and both siblings (a sister and brother) are all medical doctors. As a professional writer and English professor Monk is the oddball of the family. Although Monk rejected a career in medicine, Monk's father always encouraged his son's literary interests. A flashback to a family dinner table conversation on the finer points of James Joyce's *Finnegans Wake* is one of the many fine bits of high literary comedy sprinkled throughout the novel.[40] Monk's sister, Lisa, is a physician who works at a women's health clinic. Her murder at the hands of an antiabortion fanatic is one of the factors that leads Monk back to Washington, D.C., to care for his ailing mother. His brother,

Bill, a plastic surgeon in Arizona, is depicted as a bit of a pathetic closet case, trying to come out and live openly as a gay man. Bill is still coming to terms with his sexuality while going through a divorce from his wife and a custody battle over their children. Their ailing father has committed suicide a few years earlier, and their mother discovers some letters indicating that he may have had an affair and fathered a child. At the end of the novel Monk's attempts to track down the half-sister whom he has discovered and his plan to give her the money his father had left to her provide another comic set piece that has Monk traveling to a seedy New York neighborhood looking for her.

The upper-class status of the Ellison family is an important part of Monk's character and the source of his elitist attitude toward black culture. The children are raised by a housekeeper named Lorraine, who becomes their mother's full-time caretaker as she struggles through Alzheimer's. When Lorraine decides to marry an older male friend of the family's, Monk gives her ten thousand dollars as a kind of severance package and wedding present. At a gathering with Lorraine and the man's family, the class differences between the Ellisons and the less-wealthy African Americans comes into stark relief. As Monk says to himself, "I truly didn't understand how anyone could get so excited over a mere ten thousand dollars . . . The problem was the one I had always had, that I was not a *regular* guy and I so much wanted to be. Can you spell *bourgeois?*"[41]

Monk first encounters Juanita Mae Jenkins's novel when he sees a poster advertising a reading for the best-selling book while visiting a Borders bookstore with his sister, Lisa. Monk is once again confronted with Jenkins's novel *We's Lives in Da Ghetto* while on a plane back to Los Angeles from Washington, D.C., when he sees a review of it in a literary magazine. "The twists and turns of the novel are fascinating, but the real strength of the work is in its haunting verisimilitude. The ghetto is painted in all its exotic wonders," the review gushes.[42] The protagonist of the novel, Sharonda, is a fifteen-year-old mother of three children by three different men who becomes a hooker to make enough money to take dance classes, where she is discovered by a producer and lands in a Broadway show. She is described by the reviewer as "the epitome of the black matriarchal symbol of strength."[43] Later, Everett sees Juanita Mae Jenkins on the Kenya Dunston Show, a program not unlike the wildly popular real-life television program run by Oprah Winfrey. On the show Jenkins talks about her reasons for writing the book and asks, "Where are the books about our people? Where are our stories?"[44]

Meanwhile Monk's mother is beginning to show signs of Alzheimer's, and he has to consider moving back to Washington to take care of her. Everett's depictions of the family's struggle with the disease are full of dark humor and a poignancy that breaks through the novel's otherwise cool metafictional tone. Because of his mother's condition he decides to explore the possibility of moving back to Washington and applies for a teaching job at American University. He contacts the chair of the English department, who explains to Monk that the best they can offer him is a position as a lecturer for a course on American literature, a position that pays "thirty-nine hundred and something" for the semester.[45] The reference is a welcome reminder of the economics of academic labor in the corporate university, where adjuncts increasingly make up the majority of a department's faculty. It is a far cry from the derogatory depictions of cushy tenured radicals castigated in conservative tirades about the university, not to mention its being far below the black feminist professor April Jokujoku's laughable hundred and fifty thousand per semester in Ishmael Reed's *Japanese by Spring*.

Throughout the story Monk is in conversation with his literary agent, Yul, who is sympathetic and supportive of his writing but pushes him to consider writing more commercially viable fiction, which in Monk's case means fiction with immediately legible blackness as its subject matter. From his curriculum vitae we see the range of books and articles he has written, and the full CV is included in the novel as a touchstone of professional academic life and as a narrative device to convey some backstory about Monk's career.

Seeing Juanita Mae Jenkins's face on the cover of *Time* magazine is the final straw for Monk, and he sits down and produces the novel within a novel at the center of *Erasure*, a book he titles *My Pafology* and signs under the pen name Stagg R. Leigh. *My Pafology* is full of hood clichés culled from American popular culture. The main character, Van Go Jenkins, is nineteen years old and has four children by four different women. He lives with his mother, and the book opens with a nightmare of him stabbing her to death. "I hates my mama, I loves my mama," he repeats several times throughout the story. Van Go spends his time mostly hanging out in a pool hall fighting with his ne'er-do-well friends, watching television, and trying to avoid the mothers of his children. The chapter titles of the book are spelled phonetically "Won, Too, Free, Fo," and so on. And, most important for this discussion, the plot of the novel closely resembles that of Richard Wright's novel *Native Son*.

In Everett's parody of *Native Son* Van Go Jenkins gets a job working for a family named Dalton, but in a significant twist the Daltons are an upper-crust black family, not the rich white liberals of *Native Son*. The Daltons' daughter, Penelope, and her boyfriend, like the characters in Wright's novel, have a patronizing fascination with black culture and ask Van Go to drive them from their plush West Hollywood home into the hood for fried chicken, waffles, and beer and to score some weed. The decision to make the Daltons black calls attention to the ways in which black elites also participate in the romanticization of black hood life, a pandering fascination often born of their anxieties about being disconnected from an authentic black experience. Van Go ends up carrying the drunk Penelope back home from the excursion and, we find out later, raped her while she was passed out. He later robs and murders a Korean grocer, perhaps an allusion to the popular film *Menace II Society* but certainly related to the real-life prevalence of Korean-owned businesses in inner-city black neighborhoods. After hiding out for a while he is discovered by the police and is pursued in a high-speed chase along the highways of Los Angeles (à la O. J. Simpson) and eventually cornered and caught.

Monk understands that what he has written is a parody, but those who control the apparatus of production do not understand, don't care, and aren't even sophisticated enough to tell the difference since they didn't even recognize the rather obvious references to *Native Son*. However, what the publishers are in a position to do is to help Monk make his financial troubles disappear. Though his agent initially tries to discourage Monk from distributing the novel, Monk convinces him to send it out under the name Stagg R. Leigh, without any other qualifiers or indicators that the book was written by an academic author of literary fiction. His agent later calls with the news that he has been offered a six-figure advance for the book. When the book is later sent to a Hollywood producer, Monk receives a seven-figure offer for the film rights. Monk raises the stakes and asks his agent to change the title of the novel to *Fuck*, threatening that if the publisher does not agree he'll take it to another publisher. The publisher agrees to change the title.

In a scene toward the end of the novel Monk sits in a doctor's office and wonders if maybe he overreacted to *We's Lives in Da Ghetto*. He sees some popular novels on the table and ponders that maybe what Jenkins has produced is little more than a genre novel no different from the mystery, romance, and crime novels one might find in airports and chain bookstores.

> There were books by John Grisham and Tom Clancy, a paperback of John MacDonald and things like that. Those books didn't bother me. Though I had never read one completely through, I had peeked at pages, and although I did not find any depth of artistic expression or any abundance of irony or play with language or ideas, I found them well enough written, the way a technical manual can be well enough written. *Oh, so that's Tab A*. So why did Juanita Mae Jenkins send me running for the toilet? I imagine it was because Tom Clancy was not trying to sell his book to me by suggesting that the crew of his high-tech submarine was a representation of his race (*however fitting a metaphor*). Nor was his publisher marketing it in that way. If you didn't like Clancy's white people, you could go out and read some others.[46]

The kicker at the end of the novel is that Monk is asked to serve on a book-award committee, and *Fuck* is one of the books selected for the award. He soon finds, much to his dismay, that the four other judges on the committee all loved the book. "A gutsy piece of work," and "the strongest African-American novel I've read in a long time" are some of the comments thrown around in of the committee's conference calls.[47] As the committee decides on the finalists, Monk intensifies his arguments against the book: "It's no novel at all. It is a failed conception, an unformed fetus, seed cast into sand, a hand without fingers, a word with no vowels. It is offensive, poorly written, racist and mindless."[48] The committee members respond by telling him how real and true to life the novel must be. One of them even tells him, "I should think as an African American you'd be happy to see one of your own people get an award like this."[49] In the end, *Fuck* wins the award. Monk is in attendance at the ceremony, and in the book's final scene he confuses everyone in the room by walking up to the podium to receive the award, and the book ends with him staring into one of the television cameras and saying, "Egads, I'm on television." As Margaret Russett emphasizes in her critical essay on *Erasure*, both *My Pafology/Fuck* and *Erasure* end with the characters staring into television cameras, a gesture to the influence that television has had on the dispersal of black representations and the shaping of black identity over the course of the twentieth century.[50]

It is clear that Percival Everett is engaging with the infamous critical debate between Ralph Ellison and Irving Howe in the 1960s. Revisiting this exchange in the context of my discussion on black academic novels reveals why authenticity is such an important recurring concept in this particular set of novels, and this conversation also has implications for theorizing the form of the academic novel as a genre.

Irving Howe's 1963 *Dissent* magazine article "Black Boys and Native Sons" lauds Richard Wright as a model black writer, particularly with his award-winning novel *Native Son*, and Howe pits Wright against writers such as James Baldwin and Ralph Ellison, who, he feels, have specifically rejected this kind of protest in their work. Howe's essay was preceded in the 1950s by James Baldwin's "Everybody's Protest Novel," which was published in his 1955 collection *Notes of a Native Son*. In "Everybody's Protest Novel," Baldwin had already begun to question the efficacy of the American protest novel. Baldwin interrogated the sentimentality of Harriet Beecher Stowe's *Uncle Tom's Cabin* (a novel Baldwin admits had a deep influence on him as an emerging writer) and questioned the bitterness of Bigger Thomas in Richard Wright's *Native Son*. Howe, in response to Baldwin, Ellison, and Wright, published his article in *Dissent* as a defense of Richard Wright, writing that *Native Son* "brought out into the open, as no one ever had before, the hatred, fear and violence that have crippled and may yet destroy our culture."[51] About Ellison's *Invisible Man*, he wrote that "to simply write about the 'Negro experience,' with the esthetic distance urged by the critics of the fifties, is a moral and psychological impossibility, for plight and protest are inseparable from that experience, and even if less political than Wright and less prophetic than Baldwin, Ellison knows this quite as well as they do."[52] In 1964, Ralph Ellison responded to Howe with "The World and the Jug," which was first published in the *New Leader* and later included in an expanded form in his essay collection *Shadow and Act*. In responding to Howe, Ellison managed to produce one of the most profound statements on black art and politics. In "The World and the Jug" Ellison argued that Howe's criticism contained a nasty strain of liberal condescension that has long existed in American writing. From the days of Phillis Wheatley, to the nineteenth-century slave narratives, up to Wright's *Native Son*, black literature had often been extolled by sympathetic white critics for its sociological significance but rarely evaluated for its literary and artistic merits or with very little sense that this literature was the result of artistic creativity and intentionality of any sort. Instead of being art, it could and should be seen only as a pure expression of the Negro's sociological reality. In Howe's essay Ralph Ellison saw more of this sociological burden being placed on black literature and was perturbed by the way that this emphasis on sociology led critics to dismiss the creative aspects of his work and the work of other black artists. For these critics the work of art by a black artist could only be pure expression and never a matter of invention or skill. Ellison, being the self-righteous and supremely confident artist that he was, was especially annoyed that critics such as Howe would trivialize the artistic invention and rich literary allusions of which he was so proud in his own work. In the now-famous first lines of the essay, Ellison wrote,

> First three questions: Why is it so often true that when critics confront the American as Negro they suddenly drop their advanced critical armament and revert with an air of confident superiority to quite primitive modes of analysis? Why is it that sociology-oriented critics seem to rate literature so far below politics and ideology that they would rather kill a novel than modify their presumptions concerning a given reality which it seeks in its own terms to project? Finally why is it that so many of those who would tell us the meaning of Negro life never bother to learn how varied it really is?[53]

While there are many different issues raised by the Ellison–Howe exchange, the question of racial authenticity ranks chief among them. For in raising the question of what should be the theme of black literature, Howe and Ellison were also exploring the question of what is "real" black literature. Later in the essay, Ellison explicitly argues his belief that "Wright, for Howe, is the genuine article, the authentic Negro writer, and his tone is the only authentic tone."[54]

One paragraph of "The World and the Jug" particularly encapsulates Ellison's complicated critical vision. He writes,

> No matter how strictly Negroes are segregated socially and politically, on the level of the imagination their ability to achieve freedom is limited only by their individual aspiration, insight, energy and will. Wright was able to free himself in Mississippi because he had the imagination and the will to do so. He was as much a product of his reading as of his painful experiences, and he made himself a writer

by subjecting himself to the writer's discipline—as he understood it. The same is true of James Baldwin, who is not the product of a Negro store-front church but of the library, and the same is true of me.⁵⁵

For many years after the publication of this essay Ellison was criticized for his ideas about the Americanness of black culture and for his metaphysical vision of black artistic freedom expressed in this passage. To be fair, some of the criticism was unwarranted and came from militant black nationalists who reveled in romanticized visions of the African past and disavowed any intellectual influence from the American political culture in which they were so deeply ensconced. However, Ellison clearly deserved to be taken to task for his rose-colored vision of black life under Jim Crow.

Jerry G. Watts provides a detailed analysis of this exchange between Howe and Ellison and its significance for black intellectuals in *Heroism and the Black Intellectual*. In the process of examining this debate and Ralph Ellison's theories of art and politics, Watts also provides a much-needed corrective to the idea of Ralph Ellison as the patron saint of black artistic freedom. As he puts it,

> Mistakenly commentators have often assumed that Ellison's response to Howe in "The World and the Jug" is an argument in behalf of black artistic/intellectual freedom. In fact, Ellison implicitly accepts Howe's claim that a black novelist should articulate the views and struggles of the black masses, but he disagrees over the substance of those views and struggles and how they should be conveyed artistically.⁵⁶

He goes on to argue that Ellison's response to Howe is reflective of a major tendency on Ellison's part to use "the exceptional as the standard-bearer for a people."⁵⁷ The conditions of life in the Jim Crow South, particularly in my violent, regressive home state of Mississippi (I'm from there, so I can say that), had crushed the spirits of too many black citizens and had snuffed out the lives of so many people who possessed "will" and "imagination" but were never allowed to cultivate them because of the repressive political order in which they lived. Ellison's statement has the unfortunate consequence of suggesting that all people from the state of Mississippi who were not as successful as Richard Wright and all people in Harlem who were not as successful as James Baldwin must be stuck in their situations simply because they lacked will and imagination.

Ellison's emphasis on the discipline and practices of reading and writing must be a part of any serious analysis of black literature, and I believe that they can be extended to any form of black artistic and intellectual practice. But it would have been better for Ellison to say that James Baldwin was a product of the storefront church *and* the library. Obviously numerous black persons attended storefront churches but never reached the literary heights that Baldwin reached. Baldwin would not have been able to parlay his experiences in the church into the great literature of *Go Tell It on the Mountain* were it not for the disciplines of reading and writing that he practiced throughout his life. No matter what the subject matter of one's work, to produce artistic work one must either sit down with pen and paper, sit down with one's instrument to practice scales, or spend time in the recording studio crafting whatever it is that he or she expects to distribute.

And to some degree what Ellison is referring to here has to do with the ethics of representation in black art. In *Erasure*, Monk is able to sell *My Pafology* by concealing his actual identity as a learned man and an author of more intellectually rigorous fiction. Had he submitted the book to publishers under his own name the book would likely have been dismissed as the work of an imposter. Before the publishers could get behind the work they needed to be sure that it was the Real Thing, and Monk was able to convince them of his authenticity by concealing his identity and assuring them that his writing was the product of the streets and not the library. This reality points to the fact that the sale and marketing of authentic art as a commodity is contingent upon the "organic" quality of the author herself. Too much formal education (real or perceived) corrupts that authenticity.

Another among the many famous lines in "The World and the Jug" is Ellison's statement on the disconnect between the novelist Richard Wright and his character in *Native Son*, Bigger Thomas: "Wright could imagine Bigger, but Bigger could not possibly imagine Richard Wright. Wright saw to that."[58] Ellison's most stinging criticism of Wright was that Wright had sacrificed the complexity of his own life and intelligence for the bleak vision of *Native Son*. He went on to elaborate that "to me Wright as writer was less interesting than the enigma he personified, that he could so dissociate himself from the complexity of his background while trying so hard to improve the condition of black men everywhere; that he could be so wonderful an example of human possibility but could not for ideological reasons depict a Negro as intelligent, as creative or as dedicated as himself."[59]

Ellison's statement could be taken as a false assumption about Wright's intentions. While *Native Son* drew on his experiences living in the stark conditions of inner-city Chicago, Bigger Thomas was not meant to be a practicing intellectual with Richard Wright's intelligence and literary skills. Certainly it can and should be possible for a black writer, indeed any writer, to depict characters at any point on the socioeconomic ladder and of various intellectual capabilities, and to do so with depth and pathos.

I have made it a point to avoid the assumption that only black academics can write nuanced representations of blackademic life, or that the educated black writer must write only about other educated people. Percival Everett even throws in a joke about this correlation between the writer and his subject at the beginning of *Erasure*. "And I am a writer of fiction. This admission pains me only at the thought of my story being found and read as I have always been put off by any story which has as its main character a writer."[60] The ability to create images of characters and situations outside the self, the alterity inherent in the enterprise of writing and reading literature, is one of its most powerful and enduring qualities.

This paradigm of black authenticity can lead to simplistic caricatures of black life, and critics may make the same mistake that Ellison attributes to Howe by thinking that "unrelieved suffering is the only 'real' Negro experience, and that the true Negro writer must be ferocious."[61] Furthermore, I submit that there this is a larger lesson here about the academic novel and higher education. To some degree the academic novel is often read as an inauthentic form, and academic writing as inauthentic writing. Hidden in those accusations is an anti-intellectualism that insists real literature is something that happens outside the halls of academia and that it can come only from those who are unpolluted by formal education. To be sure, one wants to celebrate the importance of organic intellectuals and autodidacts who learn their craft outside college classrooms. Too often, however, such celebrations devolve into a series of authenticity claims in which formal education and expertise are despised in favor of the pure and intuitive. And as I write this in the wake of the 2016 election, when America elected a man of such astonishing, proud ignorance who never reads, whose entire intellectual diet is organized around televised depictions of himself, and whose followers are positively hostile to expertise, it feels like we are living in a dystopian political timeline meant to illustrate just how badly this kind of vicious anti-intellectualism can go awry.

Desire constitutes another layer in this analysis of the authentic, as the authentic is often something used to lure, it is a thing to be lusted after and pursued. I have already addressed issues of color, embodiment, and sexuality in my analysis, but a fuller understanding of the black academic novel requires a more direct engagement with a queer analysis of the black intellectual.

One of the chief contributions of queer critical practice is to draw our attention toward the ways that race and sex are interrelated, that sexuality is always already embedded in racial discourses. The politics of respectability, while often deployed as a counterdiscursive formation against degrading images of black people, must be seen as a discourse that is always operating in that same sexualized territory that it claims to disavow. Samuel R. Delany's *The Mad Man* takes on the politics of respectability and offers a unique vision of queer black intellectual practice. Placing this provocative and fantastic pornographic novel in conversation with the other novels discussed in this book, one finds a novelist who presents possibilities for black embodiment and intellectual practice that directly challenge respectability narratives (in black and gay politics) by examining the political economy that undergirds them. Delany's intervention also prompts us to think about positive and negative representations and how black artists wield them.

The Mind-Body Problem

It was years ago, when I read "The Phil Leggiere Interview" in Samuel R. Delany's *Shorter Views: Queer Thoughts and the Politics of the Paraliterary*, that I got my first intimation that there was such a thing as an academic novel. This interview was composed in Delany's preferred "written interview" style wherein the questions are submitted in writing and Delany responds back in writing with answers that often read like stand-alone essays. Leggiere asks Delany about the genre of his recently published novel *The Mad Man*, and Delany writes,

> You've mentioned pornography and mysteries as two genres my new book *The Mad Man* plays with. But the most important genre—or sub-genre—it takes to itself is the "academic novel." And, as academic novels go, it's a pretty scathing one. It's a novel that allegorizes—if you want to read it that way—the situation our contemporary graduate students (who, in most major research universities, teach 50 percent or more of our university classes) have to endure in order to survive. Jarrell's *Pictures of an Institution*, Amis's *Lucky Jim*, or Philip Roth's *Letting Go* are really the books it contests with. Exploding, or just messing with, the expectations of the academic novel is where it does its most subversive work.[62]

The Mad Man is not merely an academic narrative about the inclusion of the black gay intellectual into existing academic institutions, not just a criticism of academic capitalism, but also a reckoning with the human cost of the capitalist mode of production. Its story line about homelessness is a criticism of the optimization and productivity of capital and calls attention to how its processes produce waste. Capitalism's construction of the human being as product, as resource, necessarily means the creation of waste, the rejection of the imperfect, defective objects that must be tossed aside because they have no market value. The problem of homelessness is the problem of these very inhumane processes, and in the novel Delany challenges readers to look beyond the easy moralism ("isn't it awful what happens to those people") to understand how these processes define the society we live in. Throughout Delany's copious body of work, one finds a constant exploration of the erotic as a mode of resistance against this dehumanization.[63]

Literary critic Reed Woodhouse gave the novel one of its first serious critical readings in his 1998 book *Unlimited Embrace: A Canon of Gay Fiction, 1945–1995*, in which he writes: "Delany is on the side of the body, which means being also on the side of all its beautiful, tragic, and arbitrary concreteness—of race, age, looks. And like bodies he admires, Delany's speech is direct, funky, unhypocritical, and lively."[64] Indeed, *The Mad Man* is full of candid speech about racial identity and the body, and the characters in the novel talk about and pursue their desires for racial difference, often using racial epithets as a part of their sexual play.

Delany's family history marks him as one deeply embedded in "the talented tenth." He was born and raised in Harlem to a family of southern black educators. His father, Samuel R. Delany Sr., was the youngest of ten children in a family of black educators and professionals involved with Saint Augustine's College in Raleigh, North Carolina. Samuel Sr. moved to New York in 1924 and went on to become a successful funeral director in Harlem as the owner of Levy and Delany Funeral Home. His wife, Margaret Delany, worked for the New York Public Library. The Delany family's life in Harlem in the 1920s was fictionalized in Delany Jr.'s novella *Atlantis: Model 1924*, which is another example of a novel that sits on the borderline of being an academic novel, with its educated characters and references to Du Bois, Paul Robeson, Jean Toomer, and the literature of the Harlem Renaissance.[65]

This family history places the author in the history of black higher education and its discourses of respectability fueled by Christian civilizationism. Students at early historically black colleges were taught not only academic subjects but also table manners, grooming, and other forms of social etiquette. In Booker T. Washington's *Up from Slavery* he writes of the "gospel of the toothbrush," which he learned from General Samuel Armstrong when he was at Hampton Institute:

> It has been interesting to note the effect that the use of the toothbrush has had in bringing about a higher degree of civilization among the students. With few exceptions, I have noticed that if we can get a student to the point where, when the first or second toothbrush disappears, he of his own notion buys another, I have not been disappointed in the future of the individual. Absolute cleanliness of the body has been insisted upon from the first. The students have been taught to bathe as regularly as to take their meals.[66]

Certainly, a statement like Washington's must be read contextually: southern black colleges were filled with students from rural backgrounds. Washington was on a mission to assimilate them into middle-class bourgeois values and make them at ease with socializing in the presence of whites, a necessary skill if they were to be the ideal service workers and laborers whom Washington hailed so famously in that 1895 speech that inspired Ralph Ellison's narrator of *Invisible Man*.

However, some recent works in black studies have sought to trouble this politics of respectability, raising questions about how the paradigm of respectability also serves to reinforce notions of inherent inequality. In his book *Aberrations in Black* (2004) sociologist Roderick Ferguson proposes a "queer of color" critique positioned against sociological discourses that construct black persons as sexually abnormal and black families as inherently disorganized. By reading *The Mad Man* as an academic novel with and against earlier narratives of black higher education, I'd like to emphasize queer interpretations of blackness, such as the one Ferguson puts forth, and one that Delany himself offers in "Some Queer Notions about Race." These interpretations of black identity that are attentive to the work of gender and sexuality militate against sociological constructions of black deviancy and white normativity.

One of the ways in which Delany subverts the genre expectations of the academic novel is by setting *The Mad Man* in the city. John Marr spends most of his time in the novel away from the campus and its cloistered academic community. In the introduction to the 2004 Everyman's Library edition of Vladimir Nabokov's 1953 academic novel *Pnin*, the academic novelist and critic David Lodge discusses the relationship between *Pnin* and two other academic novels of the 1950s, Randall Jarrell's *Pictures from an Institution* and Mary McCarthy's *Groves of Academe*. Lodge states, "What the three books have in common is a pastoral campus setting, a 'small world' removed from the hustle and bustle of modern urban life, in which social and political behaviour can be amusingly observed in the interaction of characters whose high intellectual pretensions are often let down by their very human frailties."[67] *The Mad Man* rejects that pastoral setting for the metropolis, and whereas there are some scenes that take place in the halls of academe, for most of the novel the bucolic campus quad is exchanged for the gritty urban city parks where drug addicts and other street people hang out. Not only the city's setting but also its metaphysics are a significant part of the novel's narrative construction. There are many similarities between the action of *The Mad Man* and Delany's ideas about city life in his book *Times Square Red, Times Square Blue*, a work directly inspired by Jane Jacobs's influential urban study *The Death and Life of Great American Cities*, in which she suggests that the interclass contact that happens in cities is one of the things that makes city life unique, humane, and desirable. Delany rejects the typical suburban admonition that one should "never talk to strangers." In fact, talking to strangers is the very thing that one must learn to do again and again to successfully navigate city life. This contact between people of different races, classes, occupations and sexual identities happens all throughout the novel and animates John Marr's philosophical education.

One of the epigraphs in the opening chapter of *The Mad Man* comes from Michel Foucault: "The *bios philosophicus* is the animality of being human, renewed as a challenge, practiced as an exercise—and thrown in the face of others as a scandal." The quote underscores Mossman's attitude toward Hasler's sexuality and the novel's depiction of black embodiment and sexuality. Delany's engagement with Foucauldian conceptions of sexuality, language, and power, here and in all his work, is a way of neutralizing such scandalous interpretations of sexual identities and practices, which are often weaponized against marginal communities.

The ancient philosophical problem of reconciling mind and body is a thread connecting numerous works of academic fiction. In these novels the scholar is devoted to the life of the mind and works in a profession dominated by bourgeois heteronormative values. As a result, their characters find their sexual longings and desires at odds with the cerebral and respectable nature of their profession. Rebecca Goldstein's *The Mind-Body Problem* takes on this topic directly in the life of a young Jewish woman intellectual who experiences a sexual awakening in college. The novelist Philip Roth explores the concept extensively throughout nearly all his academic novels but particularly in the trilogy featuring the transgressive character David Kepesh. Over the course of the Kepesh novels, *The Breast*, *The Professor of Desire*, and *The Dying Animal*, the literature professor grapples with his unruly sexual desires, which have led him into a polyamorous relationship with two young women as a graduate student in Europe and later into a liaison with a Cuban-American student in *The Dying Animal*. The title and thematic focus of the last of these books, *The Dying Animal*, is indicative of the ideas Roth explores throughout the series when it comes to human biology, sexuality, death, and the ways that mortality and embodiment inspire and define artistic production.

Delany's *The Mad Man* was first published in 1994 by Richard Kasak Books in a hardback edition. It was released in a heavily revised 2002 paperback edition published by the now-defunct small press Voyant Publishing. The fundamental story of the novel remains the same in this newer version. There are no major characters or new plot developments added that radically change the story (though a part in the end where Marr goes to visit his partner's family in Maryland was significantly expanded in the Voyant edition). But it is important to note the novel's original publication date since it was first published in the midst of the HIV/AIDS crisis. The novel is itself a historical document of that crisis, as was his 1985 novella *The Tale of Plagues and Carnivals* and other works of queer fiction published in the 1980s and 1990s that portrayed the epidemic as it unfolded, including Randy Shilts's *And the Band Played On*, Larry Kramer's *The Normal Heart*, Tony Kushner's *Angels in America*, and Sarah Schulman's *People in Trouble*.

The Mad Man tells the story of John Marr, a black graduate student in philosophy who is working on a dissertation about Timothy Hasler, a (fictional) Korean American philosopher who was murdered in a New York City hustling bar in 1973 when he was twenty-nine years old. Delany connects Marr's research on philosophy and Hasler to the mind-body problem. Through extensive use of scatological imagery in a story about philosophical concepts and research, *The Mad Man* challenges the idea that the mental activity of the academic life is wholly separate from an erotic experience of the world.

The first section of the novel, "Part I: The Systems of the World," begins, "I do not have AIDS. I am surprised that I don't. I have had sex with men weekly, sometimes daily—without condoms—since my teens, though true, it's been overwhelmingly . . . no, more accurately, it's been since 1980—*all* oral, not anal." Such are the first words from the graduate student in philosophy at the fictional Enoch State University. As Reed Woodhouse notes, in this first paragraph Delany throws down the gauntlet and declares what the novel's relationship to the HIV/AIDS epidemic and homosexuality will be. John Marr is not an "innocent victim" but rather a "guilty victor," a promiscuous gay man in New York during the heights of the AIDS crisis who has managed to avoid contracting the disease. The paragraph speaks to Delany's ideas about the epidemiology of HIV/AIDS—namely, that oral sex is an extremely low-risk activity and that anal sex is a far more likely source of seroconversion than the medical establishment has been able to determine, largely because of what Delany interprets as methodological flaws in much of the research on HIV/AIDS transmission.

This beginning is a deliberate inversion of the opening lines of an article written during the AIDS epidemic by the writer Harold Brodkey, who remained heterosexually married throughout his life but attributed his infection to earlier homosexual encounters. The article appeared in the *New Yorker* over two issues, starting in June 1994. It began, "I have AIDS. I am surprised that I do. I have not been exposed since 1977, which is to say that my experiences, my adventures with homosexuality took place largely in the 1960s and 70s, and back then I relied on time and abstinence to indicate my degree of freedom from infection and to protect others and myself." Brodkey's article was later published in revised form in 1996 in his collection of essays titled *This Wild Darkness: The Story of My Death*. Brodkey died in January of 1996, before the book was published.[68]

The narrative of *The Mad Man* includes casual conversations about the epidemiology of HIV/AIDS, and in the back of the book Delany reprints the full text of a 1987 article in *The Lancet*, which he holds up as one of very few studies that include a detailed analysis of specific sexual acts and their rates of seroconversion, data that seem to show a strong correlation between insertive anal sex and seroconversion to HIV-positive status. The conceit of *The Mad Man*'s sexual excess is that for all its messy exchanging of bodily fluids, anal sex is the one thing that the characters *do not* do.

John Marr was born and raised on Staten Island, New York, to a working-class black family and was a bit of an intellectual prodigy, entering college at sixteen and graduate school at twenty. He earned an undergraduate degree in philosophy at the fictional Enoch State University and eventually enrolls in the school's graduate program in philosophy. "Systems of the World" was the title of the "grand Hegelian project" that Marr was considering for a dissertation but now realizes was too naively ambitious. In the opening pages of the novel Marr is back in his home city of New York and recently moved into an apartment on the Upper West Side of Manhattan. He is supporting himself by working as an office temp while trying to complete his dissertation on the life and work of Timothy Hasler.

John Marr's adviser, Irving Mossman, a forty-seven-year-old Jewish associate professor of philosophy at Enoch State, convinces John to work on a collaborative project on the life and work of Timothy Hasler. Like Marr, Hasler was also an intellectual prodigy and a product of New York. He was born to a father who was half Korean and a Korean mother. (The last name, Hasler, was from his paternal grandfather, an Englishman.) Hasler attended the prestigious Stuyvesant High School in Manhattan and went on to be accepted, at age fourteen, to Stilford University in California, where he studied philosophy as an undergraduate and graduate student. Hasler was murdered in 1973 at twenty-nine years old in a bar on Fiftieth Street and Ninth Avenue in Manhattan. (Eventually John Marr figures out that this was a hustling bar populated by older "Johns" and the young men who have sex with them for money.) At the time of his death Hasler had published sixteen refereed articles and a book, in 1967, called *Pascal, Nietzsche, Peirce*, a study tying together the thought of these three philosophers. As Marr goes on to explain, Timothy Hasler had a truncated academic career littered with periods where he dropped out of school to travel. His dissertation was never completed and existed only in the form of five chapter drafts that had been circulating through photocopies among the small cadre of philosophy academics interested in Hasler's work.

Hasler had also published some science fiction work, and John Marr was particularly taken with it. "And (my favorite) Hasler was six published (and, we discovered, two fragmentary and unpublished) science fiction stories, that, against titanic intergalactic backgrounds to dwarf *Star Trek*, *Star Wars*, and *Dune*, turned on some of the finer mathematics that informed his articles on the philosophy of natural languages."[69] The reaction of scholars to Hasler's fiction underscores Delany's criticism of science fiction and fantasy as "paraliterary" genres of literature, which are seen as beneath, outside, or beyond proper literary fiction.[70]

The plan to collaborate with Mossman on Hasler's life seems like a good one until Mossman sends a letter to John in New York saying that he had come across some unsettling material in Hasler's journals. "Hasler must have been indulging in the most degrading—and depressing—sexual 'experiments': bums on the New York City streets, destitute alcoholics in Riverside Park, white, black or Hispanic winos lounging about on the island in the middle of upper Broadway, about whom his only criterion could have been, as far as I can make out, the dirtier the better."[71] In another letter, Mossman writes, "Tell me John, how can I write a biography of someone when I find I've been walking through the streets for a couple of hours muttering to myself: 'He was an obnoxious little chink with an unbelievable nasty sex life.'"[72] It is at this point that John realizes Mossman is the wrong person to be writing Hasler's biography. It is also at this point that John begins to carry out his own Hasler-inspired sexual experimentation, venturing out into Riverside Park for sex with several homeless men and later going to the Golden Shower Association

"Wet Night" held at the Mineshaft, a leather bar in the Lower Manhattan neighborhood known as the Meatpacking District.

The activity that Mossman is referring to in Hasler's work, and the activity John engages in, forms the bulk of this novel's pornographic content: sex with and between homeless men, sometimes in the streets and parks of New York, other times in John Marr's apartment. That Hasler's murder was somehow linked to this perversion is what Mossman tunes in to. But as Ray Davis writes in his essay on Delany's pornographic novels, "Delany's Dirt," "Yes, tragedy happens to perverts. But to introduce the 'perverse' into a tragic situation is by default to imply that the perversion itself is to blame."[73] It is precisely that mythic literary archetype that Delany challenges in *The Mad Man*, both in the death of Hasler and in the AIDS pandemic that soon takes over the foreground of the novel, as it took over the lives of many gay men in the 1980s regardless of their HIV status. One of the many ways in which the book breaks convention is by neither settling for a simplistic and untroubled celebration of promiscuity nor indulging in the cliché that perversion always leads to a tragic end. Though Hasler indeed died tragically and young, it was often his sexuality that fueled his brilliant philosophy, something that Mossman cannot seem to understand when he discovers Hasler's sexual life and attempts to deal with it by separating "the sexual practice from the thinking."[74]

The story line about Mossman and his approach to Hasler dramatizes the type of resistance that existed against gay and lesbian studies in the academy. Through Mossman as a "villain" Delany shows the hypocrisy in some academics' responses to queer studies and offers a welcome corrective to the assumption of a universal "liberal bias" in higher education. It has only been in recent years that LGBT studies has received any kind of acceptance in higher education. Scholars like Mossman shunned the intrusion of queer theory and sexual-identity politics into academic discourse but thought nothing of bringing sexual gossip to discredit an intellectual whom they disagreed with. More to the point, that sexuality is often seen as the source of the tragedy. In his essay "Atlantis Rose" on the poet Hart Crane, Delany unravels this kind of rhetoric in the previous literary scholarship on the poet, particularly from "New Critics," who insisted on ignoring artistic biography as a part of their critical analysis. These critics often brought up salacious sexual gossip about Crane but refused to see the homosexual coding that was a direct part of his work.[75] At one point in *The Mad Man*, John remembers an episode with a homophobic Puerto Rican man in Riverside Park who had threatened to beat him up with a nail-adorned piece of wood when John propositioned him for sex. He connects that violence to Irving Mossman's homophobic response toward Hasler's sexual practices. Mossman was oblivious to Hasler's sexual orientation when he knew him and admitted to being disgusted enough by the things he found in Hasler's writing that he considered giving up the project. And yet he still considered writing about Hasler as an opportunity to advance his own career. As John puts it, "Faggots, I thought. Good people if you need something from them. Otherwise, bust 'em in the side with a fucking board."[76] Delany makes Mossman into a criticism of cynical academic careerism, and like Ishmael Reed in *Japanese by Spring* he includes in his novel a depiction of the exploitative relationship of academia to marginal intellectuals. In this case, Mossman is willing to appropriate Hasler's work as long as it fits into his narrative of academic respectability but backs off when he thinks it is too lurid for proper academic appropriation.

The centerpiece of the novel is a nearly seventy-page letter that John Marr writes to a graduate student classmate named Sallie. Coincidentally, Sallie has become involved in a relationship with the much older Irving Mossman. Sallie hears the stories about a gay cancer circulating through gay communities in San Francisco and New York and writes to John out of concern for his health. Her questions trigger a fit of writing for John that lasts over the course of three months in the fall where he cranks out the long letter explaining to her in vivid detail the sexual underground that he has experienced in New York. In the letter he explains to her how he has made peace with his own fears about the epidemic.

The last two sections of the novel follow John's relationship with a big tall bear of a man named Leaky Sowps. John first sees Leaky rummaging through a garbage can on Broadway and later introduces himself to Leaky and strikes up a conversation. It is only later that he realizes his friend Crazy Joey set the whole thing up because he thought John and Leaky had similar sexual interests and might get along. John and Leaky indeed hit it off famously, and their love story unfolds in the last two chapters of the novel.

The apex of the novel comes in the form of a urine-soaked, shit-covered orgy in John Marr's apartment set up by Leaky and Crazy Joey, who invite several of their homeless friends from the park, including a character named Michael Kerns, a tall, prison-muscled, light-skinned black man who goes by the name Mad Man Mike. John figures out Mad Man Mike is actually the same Michael Kerns whom Timothy Hasler had once dated, and he hilariously tries to "interview" Kerns about what he knows about Hasler but keeps being diverted by the sexual activity going on around him. The whole episode leaves John Marr's apartment a mess, much like the mess that John discovers had happened in Hasler's apartment in the same building years ago, "transforming the cozy clutter of the student and philosopher's retreat into an apocalypse of piss and shit."[77]

The orgy is animated by an inventive game of "buying" and "selling" sex that is all orchestrated by Mad Man Mike. When one character who "owns" another wants to turn his partner out, he does so in exchange for a penny, and never more than that. Mike is adamant about the fact that no one can ever turn out someone else for more than a penny. The system obviously represents an alternative mode of currency. And the novel's tragic ending comes not from all this perversity but when Crazy Joey introduces this penny-exchange system into a system of capitalist accumulation when they go out to the very same hustling bar in Hell's Kitchen where Hasler was murdered. Joey's murder becomes an allegory for what happens to the person who tries to introduce a system of free exchange into a system where people are mortally invested in selling the same commodity at a profit.

So far I have tried to convey a sense of the novel's narrative and some of the ideas that can be gleaned from it. What feels more difficult to describe, even seems out of place in this sober, rational form of academic writing, is the *experience* of reading *The Mad Man*. For Reed Woodhouse, there was the shock of recognition that Delany was writing about the weekly parties hosted by the Golden Shower Association at the Mineshaft, an actual club in Manhattan.

> When I first read this passage, my heart lurched. Was he really going to talk about that? How much? With what degree of irony? (The answers were: Yes; A lot; and None.) Mine was a self-protective question as well as a thrilled one. I, after all, had gone to GSA Nights at the Mineshaft. I have no idea whether Marr's experience is also Delany's, but does it matter? One can only assume that anyone who has written in such loving detail about the Mineshaft has been there. Furthermore, for most readers (even gay readers), even to imagine what Delany has lusciously described is to damn yourself as a pervert.[78]

Another critic who explores this lurid aspect of *The Mad Man* is Steven Shaviro, who wrote about the novel in an extensive blog essay. In particular Shaviro points to Delany's unique approach to the pornographic, one that bypasses the usual artistic strategies of "transgression." According to Shaviro, Delany "insists on the aim of physically arousing the reader ... the philosophical themes of the novel are energized and given form by the pornographic depictions, rather than standing in opposition to them."[79] The intellectual content of *The Mad Man* is what makes it possible to "redeem" the novel for the usual academic audiences, as I am doing in a monograph such as this, but as Woodhouse points out with his anecdote about the real-life experiences at the Mineshaft, the novel's subversive quality is that it seems to work on multiple rhetorical levels simultaneously, as pornography, fantasy, philosophy, HIV/AIDS activism, memoir, and any reader who encounters the novel must be prepared to encounter it on all these levels.

While John Marr may not seem especially fraught about his relationship to blackness in the ways that I have described regarding other protagonists in academic fiction, the novel does gesture to the politics of black intellectuals—in conversations with his friend Pheldon, a West Indian photo librarian and fellow "snow queen" who shares his feelings about interracial desire; with the snippets of information that he gives about his background in a middle-class black family on Staten Island; with his relationships to his academic colleagues, some of whom seem baffled by John Marr's identity as a black gay graduate student in philosophy; in conversations with his homeless white lover, Leaky, as their relationship develops and they learn to negotiate their desires for racially charged sexual fantasies.

Desire for race and class difference is specifically inscribed throughout the novel. And the book does much of its subversive work at the level of desire. Instead of some condescending bleeding-heart story about the sad plight of the homeless, Delany fetishizes and objectifies the poor and dispossessed, even daring to consider that the habits of the poor may be more humane and just than those of the bourgeoisie, including those nice, respectable academics with their rhetoric of liberal "tolerance."

In his book *Extravagant Abjection: Blackness, Power, and Sexuality in the African American Literary Imagination* (2010), literary critic Darieck Scott takes up Delany's provocation to explore the connections between transatlantic slavery, white supremacy, and black sexuality. Scott explores particularly the idea of black subjugation to white authority, a topic that comes up in *The Mad Man* through John Marr's sexual practices. Some of the sexual partners that he has in the novel are white men, and they and Marr both enjoy using racial epithets as part of their sexual play, although the sexual play in the novel is not entirely about black submission and white domination. There are various characters, black, white, Hispanic, Asian, and other, who express interracial desire, some preferring to "bottom," others preferring to "top."

Delany's revision of the academic novel as a pornographic genre encourages a reading of all black academic novels through lenses of gender and sexuality. His emphasis on visibility and embodiment in *The Mad Man* helps to illuminate why color is such an important part of the black academic novel. Delany often discusses his own skin tone, his family's mixed-race background, and how he has often been interpellated as white, Puerto Rican, or other racial identities throughout his life, though he steadfastly identifies as black, as did most of his politically conscious family. Creative critical readings of *The Mad Man*, such as the one that Darieck Scott provides in *Extravagant Abjection*, open up queer readings of chattel enslavement and offer us the opportunity for a deeper exploration of the relationship between sexuality and race, between sexual difference and black-identity formation. As Scott writes,

> Thus, if Delany's project in *The Mad Man* is anything, it is a flouting of liberal or conservative imperatives to ignore or downplay racialized roles and the part those roles play in both the suffering that results from domination and—much more predominantly, since *The Mad Man*'s world is pornotopia—in the forms of pleasure and power that can be derived from that domination as well, and to do so in such a way that the very meaning of suffering, pleasure, and power takes on very different valences than are encompassed in the understanding of our common vernacular.[80]

I think it is useful to examine these discomforting correlations between the control and domination of sadomasochistic sexual play and the very real oppression and subjugation under chattel enslavement and in its aftermath. While I am mindful of Audre Lorde's criticism of lesbian sadomasochism in "Sadomasochism: Not About Condemnation" and her warning against the "institutionalized celebration of dominant/subordinate relationships," Delany's historically informed aesthetic representations of sadomasochistic sexual practices point us toward all the underarticulated power dynamics already present in mundane social relations, in those areas of social interaction not specifically marked as sexual.[81] Delany's work reminds us that this play of power in "consensual" sadomasochistic practices may not necessarily be entirely continuous with state power but is never entirely dislinked from sociohistorical context either.

Earlier in the novel John Marr comes to a realization that he can no longer work with Irving Mossman and explains why Mossman's hedging over Hasler's work is precisely what makes him the wrong type of scholar to pursue it:

> Irving, you're doing this all wrong—and you've been doing it wrong for years. With someone like Timothy Hasler, you can't gamble on his fame! You read his work; you study it; you even teach it—and *you* decide if within the systems of the world, that work is of major importance or not. If you decide it is, you write your book, and your essays, and your articles, and your lectures—in which you *say* that! You write them because *you* believe in the work. You don't spend all your time looking around you, counting how many other people are saying this stuff is great—or not saying it. You don't keep counting the footnotes in which the name appears, wondering if you should abandon the project because there aren't as many this year as last ... The gamble, Irving Mossman, is not on Timothy Hasler. The gamble is on *you*.[82]

I have to confess that this passage has deep personal meaning for me. I have always found these words electrifying. When I first read this passage I strongly identified with Marr and realized that I'd encountered a few Irving Mossmans in my own academic life. I even read this as a kind of metafictional commentary on Delany's own critical reception, and I admit it was one of my inspirations for the statement of purpose I eventually submitted to my English Ph.D. program proposing to study Delany's work. I took it up as a personal challenge to do the work that I really believed in and not to spend all my time chasing trends and looking to conform to whatever everyone else is doing academically. To some degree Marr's commentary continues to inform my approach to my scholarly and writerly life, and it speaks to why I have written *The Blackademic Life* the way that I have, knowing that I probably should have added more theoretical name-dropping and jargon to appeal to the right academic crowds. Surely there are selfish professional reasons for writing an academic monograph (promotion, tenure, and future employability). But I decided that the long nights and many years of toil involved could be worth it to me only if I truly believed in the work, and I have often been annoyed with the way academics are so mistrustful of joy and enthusiasm in their smug performances of detached and objective theoretical interpretation. Delany's writing in particular has been personally important to me, far beyond a field of research interests for professional advancement. What drew me to his work was not just about leveraging my career but about how to live an ethical life, about the sense of possibility that I could embrace my own weird, black, queer self, and that I could learn to appreciate the differences in others. *The Mad Man* and Delany's other writings gave me strategies for how I might challenge the vicious, exclusionary thinking of racial capitalism and respectability politics. And in those terms *The Blackademic Life* is not only about my own prospects for tenure and promotion but also about finding my place in a genealogy of black intellectuals whose sacrifices and efforts made my own blackademic life possible.

Delany often writes about white supremacy as a discursive formation, that white supremacy is not merely random samples of individual attitudes but also involves sedimentations of language and the relationship of that established language to institutions, knowledge, and power. In a 2003 written interview he describes the 1994 lynching of James Byrd Jr., a black man in Jasper, Texas, who was offered a ride home by three white men who assaulted him, chained him to the back of their pickup truck, and dragged him to death until his body was torn into pieces. Observing the comments by the men and their families during their murder trial, Delany observes that the family members simply could not conceive that what the white men had done warranted capital punishment. In the discourse in which they lived, killing a black man in that fashion might be a mischievous thing to do, they had done "wrong," but the act was certainly not the equivalent of having taken a white person's life.

Delany then compares this discursive field of Byrd's murderers and their families with the one occupied by students at Columbia Law School in the 1920s who took classes with Paul Robeson and stomped their feet whenever he spoke to drown him out. To Delany, both groups of white people were operating in the same discourse, which says black people are not human, are not deserving of the same chances at life as white people, that in the scheme of things, black people do not matter. Delany concludes by saying, "If we—you and I—are to make any progress with sedimenting new discourses that promote new understandings of the relationship between groups of people, we will have an easier time if we approach it with a sense of the history and development of such discourse."[83]

The racialized and sexualized hostility directed toward Keeanga-Yamahtta Taylor, and toward any other black intellectuals who dare to speak up for black people, sits within the same discursive field that Delany describes for Byrd and Robeson. Such discourses have been dislodged just enough to allow black intellectuals to become professors, even at majority-white institutions, and even for one of them to become president of the United States, but the 2016 election should make perfectly clear that white supremacy continues to resonate with large swaths of the American public. Furthermore, one has to wonder whether the proliferation of lily-white representations of the academy actively contribute to perceptions of who belongs on campus, in front of classrooms, or on the dais as administrators.

Postscript

> I am bored with the topic of Atlantic slavery. I have come to be bored because so many boring people have talked about it. So many artists and writers and thinkers, mediocre and genius, have used it because it's a big, easy target. They appropriate it, adding no new insight or profound understanding, instead degrading it with their nothingness. They take the stink of the slave hold and make it a pungent cliché, take the blood-soaked chains of bondage and pervert them into Afrocentric bling. Parroting a vague "400 Year" slogan that underestimates for the sake of religious formality. What's even more infuriating is that, despite this stupidity, this repetitious sophistry, the topic of chattel slavery is still unavoidable for its American descendants. It is the great story, the big one, the connector that gives the reason for our nation's prosperity and for our very existence within it.
> —Mat Johnson, *Pym*[84]

Christopher Jaynes, the black English professor in Mat Johnson's academic satire *Pym*, delivers these lines as part of his irreverent take on the inescapable history of slavery and its hold on the black intellectual in America. Like Helga Crane in *Quicksand*, Jaynes is another black academic-novel character who is vexed by the subject of race. He is tired of the race question and suspicious of the way slavery functions in a twenty-first-century literary marketplace as a subject of study by black writers. And yet he cannot deny its importance in an understanding of what this American project is all about. Jaynes believes that cracking the racial code requires more than being his department's designated expert on blackness, but rather requires a serious study of whiteness in American literature and culture, an idea obviously inspired by Toni Morrison's *Playing in the Dark*, which is an important subtext to *Pym*. Jaynes wants to look directly into the heart of whiteness itself, and his dead white male of choice is Edgar Allan Poe. He's obsessed with Poe's most idiosyncratic work, his only full-length novel, *The Narrative of Arthur Gordon Pym of Nantucket*. With *Pym* Mat Johnson provides some sharp analysis on the black academic and his relationship to literary studies in the academy. And like other black academic novelists, Johnson utilizes the novel's inherent interdisciplinary malleability, melding his academic satire with bits of literary criticism. The story of slavery is unavoidable, it is "the big one" that explains so much of American history (and modern capitalism) and continues to define its identity. But in Jaynes's ironic commentary is also a realization that this horrific story can, and must, be used as a source of creativity, not in the way of being a justification for its barbarity and dehumanization but as a sign of human resilience against the forces of evil that imagined and created it. Johnson's novel is evidence of this and participates in that recuperation, taking the black academic experience and its postslavery subjectivity and spinning them into an imaginative story about American identity in a global reality.

Pym seems to be on its way to joining the canon of well-known academic novels. Released in 2011, it is now in a second printing with a new edition that includes an appendix with the full text of Poe's novel. Patricia A. Matthew incorporates *Pym* into the introduction of *Written/Unwritten: Diversity and the Hidden Truths of Tenure*, a collection of essays about minority faculty and tenure. Matthew's book is filled with some harrowing, and frankly aggravating, stories about tenure denials and microaggressions in the academy.[85] Indeed *Pym* starts with Jaynes being denied tenure, a staple plot point in the academic novel. In this case Matthew points to the main character's arguments on the futility of diversity committees. As Johnson writes, "The Diversity Committee has one primary purpose: so that the school can say it has a diversity committee . . . People find that very relaxing. It's sort of like, if you had a fire, and instead of putting it out, you formed a fire committee."[86] One of the things that Johnson does so well with *Pym* is to criticize this diversity rhetoric of the liberal academy, showing how Jaynes's replacement, the militant hip-hop scholar Mosaic Johnson, who believes he is bringing the fight to the white university, can't see how he is being used as a token and symbol to help his school avoid dealing with the underlying structural inequalities that make Jaynes and Johnson such rare birds in their white college town in the first place. Sara Ahmed addresses the academy's neoliberal appropriation of diversity in her book *On Being Included: Racism and Diversity in Institutional Life*. She writes, "People of color in white organizations are treated as guests, welcomed on the condition they return that hospitality by integrating into a common organizational culture, or by 'being' diverse, and allowing institutions to celebrate their diversity."[87] The logic of "inclusion" reveals underlying assumptions about who is centered and who belongs in these institutions. After having shown their benevolence by including such persons, the included is then required to display bottomless gratitude for being included. So that when the included begins to speak about the ongoing structures of inequality that still exist in these institutions, into which they have been "let in," their criticisms are interpreted as ungratefulness, as "biting the hand that feeds you." (Right now, this very language of ingratitude is being weaponized against NFL football players and other black athletes in amateur and professional sports who have been protesting injustice by kneeling during the national anthem.)

I share Chris Jaynes's concern about the primacy of slavery and white supremacy in my interpretation of black intellectuals. There's the risk that calling attention to white supremacy as a discursive formation and writing about the black academic novel as counternarrative serve to center whiteness and white supremacy and construct black literature as reactionary. Aida Levy-Hussen's book *How to Read African American Literature* also borrows from *Pym*, citing the same passage as that heading this section, to frame her study of post–civil rights African American fiction and the legacies of slavery.[88] Levy-Hussen also refers to the interiority of black texts, drawing on Elizabeth Alexander's *The Black Interior* and using psychoanalysis to probe into the trauma, mourning, masochism, and depression present in black literature. Ultimately I agree with Levy-Hussen's assessment that "the ability to read individuality and human complexity within blackness seems to me an irreducibly important pre-condition for politics—and a pre-condition that literature is uniquely equipped to address."[89]

In an article titled "Teach the University" published in the journal *Pedagogy*, Jeffrey J. Williams articulates the pedagogical value of academic fiction and discusses academic fiction in the context of teaching about the history and politics of the university.[90] Williams's idea for the article was inspired by Gerald Graff's popular book *Beyond the Culture Wars: How Teaching the Conflicts Can Revitalize American Education*.[91] Graff's concept of "teaching the conflicts" is often cited as a method of drawing on political conversations about higher education (around issues such as educational policy, funding, and curricula) and incorporating these critical debates into the classroom itself, using them as opportunities to help students learn about the politics of education even as they are immersed in the educational process.

In particular, Williams provides some creative ideas for using academic fiction as a way to "teach the university." Williams makes an important point that the status of the university can no longer be considered an issue that affects only a few exclusive elites. Rather, the demographic changes in the university over the course of the twentieth and twenty-first centuries have brought more people into contact with the institution in some form. As Williams writes, "If over 70 percent of American citizens attend college at some point, it is not a sideline or an intra-academic concern but a central public issue. Next to health care, it is the most significant public institution of our day that speaks to the distribution of resources and the welfare of citizens."[92] What seems lost in the debates these days is a sense of higher education as a public good and not just a private benefit. This is why in the present American political language arguments about "free college" and student loan debt relief get reduced to the pejorative of "handouts." Such language reveals the extent to which an idea of higher education as a social good has deteriorated and how successful the culture-wars rhetoric targeting "academic elites" has been. And this is frankly why I also resist the authenticity narrative that the academic novel is an automatically elitist and inauthentic literary form, because such attitudes reveal how widely an anti-intellectual narrative of higher education prevails. It's that idea that pervades the culture-wars slur that campuses are "safe spaces" and students need to toughen up and learn how things go in the "real world." The campus is a real world, and the real world is full of people who are as college educated as their peers whom they denounce as hopelessly elitist. Having grown up around fundamentalist religiosity, I recognize such claims of innocence as analogous to the claims of the devout believers who think that one is more innocent and pure if one is untouched by formal education and gets the spirit directly from God.

This is why, as Williams states, it is important to "prompt students to reflect on how [universities] are formed, where modern institutions come from," and that "it is especially important that they are briefed on the details of the case, since they will be the future judges of it, as voters in and constituents of the states that support or lease out their universities."[93] There's no guarantee that such an education will lead to the political outcomes I would like to see, but citizens should be making decisions about these institutions based on substantive information and not simplistic caricatures. In effect, Williams argues that the history and politics of the university should be a part of our common political literacy. While universities are usually separate physical spaces, their boundaries are often porous, with students, professors, staff, and community members flowing across them in both directions. In many cases the scholarship produced in the academy can have a public impact, and the quality of knowledge that universities produce is improved by public engagement.

I agree with Williams and have implemented some of his ideas in my classrooms. I talk to students about the labor of academia, explaining to them, as a practical matter, why most of their professors are on campus only a few hours a day and do not have an office and may need to rush away after class to go teach at another campus, maybe even one in a different borough or state. And generally I'm onboard with the ideas of "critical university studies." But I also think that any effort to "teach the university" must have the experiences of black students, faculty, and administrators as a central component of that narrative. We could all take notes from the exemplary work that Tressie McMillan Cottom has been doing with her work on for-profit colleges, including her book *Lower Ed: The Troubling Rise of For-Profit Colleges in the New Economy*, and all her public social media engagement on higher education.[94] *Lower Ed* is a work of advocacy scholarship that centers black women, who are the most likely to encounter for-profit colleges, but it is also a study that helps us all to understand why this expensive and risky sector of higher education has endeared itself so well to black people and built inroads into black communities, usurping the role that community colleges and HBCUs once played as public-serving institutions, where many working-class and first-generation college students first encountered higher education. Indeed, higher education's efforts toward growth and expansion necessarily mean that it must engage with the needs of students of color, many of whom are from immigrant populations, and that whatever future higher education has in America, it will be a future that is demographically dynamic.

I understand that my own study of higher education has been carried out while a very different and quite powerful narrative of higher education has also flourished. This narrative is typified not by *Dear White People* or even *Admission* or *Liberal Arts* but by academic films such as the 2014 Christian drama *God's Not Dead*, about an atheist philosophy professor daring his Christian student to prove the existence of God, or by films like *Blue Like Jazz*, a story of a Christian student struggling to hold on to his faith at the liberal Reed College. This narrative of higher education is one in which liberal elite professors, all of whom are highly paid and tenured untouchables, bully their students into accepting gay marriage, transgenderism, atheism, miscegenation, communism, evolution, and global warming. The thinking of many Americans about higher education is aligned with that of former National Rifle Association (NRA) president Wayne LaPierre, who at an April 2017 NRA leadership forum stated, "It's up to us to speak up against the three most dangerous voices in America: academic elites, political elites and media elites. These are America's greatest domestic threats."[95] That these words were spoken by the leader of one of the nation's most powerful and politically influential organizations, an organization that encourages the unfettered ownership and use of powerful, deadly weapons, and that he can get away with calling academics "domestic threats" while also encouraging states to make it legal for students to carry guns on campus at all times, is just one of the many ways that America leans perilously toward dystopian horror in these trying times.

The contemporary conservative "free speech" movement has targeted college campuses with inflammatory speakers, even dredging up a tired old race scientist like Charles Murray to poke the hornet's nest at schools like Middlebury College in Vermont, where there was a recent dustup over his invited lecture. Such spectacles are driven by a nostalgia for unchallenged white-supremacist thought and fueled by accusations of "identity politics," implicitly suggesting, as whiteness often does, that white male supremacy is not ideological at all but simply natural and normal. And for a nervous media industry, struggling to swim in the digital stream and reliant on attention data for revenue, these controversies are always a reliable hot-button topic to bring in some of those sweet, sweet clicks and comments to their sites.

One of the most recent volumes on academic fiction is *Anti-Intellectual Representations of College and Universities*, edited by Barbara F. Tobolowsky and Pauline J. Reynolds, which organizes essays on academic fiction around the theme of anti-intellectualism. Tobolowsky and Reynolds have perceptively noted the way that many popular depictions of professors and colleges are not only satirical but specifically targeted at taking the elites down a peg by portraying them as incompetent buffoons.[96]

The very presence of African Americans on campus and the efforts toward a more inclusive university curriculum are part of this right-wing narrative and its depiction of a nefarious university bent on subverting American exceptionalism from within by focusing on identity politics, gender theory, critical race theory, or whatever disciplinary bugaboo they've decided to target that week on Breitbart. But it's a narrative that black scholars have lived with for generations, and black academic novels are a documentary record of the university's history and the public's often contemptuous attitude toward demographic and disciplinary changes in higher education. Black intellectuals have many reasons to distrust the academy and the knowledge it produces, but the persistence of black scholars in working to transform the university is also an object lesson in how to critically view the university without lapsing into a destructive and counterproductive anti-intellectualism. Reading them and engaging with them can be a source of vitality for the next generation as they learn to navigate the treacherous terrain of higher education in the twenty-first century.

Conclusion

Blackademics On Screen

> Our generation—we subscribe to the old liberal doctrine of the inviolate self. It's the great tradition of realistic fiction, it's what novels are all about. The private life in the foreground, history a distant rumble of gunfire, somewhere offstage. In Jane Austen not even a rumble. Well, the novel is dying, and us with it. No wonder I can never get anything out of my novel-writing class at Euphoric State. It's an unnatural medium for their experience. Those kids (*gestures at screen*) are living a film, not a novel.
>
> —David Lodge, *Changing Places*

To conclude, I'd like to briefly turn toward cinematic and televisual representations of blackademics as an extension of the conversations from the previous pages. I'm not sure that I agree with Morris Zapp in *Changing Places* that the screen is a more "natural" medium for the kids these days, but the screen is certainly a more familiar and ubiquitous storytelling platform for our twenty-first-century students, who have grown up as "screenagers." Given the scale and influence of these televisual culture industries—now a mixture of television, film, and digital platforms—the screen becomes another important venue for blackademic representation and one in which more money, power, and influence are at stake than in the literary world.

Critics have often sparred over Hollywood's positive and negative portrayals of blackness, black culture, and black families. W. E. B. Du Bois, in his 1926 editorial in *The Crisis*, was already thinking about mass media and its role in disseminating representations of blackness. From the beginning I have been aware that this topic lends itself to a certain language of respectability. I hope I have done my due diligence in explaining how the novels taken up in this book actually provide complex images of black scholars, diverse images of black people, and engage with various strains of black political thought. The novels I have discussed in this book are not just one-dimensional caricatures of black educational striving and achievement. But I also want to take a cue from Racquel Gates in *Double Negative: The Black Image and Popular Culture*.[1] Gates argues that despite all the nuances involved, the dichotomy of "positive" and "negative" is actually useful for thinking about black cultural production, especially when it comes to television and film. I think it's safe to say that many depictions of black higher education fall into the category of the positive because they depict the lives of black intellectuals and scholars, who are often considered to be underrepresented among the available portrayals of black people in popular culture, and generally the existence of intellectuals and scholars among a people who have been denied literacy and education is considered a good thing. So I think it's worth unpacking this idea of the positive and how positive representations may provide cover for questionable ideas about black people.

A little more than twenty years after the death of W. E. B. Du Bois (August 27, 1963) and the historic March on Washington for Jobs and Freedom (August 28, 1963), television saw the arrival of *The Cosby Show* in 1984. The actor, comedian, and director William H. Cosby Jr.'s highly successful landmark sitcom was about the Huxtable family, a wealthy black heterosexual nuclear family in Brooklyn, led by a father who is a doctor and a mother who is a lawyer. Heathcliff Huxtable (played by Bill Cosby), and his wife, Clair Huxtable (Phylicia Rashad), are graduates of the fictional HBCU Hillman College. Their daughter Denise (Lisa Bonet) follows in their footsteps to Hillman, and it was the daughter's story line through which *The Cosby Show* spun off into the college-themed show *A Different World*, set at Hillman College.

These shows were celebrated as positive representations of successful, well-adjusted, law-abiding black people. They were celebrated as groundbreaking and refreshing interventions in a medium where black people were depicted mostly as social problems or reduced to buffoonish caricatures, and where depictions of educated and professionally successful black people were unfairly excluded from popular culture.

The Cosby Show and *A Different World* were both influential for their depictions of black college life in particular. Heathcliff Huxtable's college T-shirts and sweaters on *The Cosby Show* were a phenomenon unto themselves. *The Cosby Show* featured scenes shot on HBCU campuses; *A Different World*'s Hillman College, set in Virginia, was a composite HBCU that featured exterior shots from various real-life HBCU campuses and pulled story lines from the HBCU experiences of its writers and cast members, and to this day references to characters and plotlines from both shows are still legible in contemporary pop culture.

The full story of Bill Cosby is one that now complicates this narrative, to put it mildly. An evaluation of Bill Cosby's problematic legacy actually raises some of the most pressing issues in this study of black academic fiction, including matters of class, gender, sexuality, and sexual violence. It forces us to think about how black people see one another and how we are seen by others and raises questions about audience and intention when it comes to representations of black people. But even before the news about Bill Cosby's crimes became public, *The Cosby Show* was already a bit of a problem. The show won over white audiences by presenting the Huxtables as exemplary black people who had triumphed over racism and rejected victimhood. Kiese Laymon provides the most incisive description of Cosby's career when he writes that "Bill Cosby seemed obsessed with how white folks watched black folks watch ourselves watch him."[2] Laymon points to the centrality of the white gaze in Cosby's creative work and in his political rhetoric (despite his problack optics) and how *The Cosby Show* leaned toward idealized narratives of pride and prosperity while downplaying any evidence of injustice, damage, or resentment. It's important that we are vigilant about how "positive" texts like *The Cosby Show* might be propped up by antiblackness. What was subtext on *The Cosby Show* became text when Cosby decided to launch a public crusade against the style, speech, and habits of the black poor.

The downfall of Cosby as an icon really began with the "Pound Cake" speech, so called because of his riff on the police shooting of a young man who was allegedly stealing a piece of pound cake from a corner store, an image that Cosby used to symbolize a whole host of urban pathologies, including fatherlessness, drug use, loose sexual morals, and antipathy to education. We've all been forced to read that speech from a different perspective now that more than fifty women have accused Cosby of drugging and sexually assaulting them and he has been convicted and sentenced to three to ten years in a Pennsylvania state prison on three counts of aggravated and indecent sexual assault. (Which also, by the way, doesn't change the historic inequalities of an imperfect and racist American justice system.)

In the wake of his speech Cosby organized and led a series of "callout" meetings in black communities around the country to address social problems such as teenage pregnancy, drugs, and criminality, as well as the clothing styles, speech, and child-rearing practices of black people. These meetings coincided with the publication of his popular book *Come On, People: On the Path from Victims to Victors*. Ta-Nehisi Coates followed Cosby to several of these meetings and wrote a long essay about them in 2008 in which he analyzed Cosby's cultural politics, placing them in the context of a tradition of black folk conservatism that existed long before this particular flash point. Coates wrote as follows:

> Indeed, a century ago, the black brain trust was pushing the same rhetoric that Cosby is pushing today. It was concerned that slavery had essentially destroyed the black family and was obsessed with seemingly the same issues—crime, wanton sexuality, and general moral turpitude—that Cosby claims are recent developments. "The early effort of middle-class blacks to respond to segregation was, aside from a political agenda, focused on a social-reform agenda," says Khalil G.

Muhammad, a professor of American history at Indiana University. "The National Association of Colored Women, Du Bois in *The Philadelphia Negro*, all shared a sense of anxiety that African Americans were not presenting their best selves to the world. There was the sense that they were committing crimes and needed to keep their sexuality in check." Adds William Jelani Cobb, a professor of American history at Spelman College: "The same kind of people who were advocating for social reform were denigrating people because they didn't play piano. They often saw themselves as reluctant caretakers of the less enlightened."[3]

Buttressed by commentary from black thinkers like Cobb (now a professor in the Columbia Journalism School) and Muhammad (now a professor in the Harvard Kennedy School and former director of the Schomburg Center for Research in Black Culture), Coates explored how Cosby's tirades spoke to the complicated relationship between black spokespersons and the black public whom they claim to represent. Like Coates, these critics have noted that there is a genuine black audience for the politics of respectability (there are still a couple of copies of *Come On, People* on the bookshelves in my parents' home in Mississippi). But they also insist that it's a strategy that reinforces second-class citizenship for black people, and it is one based on idealized images of virtuous white people whose power emanates from their moral behavior. After all, no one questions the civil rights of all white citizens when, say, white politicians are caught cruising for sex in public bathrooms (Larry Craig), or patronizing prostitutes (Elliot Spitzer), or hitting on teenage congressional pages (Mark Foley), or sending lewd pictures of himself over the internet to teenage girls (Anthony Weiner), or repeatedly committing adultery while legislating "family values" (Newt Gingrich), or bragging about sexual assault (Donald Trump), or committing adultery by having unprotected sex with a porn star in the months after the birth of his son (Donald Trump), or paying off said porn star with campaign funds leading to his personal lawyer being charged with breaking campaign finance laws (Donald Trump).

For the loudest Cosby defenders, the goalposts have moved and moved until they are all the way off the field. No longer are we talking about some outlandishly false allegations. We're talking about someone who went around to churches and communities across the country lecturing black people on promiscuity and irresponsibility while knowing that he had drugged and raped women. This is a moment of reckoning with the consequences of Cosby's respectability politics. And it is a referendum on the way that heteronormative respectability politics have too often marginalized black women, the black poor, and black LGBTQ persons and made them scapegoats for systemic inequalities. Whenever I think of Cosby, I come back to Marlon Ross's trenchant insights about the paradox of Jim Crow masculinity. "The more black men attempt to man the race through a fit masculinity patterned on dominant gender norms, the more they risk emulating the white ruling men whose Jim Crow racial/sexual codes unman them."[4] By attempting to man the race through a rigid heteropatriarchy Cosby emulated the worst aspects of white supremacy's norms, which have included the routine, uncontested rape and abuse of black women, men, boys, and girls, and he emulated the sanctimonious morality lectures that white men have dished out to us to hide their own unethical and immoral behavior.

In *Double Negative*, Racquel Gates calls for more sophisticated readings of positive and negative portrayals of blackness, readings that take into account the economics and labor of the entertainment industry as well as the context of the portrayals. As she states, "When we refer to media as either positive or negative, we imply that the images push perceptions of blackness in one of two directions: either forward or backward. But is that their only function? What about resistant reading? And irony? And pleasure? Where do these factor into the equation?"[5] To go back to Brittney Cooper's idea of "embodied discourses," criticism related to "negative" portrayals of blackness are often connected to shame about black bodies, black sexuality, black expression, and about the inadequacies of black people to fully conform to white aesthetic ideals.

Another reason to contextualize positive portrayals is that I do not want to rule out the value of "strategic negativity."[6] Black performers have been known to embrace stereotypes in order to wield them as weapons, subvert them through satire and irony, and yes, to profit from them. The subversion is (partly) what Samuel R. Delany accomplishes with "nigger," "cocksucker," and other slurs in his academic novel *The Mad Man* (and in others of his works). This is what rappers have done by dubbing themselves niggas and bad bitches. It's what black comedians have done by spinning negative stereotypes into comic routines that win them audiences and advance their performing careers. It's what Spike Lee did in *School Daze*, airing out dirty-laundry topics of colorism, misogyny, and classism in a black college film that otherwise shows pride in HBCUs. I can't say with confidence that this strategy is always desirable or empowering. But it can be read as an act of agency. People from marginalized groups have often strategically appropriated the words and images that have been used to hurt them. The etymology of commonly used terms like "black" and "queer" prove that repurposing these terms for empowerment is possible, even if not everyone from such groups always agrees on the strategy. The results may not be noble, but they are examples of oppressed people doing what they can with what they are given, by taking the negative word or image and redirecting it outward as a sign of defiance and empowerment. I admit this is partly my own strategy by utilizing the term the "overeducated Negro" as the title of my blog and talking about discourses of overeducation in this book.

Look, if it were as simple as just saying, "Hey, negative stereotypes are bad and they can only hurt people in the end," then it would be easy for me to say, "You know, let's stop using these negative images and focus on the positive, empowering ones instead." But what Racquel Gates shows in *Double Negative* and what the academic novels together show in their narratives is an ongoing dialogue among black artists and thinkers about representations and how best to use them. And sometimes negative representations actually have their good uses, and sometimes positive representations mask deeply problematic ideas about black people.

The Cosby Show is an example of what I'd call a false positive, where so-called positive images of blackness can actually be riddled with antiblackness and do harm to black people who are unassimilable to white ideals (which, let's face it, is most of us).[7] This is especially true if we center black women in our thinking about black representations. Gates analyzes "trash TV" as a negative genre that actually allows space for black women's expression in ways that more positive and respectable shows might not be able to do. She writes,

> What I want to offer here is the idea that shows like *Love & Hip Hop*, *Basketball Wives*, and other unapologetically trashy reality TV programs provide a safe space for emotional and psychological catharsis and the exploration of complicated, messy, or "negative" feelings. These feelings are particularly complicated because of black women's intersectionality and, thus, the ways that they experience everyday life from specifically gendered, racialized (but also classed and sexualized) points of view.[8]

Here is where shows like *A Different World* and *Dear White People* have made interventions by centering black women. Although *A Different World* was produced by Bill Cosby, its chief creative force and director was Debbie Allen; it had episodes written by women and featured a cast populated with actresses including Jasmine Guy, Dawnn Lewis, and Cree Summer. Its story lines included topics such as date rape, sexual harassment, skin color, body image, depictions of black women in popular culture, gender roles, class status, and other topics pertinent to black women. Likewise, both the film version and the Netflix TV show of *Dear White People* are centered around a black woman student activist, feature black women characters prominently, and pay attention to feminist politics in their story lines. There are many examples from both shows where the concerns of black women are central, where black women's gender, sexuality, and embodiment are represented and embraced. This is not to say that both shows are above reproach, and both have received plenty of criticism (including my 2014 review of the film version of *Dear White People*).[9] But these shows offer us alternative possibilities for representing blackademics beyond Cosby's patriarchal conservatism.

Cosby's conviction is a tragedy on many levels. It is personally painful for someone like myself who grew up with those Thursday nights gathered around the television to watch the antics of the Huxtable family and believed in his mission of positive representation and supporting black higher education. His actions ruined the lives of the women who were abused by him, women who were ashamed to come forward given his stature and the blowback they would face for publicly accusing him. Jewel Allison, one of his victims, wrote in a 2015 article that she "feared it would undermine the entire African American community" if she revealed her story.[10] It has destroyed the reputation of a black celebrity who, despite his political statements, was still respected as a pioneer in entertainment and who was a philanthropist of black higher education, including generous gifts to Spelman College and Morehouse College, my alma mater and the alma mater of his late son, Ennis.

His actions have left an unfortunate stain on the history of black academic representations. His shows really did celebrate the cause of black education like no other. Yet there were many more people involved in them who had nothing to do with his violent acts, and the legacy of their presence on television can't entirely be erased. Despite what has transpired, it seems that there are audiences who are still celebrating the good parts about these blackademic shows. Blogger and journalist Tyler Young hosts a fan account for *A Different World* under the Twitter handle @hillmantoday and in 2015–16 held weekly online chats about episodes in the series. In 2017 sports reporters Jemele Hill and Michael Smith gathered some of the original cast members of *A Different World* to re-create its iconic opening credits for their ESPN show. The novelist Mark Luckie wrote about how his love for *A Different World* encouraged him to attend Florida A&M University and compose his HBCU novel *Do U*.[11] *Dear White People* screenwriter Lena Waithe was also inspired by *A Different World*, once using the Twitter handle @hillmangrad and calling her production company Hillman Grad Productions.

It would be foolhardy to think a few novels, TV shows, and films about black higher education can topple white supremacy, regardless of how nuanced the portrayals are, and I make no such claim. However, by placing works of blackademic fiction together in a field of study, I have sought to lift up an archive that shows a sustained engagement with the inner lives of black scholars, and I have hopefully provided a road map for other critics to find these works and engage with them as narratives of higher education. The blackademic novel is a vital form because it reacts—to slavery, white supremacy, antiblackness, misogyny, homophobia—but also because it refuses the limitations of being a reactionary form. Ralph Ellison hit the nail on the head when he praised J. Saunders Redding's *Stranger and Alone* by saying "at least we're going to have a group of writers who are aware that their task is not that of pleading Negro humanity, but of examining and depicting the forms and rituals of that humanity."[12] These are works that examine the complexities of black intellectuals in all their permutations. To borrow a formulation Samuel Delany uses in *The Mad Man*, blackademic novels are often the novels of "guilty victors," of those who have somehow managed to outlive the antiblack violence of America, who managed to overcome the impediments to education that many black Americans faced historically, who have defied narratives that black people are uneducable. The conscious black intellectual understands that her exceptionality and survival will be weaponized against other black people, no matter how nuanced she makes her statements, that her professional "success" can, and often will, be misused against her and others like her, and that despite all this she must continue to depict and examine black humanity as forcefully and creatively as she knows how.

My own blackademic life has been shaped by these narratives. I didn't become a professor just because I was interested in history and literature. I didn't realize it at the time, but in my undergraduate days I was developing my own romantic images of a blackademic life. These images were available to me because of black intellectuals who dared to tell their stories. These affirming stories of blackademic life were in films (like *School Daze*, which I watched before my freshman year in college) and in books (like *Invisible Man*, which I discovered as a graduate student and which gave me a model for defusing racism with irony) and in the real-life stories of academic life passed down from my professors and others in the profession. For me, many of these stories were about the students, professors, and administrators of historically black colleges and the sacrifices they made for the education of our people. And yes, sometimes those sacrifices meant playing the respectability game and conforming to what white people expected them to be in order to get a foot in the door.

In the spring of 2017 as an assistant professor of English at New York City College of Technology I taught an introduction to fiction course built around Ralph Ellison's *Invisible Man* and Chimamanda Adichie's *Americanah*. On the first day of class I explained my research topic on black academic fiction and why I had chosen these particular novels for a fiction course that could have accommodated many possible texts. (I wanted to have the opportunity to explore *Invisible Man* more closely, and I was fascinated by Adichie's depiction of diasporic blackness, immigration, college life, and black hair in *Americanah*.) A black male student, who I would later come to find was one of the smartest and most well-read in the bunch, raised his hand and asked me a pointed question. "You say you're studying representations of black higher education. Why not just write about black higher education directly?" It seems to me now that this book is a very long-winded, detailed answer to his rather perceptive question. I can only hope I have answered it sufficiently.

NOTES

Introduction

1. "A statement from Keeanga-Yamahtta Taylor," Facebook, May 31, 2017, https://www.facebook.com/haymarketbooks/posts/1494045207312386.
2. Tressie McMillan Cottom, "Using Social Media to Rage Against the Machine: The Chronicle of Higher Education, Naomi Schaefer Riley, and Black Studies," *Academia.edu*, May 2012, accessed October 25, 2017, http://www.academia.edu/4165272/Using_Social_Media_to_Rage_Against_The_Machine.
3. Tressie McMillan Cottom, Twitter, October 22, 2017, https://twitter.com/tressiemcphd/status/922114047826386944.
4. Vincent Harding, "The Vocation of the Black Scholar and the Struggles of the Black Community," in *Education and Black Struggle: Notes from the Colonized World*, ed. Institute of the Black World, 3–29 (Cambridge, Mass.: Harvard Educational Review, 1974).
5. Fast Facts, National Center for Education Statistics, https://nces.ed.gov/fastfacts/.
6. Cynthia Franklin, *Academic Lives: Memoir, Cultural Theory, and the University Today* (Athens: University of Georgia Press, 2010).
7. Margaret Edson, *Wit: A Play* (New York: Farrar, Straus and Giroux, 1999).
8. Thomas Jefferson, *Notes on the State of Virginia* (1785; repr., New York: Penguin Books, 1999), Query IV, 137–55.
9. Craig Steven Wilder, *Ebony and Ivy: Race, Slavery, and the Troubled History of America's Universities* (New York: Bloomsbury Press, 2013).
10. Samuel R. Delany, "Racism and Science Fiction," *New York Review of Science Fiction*, issue 120, August 1998, accessed February 4, 2019, www.nyrsf.com/racism-and-science-fiction-.html.

Chapter 1

1. Frederick Douglass, *Narrative of the Life of Frederick Douglass*, ed. David W. Blight (1845; repr., Boston: Bedford/St. Martin's, 2003), 63–64.
2. Douglass, *Narrative*, 106.
3. "Southern Press on Negro Education," *Literary Digest* 28, no. 12 (February 6, 1904): 168, Google Books, accessed February 4, 2019, https://books.google.com/books?id=yJgXAQAAIAAJ&printsec=frontcover&source=gbs_ge_summary_r&cad=0#v=onepage&q&f=false.
4. William F. Holmes, *The White Chief: James K. Vardaman* (Baton Rouge: Louisiana State University Press, 1970), 215.
5. Wilbur Thirkield, "The Higher Education of the Negro," in *The Negro*

Problem, comp. Julia E. Johnsen (New York: Wilson, 1921), 193, Google Books, accessed March 2, 2017, https://books.google.com/books?id=QroTAAAAYAAJ&pg=PR4#v=onepage&q&f=false.

6. W. E. B. Du Bois, *The Quest of the Silver Fleece: A Novel* (1911; repr., New York: Random House, 2004), 149.

7. James Anderson, *The Education of Blacks in the South, 1860–1935* (Chapel Hill: University of North Carolina Press, 1988), 3.

8. Booker T. Washington, *Up from Slavery: An Autobiography*, ed. William L. Andrews (1901; repr., Oxford: Oxford University Press, 1995), 58.

9. I borrow the phrase "scholar as buffoon" from Wilson J. Moses, *Afrotopia: The Roots of African American Popular History* (Cambridge: Cambridge University Press, 1998), 169–70, in which he discusses how the black intellectual William Ferris was depicted in prior assessments of his life. Moses's chapter on Ferris and the American Negro Academy is a good treatment of how overeducation language gets applied to black intellectuals.

10. William Sanders Scarborough, *The Educated Negro and His Mission*, Occasional Papers, no. 8 (Washington, D.C.: American Negro Academy, 1903; repr., New York: AMS Press, 1970), 3.

11. Carter G. Woodson, *The Mis-Education of the Negro* (1933; repr., Trenton, N.J.: Africa World Press, 1990), xiii.

12. There are many treatments of *The Crisis of the Negro Intellectual*, but the most relevant ones here (besides from Jerry Watts) are Hortense J. Spillers, "*The Crisis of the Negro Intellectual*: A Post-Date," in *Black, White, and in Color: Essays on American Literature and Culture*, 428–70 (Chicago: University of Chicago Press, 2003), and Winston James's critique of Cruse in *Holding Aloft the Banner of Ethiopia: Caribbean Radicalism in Early-Twentieth Century America* (New York: Verso, 1999).

13. Jerry Watts, *Heroism and the Black Intellectual: Ralph Ellison, Politics, and Afro-American Intellectual Life* (Chapel Hill: University of North Carolina Press, 1994), 14.

14. Watts, *Heroism*, 14.

15. Jerry Watts, *Amiri Baraka: The Politics and Art of a Black Intellectual* (New York: New York University Press, 2001), 8.

16. W. E. B. Du Bois, "Opinion of W. E. B. Du Bois: A Questionnaire," *The Crisis*, February 1926; reprinted in Henry Louis Gates Jr., "The Black Person in Art: How Should S/He Be Portrayed? (Part II)," *Black American Literature Forum* 21, no. 3 (1987): 317–32, doi:10.2307/2904034. The article features a roundtable of intellectuals responding to the original Du Bois "Questionnaire." The subsequent *Crisis* issue, of March 1926, contained "The Negro in Art: A Symposium," with responses from Carl Van Vechten, H. L. Mencken, DuBose Heyward, and Mary Ovington.

17. W. E. B. Du Bois, "Tom Brown at Fisk in Three Chapters" (1888), in *Creative Writings by W. E. B. Du Bois: A Pageant, Poems, Short Stories, and Playlets*, ed. Herbert Aptheker (White Plains, N.Y.: Kraus-Thomson, 1985).

18. W. E. B. Du Bois, "A fellow of Harvard, ca. 1892," W. E. B. Du Bois Papers (MS 312), Special Collections and University Archives, University of Massachusetts Amherst Libraries, http://credo.library.umass.edu/view/full/mums312-b231-i104.

19. Alison Bechdel, *Dykes to Watch Out For* (Ithaca, N.Y.: Firebrand Books, 1986).
20. Manohla Dargis, "Sundance Fights Tide with Films Like *The Birth of a Nation*," *New York Times*, January 29, 2016, https://nyti.ms/2nyL9Sg.
21. Elizabeth Alexander, *The Black Interior: Essays* (Saint Paul, Minn.: Graywolf Press, 2004), x.
22. Karen E. Fields and Barbara J. Fields, *Racecraft: The Soul of Inequality in American Life* (New York: Verso, 2012).
23. Michel Foucault, *"The Archaeology of Knowledge" and "The Discourse on Language,"* trans. A. M. Sheridan Smith (New York: Pantheon Books, 1972), 219.
24. Elaine Showalter, *Faculty Towers: The Academic Novel and Its Discontents* (Philadelphia: University of Pennsylvania Press, 2005), 23.
25. Kingsley Amis, *Lucky Jim* (New York: Penguin, 1954), 14.
26. John O. Lyons, *The College Novel in America* (Carbondale: Southern Illinois University Press, 1962), xxii.
27. Merritt Moseley, ed., *The Academic Novel: New and Classic Essays* (Chester, U.K.: Chester Academic Press, 2007), 99–113.
28. Showalter adopted the term "professorromane" from a dissertation by Richard C. Caram; see Showalter, *Faculty Towers*, 2.
29. George Saintsbury, "Novels of University Life," *Macmillan's Magazine*, no. 77 (March 1898): 343.
30. Matthew H. G. Fullerty, "The British and American Academic Novel. The 'Professorromane': The Comic Campus, The Tragic Self" (Ph.D. diss., George Washington University, 2008, ProQuest), 2.
31. Mark McGurl, *The Program Era: Postwar Fiction and the Rise of Creative Writing* (Cambridge, Mass.: Harvard University Press, 2011).
32. Gore Vidal, *At Home: Essays, 1982–1988* (New York: Random House, 1988), 180.
33. Quoted in Aida Edemariam, "Who's Afraid of the Campus Novel?," in Moseley, *The Academic Novel*, 159.
34. Henry Louis Gates Jr., *Figures in Black: Words, Signs, and the "Racial" Self* (Oxford: Oxford University Press, 1988), 26.
35. Henry Louis Gates, *Figures in Black*, 26.
36. Henry Louis Gates, *Figures in Black*, 105.
37. W. E. B. Du Bois, "The Talented Tenth," in *W. E. B. Du Bois: Writings*, ed. Nathan Huggins (New York: Library of America, 1987), 842.
38. Gene Andrew Jarrett, *Representing the Race: A New Political History of African American Literature* (New York: New York University Press, 2011), 5–6.
39. Henry Louis Gates Jr., *Thirteen Ways of Looking at a Black Man* (New York: Random House, 1997), xvii.
40. Ralph Ellison, "The World and the Jug," in *The Collected Essays of Ralph Ellison*, ed. John F. Callahan (New York: Random House, 1995), 162.
41. Henry Louis Gates, *Figures in Black*, 40.
42. Christina Sharpe, *Monstrous Intimacies: Making Post-Slavery Subjects* (Durham, N.C.: Duke University Press, 2009), 26.
43. Tal Kopan, "Scalia Questions Place of Some Black Students in Elite Colleges," *CNN*, December 7, 2015, accessed January 14, 2018, http://www.cnn.com/2015/12/09/politics/scalia-black-scientists-scotus/.

Chapter 2

1. See Marlon Riggs, dir., *Ethnic Notions* (California Newsreel, 1987), https://www.kanopy.com/product/ethnic-notions-0, for a compelling visual narrative of how racist images were deployed in popular culture to romanticize the South and depict unfettered black men as a dangerous social element.

2. Thomas Dixon Jr., "Booker T. Washington and the Negro," *Saturday Evening Post*, August 19, 1905, 1.

3. Sutton Elbert Griggs, *The Hindered Hand; or, The Reign of the Repressionist* (1905; repr., New York: AMS Press, 1969), 331.

4. Anna Julia Cooper, *The Voice of Anna Julia Cooper: Including "A Voice from the South" and Other Important Essays, Papers, and Letters*, ed. Charles Lemert and Esme Bhan (Lanham, Md.: Rowman and Littlefield, 1998), 57.

5. Anna Cooper, *Voice of Anna Julia Cooper*, 31.

6. Brittney C. Cooper, *Beyond Respectability: The Intellectual Thought of Race Women* (Champaign: University of Illinois Press, 2017), 3; emphasis in original.

7. William L. Andrews, introduction to *Up from Slavery*, by Booker T. Washington (1901; repr., Oxford: Oxford University Press, 1995), xii.

8. Letter from W. E. B. Du Bois to Rev. Sutton E. Griggs, November 13, 1909, W. E. B. Du Bois Papers (MS 312), Special Collections and University Archives, University of Massachusetts Amherst Libraries, http://credo.library.umass.edu/view/full/mums312-b002-i316.

9. Sutton E. Griggs, *Imperium in Imperio: A Study of the Negro Race Problem* (1899; repr., New York: Modern Library, 2003), 4.

10. Griggs, *Imperium in Imperio*, 23.

11. Griggs, *Imperium in Imperio*, 26.

12. Griggs, *Imperium in Imperio*, 53–54.

13. Griggs, *Imperium in Imperio*, 55.

14. Griggs, *Imperium in Imperio*, 57.

15. Griggs, *Imperium in Imperio*, 61.

16. Griggs, *Imperium in Imperio*, 62.

17. Finnie D. Coleman, *Sutton E. Griggs and the Struggle Against White Supremacy* (Knoxville: University of Tennessee Press, 2007), 42.

18. Griggs, *Imperium in Imperio*, 244.

19. Griggs, *Imperium in Imperio*, 129–30.

20. Griggs, *Imperium in Imperio*, 130.

21. Griggs, *Imperium in Imperio*, 145

22. See Siobhan B. Somerville, *Queering the Color Line: Race and the Invention of Homosexuality in American Culture* (Durham, N.C.: Duke University Press, 2000); Jennifer L. Morgan, "'Some Could Suckle Over Their Shoulder': Male Travelers, Female Bodies, and the Gendering of Racial Ideology, 1500–1770," *William and Mary Quarterly* 54, no. 1 (January 1997): 167–92.

23. Wilder, *Ebony and Ivy*, 239. See chapter 7, "Bodily and Mental Inferiority of the Negro," for a discussion of race science and the university.

24. Griggs, *Imperium in Imperio*, 210.

25. Griggs, *Imperium in Imperio*, 220.

26. Griggs, *Imperium in Imperio*, 212.

27. Griggs, *Imperium in Imperio*, 244.

28. See Wilson J. Moses, ed., *Classical Black Nationalism: From the American Revolution to Marcus Garvey* (New York: New York University Press, 1996), for analysis and documents of nineteenth-century black nationalist thought.
29. W. E. B. Du Bois, *The Quest of the Silver Fleece: A Novel* (1911; repr., New York: Random House, 2004), 214.
30. Derrick P. Alridge, *The Educational Thought of W. E. B. Du Bois: An Intellectual History* (New York: Teachers College Press, 2008), 46
31. Mortimer Proctor, *The English University Novel* (Berkeley: University of California Press, 1957), 111.
32. W. E. B. Du Bois, *The Souls of Black Folk* (New York: Penguin Random House, 2018), 181.
33. Arnold Rampersad, *The Art and Imagination of W. E. B. Du Bois* (Cambridge, Mass.: Harvard University Press, 1976), 13.
34. Jarvis McInnis, "'Behold the Land': W. E. B. Du Bois, Cotton Futures, and the Afterlife of the Plantation in the U.S. South," *Global South* 10, no. 2 (Fall 2016): 73.
35. Du Bois, *Quest of the Silver Fleece*, 35.
36. Nellie McKay, "W. E. B. Du Bois: The Black Women in His Writings—Selected Fictional and Autobiographical Portraits," in *Critical Essays on W. E. B. Du Bois*, ed. William L. Andrews (Boston: Hall, 1985), 244.
37. Du Bois, *Quest of the Silver Fleece*, 33.
38. Du Bois, *Quest of the Silver Fleece*, 58.
39. Du Bois, *Quest of the Silver Fleece*, 67.
40. Du Bois, *Quest of the Silver Fleece*, 72–73.
41. Du Bois, *Quest of the Silver Fleece*, 149.
42. Du Bois, *Quest of the Silver Fleece*, 160–61.
43. Du Bois, *Quest of the Silver Fleece*, 364.
44. Rampersad, *Art and Imagination*, 129.
45. Du Bois, *Quest of the Silver Fleece*, 348.

Chapter 3

1. See David Levering Lewis, *When Harlem Was in Vogue* (New York: Penguin Books, 1997), and David Levering Lewis, ed., *The Portable Harlem Renaissance Reader* (New York: Penguin Books, 1995).
2. Lawrence P. Jackson, *The Indignant Generation: A Narrative History of African American Writers and Critics, 1934–1960* (Princeton, N.J.: Princeton University Press, 2013).
3. That said, Arja Engstrom's dissertation, "A Novel Way to Learn: Black Educational Fiction from Reconstruction to the Harlem Renaissance" (University of Illinois at Urbana–Champaign, 2014), contains inventive readings of the educational and intellectual themes in Fauset's *There Is Confusion* (1924) and *Plum Bun* (1928).
4. Keguro Macharia, "Queering Helga Crane: Black Nativism in Nella Larsen's *Quicksand*," *Modern Fiction Studies* 57, no. 2 (Summer 2011): 262.
5. Erika Renée Williams, "A Lie of Omission: Plagiarism in Nella Larsen's *Quicksand*," *African American Review* 45, nos. 1–2 (Spring–Summer 2012): 205–16.

6. Erika Williams, "A Lie of Omission," 208.
7. See George Hutchinson, *In Search of Nella Larsen: A Biography of the Color Line* (Cambridge, Mass.: Harvard University Press, 2006), 343–46.
8. Deborah McDowell, introduction to *Quicksand/Passing*, by Nella Larsen (New Brunswick, N.J.: Rutgers University Press, 1986), xxxiv.
9. Larsen, *Quicksand*, 1.
10. Larsen, *Quicksand*, 4.
11. Larsen, *Quicksand*, 3.
12. Larsen, *Quicksand*, 3.
13. Larsen, *Quicksand*, 18.
14. For more on the history of colorism and the "brown paper bag test," see Kathy Russell-Cole, Midge Wilson, and Ronald E. Hall, *The Color Complex: The Politics of Skin Color in a New Millennium*, rev. ed. (New York: Anchor Books, 2013).
15. Larsen, *Quicksand*, 48.
16. Larsen, *Quicksand*, 52.
17. Larsen, *Quicksand*, 55.
18. Larsen, *Quicksand*, 83.
19. Larsen, *Quicksand*, 103.
20. Larsen, *Quicksand*, 81.
21. Larsen, *Quicksand*, 133.
22. Ralph Ellison, *Invisible Man* (1952; repr., New York: Vintage Books, 1995), 355.
23. Homi K. Bhabha, introduction to *Dark Princess*, by W. E. B. Du Bois (1928; repr., New York: Oxford University Press, 2007), xxxi.
24. Rebecka Rutledge Fisher, "The Anatomy of a Symbol: Reading W. E. B. Du Bois's *Dark Princess: A Romance*," *CR: The New Centennial Review* 6, no. 3 (Winter 2006): 91–128.
25. "Race Discrimination," *New York Times*, May 13, 1928.
26. Langston Hughes, "Professor" (1935), in *Short Stories: Langston Hughes*, ed. Akiba Sullivan Harper (New York: Hill and Wang, 1996).
27. Hughes, "Professor," 102.
28. Hughes, "Professor," 106.
29. Stephanie Brown, *The Postwar African American Novel: Protest and Discontent, 1945–1950* (Jackson: University Press of Mississippi, 2011), 150–51.
30. Brown, *Postwar African American Novel*, 151.
31. Dorothy Sayers, *Gaudy Night* (1936; repr., New York: HarperCollins, 2012).
32. Elaine Showalter, *Faculty Towers: The Academic Novel and Its Discontents* (Philadelphia: University of Pennsylvania Press, 2005), 7.
33. J. Saunders Redding, *Stranger and Alone* (1950; repr., Boston: Northeastern University Press, 1989), 25.
34. Redding, *Stranger and Alone*, 119.
35. Redding, *Stranger and Alone*, 120.
36. Ellison, *Invisible Man*, 30–31.
37. Louis R. Harlan, ed., *The Booker T. Washington Papers*, vol. 3 (Urbana: University of Illinois Press, 1974), 583–87, as cited at http://historymatters.gmu.edu/d/39/.

38. Ralph Ellison, review of *Stranger and Alone*, by Redding, J. Saunders, *New York Times*, February 19, 1950.
39. Paul Venable Turner, *Campus: An American Planning Tradition* (Cambridge, Mass.: MIT Press, 1984); see "The American Campus as Academical Village," 1–7.
40. Ellison, *Invisible Man*, 116.
41. Ellison, *Invisible Man*, 111.
42. Ellison, *Invisible Man*, 134.
43. Ellison, *Invisible Man*, 134.
44. Ellison, *Invisible Man*, 264–65.
45. Ellison, *Invisible Man*, 303.
46. Ellison, *Invisible Man*, 312.
47. Ellison, *Invisible Man*, 313.
48. Ellison, *Invisible Man*, 306.
49. Eric Lott, *Love and Theft: Blackface Minstrelsy and the American Working Class* (Oxford: Oxford University Press, 1993); Camille F. Forbes, *Introducing Bert Williams: Burnt Cork, Broadway, and the Story of America's First Black Star* (New York: Basic Books, 2008).
50. Ellison, *Invisible Man*, 354.
51. Ellison, *Invisible Man*, 355.
52. Ellison, *Invisible Man*, 579.
53. Lawrence P. Jackson, *Chester B. Himes: A Biography* (New York: Norton, 2017).
54. Chester Himes, *The Third Generation* (1954; repr., New York: Thunder's Mouth Press, 1989), 68.
55. Himes, *The Third Generation*, 159.
56. Himes, *The Third Generation*, 226.
57. Himes, *The Third Generation*, 234.
58. Himes, *The Third Generation*, 258.
59. Himes, *The Third Generation*, 258.
60. Himes, *The Third Generation*, 259.

Chapter 4

1. Roderick Ferguson, *The Reorder of Things: The University and Its Pedagogies of Minority Difference* (Minneapolis: University of Minnesota Press, 2012), 29.
2. Brent Edwards, introduction to *The Ordeal of Mansart*, by W. E. B. Du Bois (Oxford: Oxford University Press, 2007), xxv.
3. June Cara Christian, *Understanding the Black Flame and Multigenerational Educational Trauma: Toward a Theory of the Dehumanization of Black Students* (Lanham, Md.: Rowman and Littlefield, 2014), 6.
4. Crystal deGregory, "We Speak Their Names: HBCU Alumni Killed in Charleston Massacre," *HBCU Story*, June 18, 2015, https://hbcustory.wordpress.com/2015/06/18/we-speak-their-names-hbcu-alumni-killed-in-charleston-massacre/.
5. W. E. B. Du Bois, "Bethesda A. M. E.: A romance of Negro religion table of contents, ca. 1928," W. E. B. Du Bois Papers (MS 312), Special Collections and University Archives, University of Massachusetts Amherst Libraries, http://credo.library.umass.edu/view/full/mums312-b231-i076.

6. Keisha Blain, Chad Williams, and Kidada Williams, eds., *Charleston Syllabus: Readings on Race, Racism, and Racial Violence* (Athens: University of Georgia Press, 2016).

7. Rayford Logan, *The Betrayal of the Negro: From Rutherford B. Hayes to Woodrow Wilson* (New York: Da Capo Press, 1997). (*Betrayal* is an expanded and revised version of the book originally published in 1954 as *The Negro in American Life and Thought: The Nadir, 1877–1901*.)

8. For a prescient look at the world of white supremacy on the internet before the 2016 election, see Jesse Daniels, *Cyber Racism: White Supremacy Online and the New Attack on Civil Rights* (Lanham, Md.: Rowman and Littlefield, 2009).

9. Du Bois, *Ordeal of Mansart*, 3.

10. Du Bois, *Ordeal of Mansart*, 45.

11. Du Bois, *Ordeal of Mansart*, 227.

12. Du Bois, *Ordeal of Mansart*, 34.

13. Du Bois, *Ordeal of Mansart*, 115.

14. W. E. B. Du Bois, *The Souls of Black Folk* (1903; repr., Boulder, Colo.: Paradigm Publishers, 2004), xiii.

15. Du Bois, *Souls of Black Folk*, 124.

16. Du Bois, *Souls of Black Folk*, 116.

17. Du Bois, *Souls of Black Folk*, 165.

18. Du Bois, *Souls of Black Folk*, 145.

19. Du Bois, *Souls of Black Folk*, 145.

20. Du Bois, *Souls of Black Folk*, 166.

21. Du Bois, *Mansart Builds a School*, 117.

22. Patricia Hill Collins, *Black Feminist Thought: Knowledge, Consciousness, and the Politics of Empowerment* (New York: Routledge, 2000).

23. W. E. B. Du Bois, *Mansart Builds a School*, Book 2 of *The Black Flame Trilogy* (1959; repr., New York: Oxford University Press, 2007), 228.

24. Celena Simpson, "Du Bois's Dubious Feminism: Evaluating through The Black Flame Trilogy," *The Pluralist* 10, no. 1 (Spring 2015): 48–63.

25. Kevin Wallsten, Tatishe M. Nteta, Lauren A. McCarthy, and Melinda R. Tarsi, "Prejudice or Principled Conservatism? Racial Resentment and White Opinion toward Paying College Athletes," *Political Research Quarterly* 70, no. 1., 209–22, https://doi.org/10.1177%2F1065912916685186.

26. Wallsten, Nteta, McCarthy, and Tarsi, "Prejudice or Principled Conservatism?," 266.

27. Wallsten, Nteta, McCarthy, and Tarsi, "Prejudice or Principled Conservatism?," 242.

28. W. E. B. Du Bois, *Worlds of Color*, Book 3 of *The Black Flame Trilogy* (1961; repr., New York: Oxford University Press, 2007), 15.

29. Du Bois, *Worlds of Color*, 17.

30. Du Bois, *Worlds of Color*, 36.

31. Du Bois, *Worlds of Color*, 51.

32. Du Bois, *Worlds of Color*, 169.

33. Du Bois, *Worlds of Color*, 229–30.

34. David Lodge, *After Bakhtin: Essays on Fiction and Criticism* (New York: Routledge, 1990), 49.

35. John Gardner, *The Art of Fiction: Notes on Craft for Young Writers* (New York: Vintage Books, 1983), 30–31.
36. Gardner, *The Art of Fiction*, 45.
37. W. E. B. Du Bois, "Two Novels," *The Crisis* 35 (June 1928): 202.
38. Arnold Rampersad, *The Art and Imagination of W. E. B. Du Bois* (Cambridge, Mass.: Harvard University Press, 1976), 196–97.
39. Keith Byerman, *Seizing the Word: History, Art, and Self in the Work of W. E. B. Du Bois* (Athens: University of Georgia Press, 2010), 114.
40. Byerman, *Seizing the Word*, 114.
41. See Roderick Ferguson's criticism of social science discourses in *Aberrations in Black: Toward a Queer of Color Critique* (Minneapolis: University of Minnesota Press, 2003).
42. Paule Marshall, *Conversations with Paule Marshall* (Jackson: University Press of Mississippi, 2010), 184–85.
43. Marshall, *Conversations*, 187.
44. I have also written about "Brooklyn" and its connections to the #MeToo movement; see Lavelle Porter, "Paule Marshall's 'Brooklyn' and the #MeToo Movement," *Black Perspectives*, July 18, 2018, https://www.aaihs.org/paule-marshalls-brooklyn-and-the-metoo-movement/.
45. Paule Marshall, *The Chosen Place, the Timeless People* (1969; repr., New York: Vintage Books, 1984), 58.
46. These ideas are also taken up by historians such as Sterling Stuckey, *Slave Culture: Nationalist Theory and the Foundations of Black America* (Oxford: Oxford University Press, 1987).
47. See Johannes Fabian, *Time and the Other: How Anthropology Makes Its Object* (New York: Columbia University Press, 2014), for an analysis of social scientific research and temporality.
48. Michelle M. Wright, *Physics of Blackness: Beyond the Middle Passage Epistemology* (Minneapolis: University of Minnesota Press, 2015), 3.
49. Reginald McKnight, *He Sleeps: A Novel* (New York: Macmillan, 2002).
50. Craig Steven Wilder, *Ebony and Ivy: Race, Slavery, and the Troubled History of America's Universities* (New York: Bloomsbury Press, 2013), 79.
51. Wilder, *Ebony and Ivy*, 222.
52. Wilder, *Ebony and Ivy*, 218.
53. Wilder, *Ebony and Ivy*, 232–36.
54. Wilder, *Ebony and Ivy*, 316.
55. Wilder, *Ebony and Ivy*, 401–2.
56. Wilder, *Ebony and Ivy*, 61.
57. Wilder, *Ebony and Ivy*, 424.
58. Wilder, *Ebony and Ivy*, 438.
59. Marshall, *Conversations*, 53.
60. Ibram H. Rogers, *The Black Campus Movement: Black Students and the Racial Reconstitution of Higher Education, 1965–1972* (New York: Palgrave Macmillan, 2012).
61. Gil-Scott Heron, *The Nigger Factory* (1972; repr., Edinburgh: Cannongate Press, 2001), 246.
62. Heron, *The Nigger Factory*, 246.

63. Alice Walker, *Meridian* (New York: Simon and Schuster, 1976), 97.
64. Walker, *Meridian*, 39.
65. Walker, *Meridian*, 186.
66. Walker, *Meridian*, 185.

Chapter 5

1. Andrew Hartman, *A War for the Soul of America: A History of the Culture Wars* (Chicago: University of Chicago Press, 2003), 6.
2. Though this period extends into these first two decades of the twenty-first century. I should mention here that novels I cover in this chapter all come before September 11, 2001. Perhaps a more detailed chronology of this period would include a post-9/11 section with the war on terror and escalation of the domestic security state. However, some of the most recent post-9/11 academic fiction is addressed in the concluding chapter.
3. I should also note here that there are some black academic novels of the culture wars era that predate *Japanese by Spring* (1993), where my discussion begins, such as David Bradley's powerful and unsettling novel *The Chaneysville Incident* (1981), which features a historian and deals with the practice of history, and Cyrus Colter's underappreciated historical and academic novel *A Chocolate Soldier* (1988). I'm not sure it is desirable to superficially cover every novel in this period. Therefore, I had to make some critical judgments about which ones to emphasize, and I accept that these judgments may be flawed. I've taken into account which novels are the most stylistically interesting and critically influential and which best encapsulate the thematic focus of this era, with hopes that the issues I raise in this chapter and in previous chapters can be related with some benefit to other recent black academic novels.
4. David Levering Lewis, *W. E. B. Du Bois: Biography of a Race, 1868–1919*. (New York: Holt, 1993), 96.
5. Ishmael Reed, *Japanese by Spring* (New York: Atheneum, 1993), 3–4.
6. Ishmael Reed, *Conversations with Ishmael Reed*, ed. Bruce Dick and Amritjit Singh (Jackson: University Press of Mississippi, 1995), 349.
7. Reed, *Japanese by Spring*, 182.
8. Reed, *Japanese by Spring*, 128.
9. Darryl Dickson-Carr, *African American Satire: The Sacredly Profane Novel* (Columbia: University of Missouri Press, 2001), 196.
10. David Palumbo-Liu, "Introduction," in *The Ethnic Canon: Histories, Institutions, and Interventions*, ed. David Palumbo-Liu (Minneapolis: University of Minnesota Press, 1995), 5.
11. Michele Wallace, "Ishmael Reed's Female Troubles," in *Invisibility Blues: From Pop to Theory* (New York: Verso, 1994), 149.
12. Wallace, "Ishmael Reed's Female Troubles," 146.
13. Derrick Bell, *Faces at the Bottom of the Well: The Permanence of Racism* (New York: Basic Books, 1992), 114.
14. Reed, *Japanese by Spring*, 10.
15. Reed, *Japanese by Spring*, 3.
16. Reed, *Japanese by Spring*, 5.
17. Reed, *Japanese by Spring*, 6–7.
18. Reed, *Japanese by Spring*, 7.

19. Reed, *Japanese by Spring*, 13.
20. Ishmael Reed, "Should America Ever Forgive Paula Deen?," *Wall Street Journal*, July 6, 2013, https://blogs.wsj.com/speakeasy/2013/07/06/should-america-ever-forgive-paula-deen/.
21. Janice Rossen, *The University in Modern Fiction: When Power Is Academic* (New York: St. Martin's Press, 1993), 6.
22. Rossen, *University in Modern Fiction*, 171.
23. Reed, *Japanese by Spring*, 49.
24. Reed, *Japanese by Spring*, 35.
25. Reed, *Japanese by Spring*, 35.
26. Reed, *Japanese by Spring*, 57.
27. Wallace, "Ishmael Reed's Female Troubles," 147.
28. Wallace, "Ishmael Reed's Female Troubles," 70.
29. Reed, *Japanese by Spring*, 143.
30. Reed, *Japanese by Spring*, 144.
31. Reed, *Japanese by Spring*, 155.
32. Nikhil Pal Singh, *Black Is a Country: Race and the Unfinished Struggle for Democracy* (Cambridge, Mass.: Harvard University Press, 2004), 173. Other works in the Afro-Orientalism field include Bill V. Mullen, *Afro-Orientalism* (Minneapolis: University of Minnesota Press, 2004); Vijay Prashad, *The Karma of Brown Folk* (Minneapolis: University of Minnesota Press, 2001); Helen Heran Jun, *Race for Citizenship: Black Orientalism and Asian Uplift from Pre-Emancipation to Neoliberal America* (New York: New York University Press, 2011); and Julia Lee, *Interracial Encounters: Reciprocal Representations in African and Asian American Literatures, 1896–1937* (New York: New York University Press, 2011).
33. Crystal S. Anderson, *Beyond "The Chinese Connection": Contemporary Afro-Asian Cultural Production* (Jackson: University Press of Mississippi, 2013), 393.
34. Samuel R. Delany, *About Writing: Seven Essays, Four Letters, and Five Interviews* (Middletown, Conn.: Wesleyan University Press, 2006), 268.
35. "Angela Bassett's *Erasure* Adaptation Is Still Alive," *Shadow and Act: On Cinema of the African Diaspora*, April 10, 2013, accessed February 4, 2019, https://www.indiewire.com/2013/04/angela-bassetts-erasure-adaptation-is-still-alive-t-d-jakes-onboard-as-producer-136542/.
36. Percival Everett, *Erasure* (New York: Hyperion, 2001), 2.
37. Louis Althusser, *Lenin and Philosophy and Other Essays*, trans. Ben Brewster (New York: Monthly Review Press, 2001), 174.
38. Everett, *Erasure*, 2.
39. For an extended analysis of this phenomenon, see Stuart Buck, *Acting White: The Ironic Legacy of Desegregation* (New Haven, Conn.: Yale University Press, 2010).
40. Everett, *Erasure*, 185.
41. Everett, *Erasure*, 195.
42. Everett, *Erasure*, 39.
43. Everett, *Erasure*, 40.
44. Everett, *Erasure*, 53.
45. Everett, *Erasure*, 58.

46. Everett, *Erasure*, 214.
47. Everett, *Erasure*, 238.
48. Everett, *Erasure*, 261.
49. Everett, *Erasure*, 261.
50. Margaret Russett, "Race Under Erasure," *Callaloo* 28, no. 2 (Spring 2005): 363.
51. Irving Howe, *Selected Writings, 1950–1990* (San Diego: Harcourt Brace Jovanovich, 1990), 125.
52. Howe, *Selected Writings*, 131.
53. Ralph Ellison, "The World and the Jug," in *The Collected Essays of Ralph Ellison*, ed. John F. Callahan (New York: Random House, 1995), 155.
54. Ellison, "The World and the Jug," 165.
55. Ellison, "The World and the Jug," 163.
56. Jerry Watts, *Heroism and the Black Intellectual: Ralph Ellison, Politics, and Afro-American Intellectual Life* (Chapel Hill: University of North Carolina Press, 1994), 73.
57. Watts, *Heroism*, 89.
58. Ellison, "The World and the Jug," 162.
59. Ellison, "The World and the Jug," 167.
60. Everett, *Erasure*, 1.
61. Ellison, "The World and the Jug," 159.
62. Samuel R. Delany, "The Phil Leggiere Interview," in *Shorter Views: Queer Thoughts and the Politics of the Paraliterary* (Middletown, Conn.: Wesleyan University Press, 1996), 312.
63. For a trenchant analysis of capitalism, excrement, and waste in the novel, see Mary Catherine Foltz, "The Excremental Ethics of Samuel R. Delany," *SubStance* 37, no. 2 (2008): 41–55.
64. Reed Woodhouse, *Unlimited Embrace: A Canon of Gay Fiction, 1945–1995* (Amherst: University of Massachusetts Press, 1998), 220.
65. Delany also discusses his family's history in the memoir *The Motion of Light in Water* (1988).
66. Booker T. Washington, *Up from Slavery: An Autobiography*, ed. William L. Andrews (1901; repr., Oxford: Oxford University Press, 1995), 81.
67. David Lodge, introduction to *Pnin*, by Vladimir Nabokov (New York: Random House, 2004), xiii.
68. Harold Brodkey, *This Wild Darkness: The Story of My Death* (New York: Holt, 1996).
69. Delany, *The Mad Man*, 9.
70. Delany, *Shorter Views*.
71. Delany, *The Mad Man*, 18.
72. Delany, *The Mad Man*, 40.
73. Ray Davis, "Delany's Dirt," in *Ash of Stars: On the Writing of Samuel R. Delany*, ed. James Sallis (Jackson: University Press of Mississippi, 1996), 178.
74. Delany, *The Mad Man*, 40.
75. Samuel R. Delany, "Atlantis Rose: Some Notes on Hart Crane," in *Longer Views: Extended Essays* (Middletown Conn.: Wesleyan University Press, 1996).
76. Delany, *The Mad Man*, 65.
77. Delany, *The Mad Man*, 277.

78. Reed Woodhouse, *Unlimited Embrace: A Canon of Gay Fiction, 1945–1995* (Amherst: University of Massachusetts Press, 1998), 221.
79. Steven Shaviro, "The Mad Man," *The Pinocchio Theory* (blog), November 30, 2006, accessed February 4, 2019, http://www.shaviro.com/Blog/?p=528.
80. Darieck Scott, *Extravagant Abjection: Blackness, Power, and Sexuality in the African American Literary Imagination* (New York: New York University Press, 2010), 223.
81. Audre Lorde, *A Burst of Light: Essays by Audre Lorde* (Ithaca, N.Y.: Firebrand Books, 1988), 14.
82. Lorde, *A Burst of Light*, 70.
83. Samuel R. Delany, *Conversations with Samuel R. Delany*, ed. Carl Freedman (Jackson: University Press of Mississippi), 105.
84. Mat Johnson, *Pym: A Novel* (New York: Spiegel and Grau, 2011), 159.
85. Patricia A. Matthew, ed., *Written/Unwritten: Diversity and the Hidden Truths of Tenure* (Chapel Hill: University of North Carolina Press, 2016).
86. Johnson, *Pym*, 18.
87. Sara Ahmed, *On Being Included: Racism and Diversity in Institutional Life* (Durham, N.C.: Duke University Press, 2012), 43.
88. Aida Levy-Hussen, *How to Read African American Literature: Post–Civil Rights Fiction and the Task of Interpretation* (New York: New York University Press, 2016), 131.
89. Levy-Hussen, *African American Literature*, 171.
90. Jeffrey Williams, "Teach the University," *Pedagogy* 8, no. 1 (Winter 2008): 25–42, accessed August 10, 2016, https://muse.jhu.edu/.
91. Gerald Graff, *Beyond the Culture Wars: How Teaching the Conflicts Can Revitalize American Higher Education* (New York: Norton, 1993).
92. Jeffrey Williams, "Teach the University," 26.
93. Jeffrey Williams, "Teach the University," 26.
94. Tressie McMillan Cottom, *Lower Ed: The Troubling Rise of For-Profit Colleges in the New Economy* (New York: New Press, 2017).
95. "'I Agree 100%': NRA Members Back Wayne LaPierre Attack on 'Leftist Zealots,'" *The Guardian*, May 1, 2017, https://www.theguardian.com/us-news/2017/may/01/nra-wayne-lapierre-guns-leftist-zealots.
96. Barbara F. Tobolowsky and Pauline J. Reynolds, eds., *Anti-Intellectual Representations of Colleges and Universities: Fictional Higher Education* (New York: Palgrave Macmillan, 2017).

Conclusion

EPIGRAPH: David Lodge, *Changing Places: A Tale of Two Campuses* (New York: Penguin Books, 1975), 250.
1. Racquel J. Gates, *Double Negative: The Black Image and Popular Culture* (Durham, N.C.: Duke University Press, 2018).
2. Kiese Laymon, "What Bill Cosby Taught Me about Sexual Violence and Flying," *Literary Hub*, February 16, 2016, http://lithub.com/what-bill-cosby-taught-me-about-sexual-violence-and-flying/.
3. Ta-Nehisi Coates, "This Is How We Lost to the White Man: The Audacity of Bill Cosby's Conservatism," *The Atlantic*, May 2008, https://www.theatlantic.com/magazine/archive/2008/05/-this-is-how-we-lost-to-the-white-man/306774/.

4. Marlon Ross, *Manning the Race: Reforming Black Men in the Jim Crow Era* (New York: New York University Press, 2004), 395.

5. Racquel Gates, *Double Negative*, 14.

6. Racquel Gates, *Double Negative*, chap. 4.

7. Here I'm using Racquel Gates's schematic in *Double Negative*, which refers to the TV show *Empire* as a "false negative."

8. Racquel Gates, *Double Negative*, 167.

9. Lavelle Porter, "The Souls of Ivy Folk," *New Inquiry*, November 13, 2014, https://thenewinquiry.com/the-souls-of-ivy-folk/.

10. Jewel Allison, "Bill Cosby Sexually Assaulted Me. I Didn't Tell Because I Didn't Want to Let Black America Down," *Washington Post*, March 6, 2015, https://www.washingtonpost.com/posteverything/wp/2015/03/06/bill-cosby-sexually-assaulted-me-i-didnt-tell-because-i-didnt-want-to-let-black-america-down/.

11. Mark S. Luckie, "I Went to a Black College Because of 'A Different World,'" *BuzzFeed*, October 26, 2015, https://www.buzzfeed.com/marksluckie/i-went-to-an-hbcu-because-of-a-different-world.

12. Ralph Ellison, review of *Stranger and Alone*, by J. Saunders Redding, *New York Times*, February, 19, 1950.

BIBLIOGRAPHY

Black Academic Fiction

Novels
Adichie, Chimamanda Ngozi. *Americanah*. New York: Penguin Random House, 2013.
Anderson, Walter "Big Walt." *Pledge Brothers*. Arlington, Tex.: Milk and Honey, 2001.
Appiah, Kwame Anthony. *Avenging Angel*. New York: St. Martin's Press, 1991.
Beatty, Paul. *The White Boy Shuffle*. New York: Picador, 1996.
Bradley, David. *The Chaneysville Incident*. New York: Harper and Row, 1981.
Briscoe, Connie. *Big Girls Don't Cry*. New York: HarperCollins, 1996.
Butler, Tajuana "TJ." *Sorority Sisters*. New York: Villard, 2001.
Carter, Stephen. *The Emperor of Ocean Park*. New York: Vintage Books, 2002.
———. *New England White: A Novel*. New York: Vintage Books, 2007.
Colter, Cyrus. *A Chocolate Soldier*. New York: Thunder's Mouth Press, 1988.
Delany, Samuel R. *Dark Reflections*. New York: Carroll and Graf, 2007.
———. *The Mad Man*. Rutherford, N.J.: Voyant Publishing, 2002.
Du Bois, W. E. B. *Dark Princess: A Romance*. 1928. Reprint, New York: Oxford University Press, 2007.
———. *Mansart Builds a School, Book 2 of The Black Flame Trilogy*. 1959. Reprint, New York: Oxford University Press, 2007.
———. *The Ordeal of Mansart, Book 1 of The Black Flame Trilogy*. 1957. Reprint, New York: Oxford University Press, 2007.
———. *The Quest of the Silver Fleece: A Novel*. 1911. Reprint, New York: Random House, 2004.
———. *Worlds of Color, Book 3 of The Black Flame Trilogy*. 1961. Reprint, New York: Oxford University Press, 2007.
Ellison, Ralph. *Invisible Man*. 1952. Reprint, New York: Vintage Books, 1995.
Emecheta, Buchi. *Double Yoke*. New York: Braziller, 1983.
Everett, Percival. *Erasure*. New York: Hyperion, 2001.
———. *Glyph*. Minneapolis: Graywolf Press, 1999.
Gay, Phillip. *Academic Affairs: Love and Murder in Academia*. Bloomington, Ind.: 1st Books, 2003.
Grant, Tracy. *Hellified*. New York: Visao, 1993.
Griggs, Sutton E. *Imperium in Imperio: A Study of the Negro Race Problem*. 1899. Reprint, New York: Modern Library, 2003.
Hedden, Worth Tuttle. *The Other Room*. New York: Crown, 1947.
Heron, Gil-Scott. *The Nigger Factory*. 1972. Reprint, Edinburgh: Cannongate Press, 2001.

Himes, Chester. *The Third Generation*. 1954. Reprint, New York: Thunder's Mouth Press, 1989.
Hughes, Althea. *Walking the Line*. Arlington, Va.: E.R.L., 2000.
Jackson, C. R. *Mistrustful*. College Park, Ga.: Media Management International, 2000.
Johnson, Mat. *Pym: A Novel*. New York: Spiegel and Grau, 2011.
Marshall, Paule. *The Chosen Place, the Timeless People*. 1969. Reprint, New York: Vintage Books, 1984.
McKnight, Reginald. *He Sleeps: A Novel*. New York: Macmillan, 2002.
Moon, Bucklin. *Without Magnolias*. New York: Doubleday, 1949.
Murray, Albert. *The Spyglass Tree*. New York: Pantheon Books, 1991.
Peterson, Brian. *Move Over, Girl*. New York: Villard, 1998.
Raboteau, Emily. *The Professor's Daughter*. New York: Holt, 2005.
Randall, Alice. *Pushkin and the Queen of Spades*. New York: Houghton Mifflin, 2004.
Redding, J. Saunders. *Stranger and Alone*. 1950. Reprint, Boston: Northeastern University Press, 1989.
Reed, Ishmael. *Japanese by Spring*. New York: Atheneum, 1993.
Robinson, C. Kelly. *Between Brothers*. New York: Villard, 1999.
Rosenman, John B. *The Best Laugh Last*. New Paltz, N.Y.: Treacle Press, 1981.
Roth, Philip. *The Human Stain*. New York: Vintage Books, 2000.
Smith, Zadie. *On Beauty: A Novel*. New York: Penguin Press, 2005.
Thomas, Michael. *Man Gone Down: A Novel*. New York: Grove/Atlantic, 2007.
Thomas-Graham, Pamela. *Blue Blood*. New York: Simon and Schuster, 1999.
———. *A Darker Shade of Crimson*. New York: Simon and Schuster, 1999.
———. *Orange Crushed*. New York: Simon and Schuster, 2004.
Thomason, Caroline. *Youth of Color*. New York: Exposition Press, 1952.
Tyree, Omar. *Colored, on White Campus: The Education of a Racial World*. Washington, D.C.: Mars Productions, 1992. Reprinted as *Battlezone*. Wilmington, Del.: Mars Productions, 1994.
Walker, Alice. *Meridian*. New York: Simon and Schuster, 1976.
Whitehead, Colson. *The Intuitionist*. New York: Random House, 1999.
Williams, Dennis A. *Crossover*. New York: Summit Books, 1992.
Williams, Robyn. *Preconceived Notions*. Chicago: Lushena Books, 1991.
Woodson, Jon. *Endowed, a Comic Novel*. CreateSpace, 2012.

Plays

Jones, LeRoi [Amiri Baraka]. *The Slave*. 1964. In *"Dutchman" and "The Slave": Two Plays*. New York: Morrow, 1967.
Kennedy, Adrienne. *The Ohio State Murders*. New York: Samuel French, 2009.
Rux, Carl Hancock. *Talk*. New York: Theater Communications Group, 2004.

Films

Birthright. Dir. Oscar Micheaux. 1939. Kino Lorber, 2016.
Brother to Brother. Dir. Rodney Evans. Wolf Releasing, 2004. DVD.
Dear White People. Dir. Justin Simien. Lionsgate, 2014.
Drumline. Dir. Charles Stone III. 2002. 20th Century Fox, 2003. DVD.
The Great Debaters. Dir. Denzel Washington. 2007. Harpo Films, 2008. DVD.

Higher Learning. Dir. John Singleton. 1995. Sony Pictures, 2001. DVD.
Mooz-lum. Dir. Qasim Basir. 2010. Rising Pictures, 2011. DVD.
The Nutty Professor. Dir. Tom Shadyac. 1996. Universal Pictures, 2007. DVD.
School Daze. Dir. Spike Lee. 1988. Sony Pictures, 2001. DVD.
Something the Lord Made. Dir. Joseph Sargent. 2004. HBO Films, 2004. DVD.
Train Ride. Dir. Rel Dowdell. Ruff Nation Films. 2000.

Television

Dear White People. Netflix, 2017–.
A Different World. Exec. prod., Bill Cosby. Carsey-Werner Productions, 1987–93.
Grown-ish. ABC Studios, 2018–.
The Quad. Black Entertainment Television, 2016–17.

Short Stories

Du Bois, W. E. B. "Of the Coming of John." In *The Souls of Black Folk.* 1903. Boulder, Colo.: Paradigm Publishers, 2004.
———. "Tom Brown at Fisk in Three Chapters." 1888. In *Creative Writings by W. E. B. Du Bois: A Pageant, Poems, Short Stories, and Playlets,* ed. Herbert Aptheker. White Plains, N.Y.: Kraus-Thomson, 1985.
Dumas, Henry. "The University of Man." In *Echo Tree: The Collected Short Fiction of Henry Dumas,* edited by Eugene B. Redmond, 176–88, Minneapolis: Coffee House Press, 2003.
Hughes, Langston. "Professor." 1935. In *Short Stories: Langston Hughes,* edited by Akiba Sullivan Harper. New York: Hill and Wang, 1996.
Marshall, Paule. "Brooklyn." In *Reena and Other Stories.* 1961. Reprint, New York: Feminist Press, 1983.
McPherson, James Alan. *Hue and Cry.* New York: Little, Brown, 1968.

Other

Bell, Derrick. *And We Are Not Saved: The Elusive Quest for Racial Justice.* New York: Basic Books, 1987.
———. *Faces at the Bottom of the Well: The Permanence of Racism.* New York: Basic Books, 1992.

Secondary Works

Alridge, Derrick P. *The Educational Thought of W. E. B. Du Bois: An Intellectual History.* New York: Teachers College Press, 2008.
Althusser, Louis. *Lenin and Philosophy and Other Essays.* Translated by Ben Brewster. New York: Monthly Review Press, 2001.
Anderson, Crystal S. *Beyond "The Chinese Connection": Contemporary Afro-Asian Cultural Production.* Jackson: University Press of Mississippi, 2013.
Anderson, James. *The Education of Blacks in the South, 1860–1935.* Chapel Hill: University of North Carolina Press, 1988.
Andrews, William L. Introduction to *Up from Slavery,* by Booker T. Washington. 1901. Reprint, Oxford: Oxford University Press, 1995.
Bakhtin, Mikhail. *The Dialogic Imagination: Four Essays.* Translated by Caryl Emerson and Michael Holquist. 1981. Reprint, Austin: University of Texas Press, 2004.

Bourdieu, Pierre. *Homo Academicus*. Translated by Peter Collier. Palo Alto, Calif.: Stanford University Press, 1988.
Brodkey, Harold. *This Wild Darkness: The Story of My Death*. New York: Holt, 1996.
Brown, Stephanie. *The Postwar African American Novel: Protest and Discontent, 1945–1950*. Jackson: University Press of Mississippi, 2011.
Byerman, Keith. *Seizing the Word: History, Art, and Self in the Work of W. E. B. Du Bois*. Athens: University of Georgia Press, 2010.
Caram, Richard G. "The Secular Priests: A Study of the College Professor as Hero in Selected American Fiction, 1955–1977." Ph.D. diss., Saint Louis University, 1980.
Carter, Ian. *Ancient Cultures of Conceit: British University Fiction in the Post-War Years*. London: Routledge, 1990.
Christian, June Cara. *Understanding the Black Flame and Multigenerational Educational Trauma: Toward a Theory of the Dehumanization of Black Students*. Lanham, Md.: Rowman and Littlefield, 2014.
Coates, Ta-Nehisi. "This Is How We Lost to the White Man: The Audacity of Bill Cosby's Conservatism." *The Atlantic*, May 2008. https://www.theatlantic.com/magazine/archive/2008/05/-this-is-how-we-lost-to-the-white-man/306774/.
Coleman, Finnie D. *Sutton E. Griggs and the Struggle Against White Supremacy*. Knoxville: University of Tennessee Press, 2007.
Collins, Patricia Hill. *Black Feminist Thought: Knowledge, Consciousness, and the Politics of Empowerment*. New York: Routledge, 2000.
Conklin, John E. *Campus Life in the Movies: A Critical Survey from the Silent Era to the Present*. Jefferson, N.C.: McFarland, 2008.
Cooper, Anna Julia. *The Voice of Anna Julia Cooper: Including "A Voice from the South" and Other Important Essays, Papers, and Letters*. Edited by Charles Lemert and Esme Bhan. Lanham, Md.: Rowman and Littlefield, 1998.
Cooper, Brittney C. *Beyond Respectability: The Intellectual Thought of Race Women*. Champaign: University of Illinois Press, 2017.
Cruse, Harold. *The Crisis of the Negro Intellectual: A Historical Analysis of the Failure of Black Leadership*. New York: Morrow, 1967.
Davis, Ray. "Delany's Dirt." In *Ash of Stars: On the Writing of Samuel R. Delany*, edited by James Sallis, 162–88. Jackson: University Press of Mississippi, 1996.
Delany, Samuel R. *About Writing: Seven Essays, Four Letters, and Five Interviews*. Middletown, Conn.: Wesleyan University Press, 2006.
———. "The Gamble." *Corpus* 3, no. 1 (2005): 140–69. http://aplahealth.org/publications/corpus/fall2005/Corpus4.pdf.
———. *1984: Selected Letters*. Rutherford, N.J.: Voyant Publishing, 2000.
———. *Phallos: Enhanced and Revised Edition*. 2004. Middletown, Conn.: Wesleyan University Press, 2013.
———. "Racism and Science Fiction." *New York Review of Science Fiction*. Issue 120, August 1998. Accessed February 4, 2019. https://www.nyrsf.com/racism-and-science-fiction-.html.
———. *Shorter Views: Queer Thoughts and the Politics of the Paraliterary*. Middletown, Conn.: Wesleyan University Press, 1996.
———. *Times Square Red, Times Square Blue*. New York: New York University Press, 1999.

Dickson-Carr, Darryl. *African American Satire: The Sacredly Profane Novel.* Columbia: University of Missouri Press, 2001.
Douglass, Frederick. *Narrative of the Life of Frederick Douglass.* 1845. Edited by David W. Blight. Reprint, Boston: Bedford/St. Martin's, 2003.
Duberman, Martin B., ed. *Queer Representations: Reading Lives, Reading Cultures.* A Center for Lesbian and Gay Studies Book. New York: New York University Press, 1997.
Ducille, Ann. *Skin Trade.* Cambridge, Mass.: Harvard University Press, 1996.
Edwards, Brent. *The Practice of Diaspora: Literature, Translation, and the Rise of Black Internationalism.* Cambridge, Mass.: Harvard University Press, 2003.
Ellison, Ralph. *The Collected Essays of Ralph Ellison.* Revised and Edited by John F. Callahan. New York: Random House, 1995.
Evans, Stephanie Y. *Black Women in the Ivory Tower, 1850–1954: An Intellectual History.* Gainesville: University Press of Florida, 2007.
Eversley, Shelly. *The Real Negro: The Question of Authenticity in Twentieth-Century African American Literature.* New York: Routledge, 2004.
Ferguson, Roderick A. *Aberrations in Black: Toward a Queer of Color Critique.* Minneapolis: University of Minnesota Press, 2003.
Foltz, Mary Catherine. "The Excremental Ethics of Samuel R. Delany." *SubStance* 37, no. 2 (2008): 41–55.
Foucault, Michel. *The History of Sexuality, Volume 1: An Introduction.* Translated by New York: Vintage Books, 1990.
———. *Madness and Civilization: A History of Insanity in the Age of Reason.* New York: Vintage Books, 1988.
Fullerty, Matthew H. G. "The British and American Academic Novel. The 'Professorromane': The Comic Campus, The Tragic Self." Ph.D. diss., George Washington University, 2008. ProQuest (3297121).
Gates, Henry Louis, Jr. *Figures in Black: Words, Signs, and the "Racial" Self.* Oxford: Oxford University Press, 1988.
———. *Thirteen Ways of Looking at a Black Man.* New York: Random House, 1997.
Gates, Racquel J. *Double Negative: The Black Image and Popular Culture.* Durham, N.C.: Duke University Press, 2018.
Graff, Gerald. *Beyond the Culture Wars: How Teaching the Conflicts Can Revitalize American Higher Education.* New York: Norton, 1993.
Griggs, Sutton Elbert, *The Hindered Hand; or, The Reign of the Repressionist.* 1905. Reprint, New York: AMS Press, 1969.
Holmes, William F. *The White Chief: James K. Vardaman.* Baton Rouge: Louisiana State University Press, 1970.
Howe, Irving. *Selected Writings, 1950–1990.* San Diego: Harcourt Brace Jovanovich, 1990.
Hughes, Langston. *The Weary Blues.* New York: Knopf, 1926.
Jackson, Lawrence. "Bucklin Moon and Thomas Sancton in the 1940s: Crusaders for the Racial Left." *Southern Literary Journal* 40, no. 1 (2007): 76–97.
James, Kenneth R. Introduction to *1984: Selected Letters*, by Samuel R. Delany. Rutherford, N.J.: Voyant Publishing, 2000.
James, Winston. *Holding Aloft the Banner of Ethiopia: Caribbean Radicalism in Early Twentieth-Century America.* New York: Verso, 1999.

Jarrett, Gene Andrew. *Representing the Race: A New Political History of African American Literature*. New York: New York University Press, 2011.

Johnson, E. Patrick. *Appropriating Blackness: Performance and the Politics of Authenticity*. Durham, N.C.: Duke University Press, 2003.

Kramer, John E., Jr. *Academe in Mystery and Detective Fiction*. 2nd ed. Lanham, Md.: Scarecrow Press, 2000.

———. *The American College Novel: An Annotated Bibliography*. 1981. Reprint, New York: Scarecrow Press, 2004.

Levy-Hussen, Aida. *How to Read African American Literature: Post–Civil Rights Fiction and the Task of Interpretation*. New York: New York University Press, 2016.

Lewis, David Levering. *W. E. B. Du Bois: Biography of a Race, 1868–1919*. New York: Holt, 1993.

———. *W. E. B. Du Bois, 1919–1963: The Fight for Equality and the American Century*. New York: Holt, 2000.

———. *When Harlem Was in Vogue*. New York: Penguin Books, 1979.

Lodge, David. *After Bakhtin: Essays on Fiction and Criticism*. New York: Routledge, 1990.

———. Introduction to *Pnin*, by Vladimir Nabokov. New York: Random House, 2004.

Lorde, Audre. *A Burst of Light: Essays by Audre Lorde*. Ithaca, N.Y.: Firebrand Books, 1988.

Lyons, John O. *The College Novel in America*. Carbondale: Southern Illinois University Press, 1962.

Macharia, Keguro. "Queering Helga Crane: Black Nativism in Nella Larsen's *Quicksand*." *Modern Fiction Studies* 57, no. 2 (Summer 2011): 254–75.

McDowell, Deborah. Introduction to *Quicksand/Passing*, by Nella Larsen. New Brunswick, N.J.: Rutgers University Press, 1986.

McGurl, Mark. *The Program Era: Postwar Fiction and the Rise of Creative Writing*. Cambridge, Mass.: Harvard University Press, 2011.

McInnis, Jarvis. "'Behold the Land': W. E. B. Du Bois, Cotton Futures, and the Afterlife of the Plantation in the U. S. South." *Global South* 10, no. 2 (Fall 2016): 70–98.

McMillan Cottom, Tressie. *Lower Ed: The Troubling Rise of For-Profit Colleges in the New Economy*. New York: New Press, 2017.

Moseley, Merritt, ed. *The Academic Novel: New and Classic Essays*. Chester, U.K.: Chester Academic Press, 2007.

Moses, Wilson J. *Afrotopia: The Roots of African American Popular History*. Cambridge: Cambridge University Press, 1998.

Palumbo-Liu, David. "Introduction." In *The Ethnic Canon: Histories, Institutions, and Interventions*, edited by David Palumbo-Liu, 1–30. Minneapolis: University of Minnesota Press, 1995.

Posnock, Ross. *Color and Culture: Black Writers and the Making of the Modern Intellectual*. Cambridge, Mass.: Harvard University Press, 1998.

Proctor, Mortimer. *The English University Novel*. Berkeley: University of California Press, 1957.

Rampersad, Arnold. *The Art and Imagination of W. E. B. Du Bois*. Cambridge, Mass.: Harvard University Press, 1976.

Reed, Ishmael. *Conversations with Ishmael Reed*. Edited by Bruce Dick and Amritjit Singh. Jackson: University Press of Mississippi, 1995.

———. *Reckless Eyeballing*. Chicago: Dalkey Archive Press, 1986.

Reid-Pharr, Robert. *Once You Go Black: Choice, Desire, and the Black American Intellectual*. New York: New York University Press, 2007.

———. "Tarrying with the 'Private Parts.'" *Feminist Formations* 25, no. 3 (Winter 2013): 149–53. Accessed February 23, 2014. https://muse.jhu.edu/.

Riggs, Marlon, dir. *Ethnic Notions*. California Newsreel, 1987. Retrieved January 14, 2018, from Kanopy. https://www.kanopy.com/product/ethnic-notions-0.

Rogers, Ibram H. *The Black Campus Movement: Black Students and the Racial Reconstitution of Higher Education, 1965–1972*. New York: Palgrave Macmillan, 2012.

Rojas, Fabio. *From Black Power to Black Studies: How a Radical Social Movement Became an Academic Discipline*. Baltimore: Johns Hopkins University Press, 2007.

Ross, Marlon. *Manning the Race: Reforming Black Men in the Jim Crow Era*. New York: New York University Press, 2004.

Russell-Cole, Kathy, Midge Wilson, and Ronald E. Hall. *The Color Complex: The Politics of Skin Color in a New Millennium*. Rev. ed. New York: Anchor Books, 2013.

Russett, Margaret. "Race Under Erasure." *Callaloo* 28, no. 2 (Spring 2005): 358–68. Accessed August 10, 2016. https://muse.jhu.edu/.

Saintsbury, George. "Novels of University Life." *Macmillan's Magazine*, no. 77 (March 1898): 340–62.

Scarborough, William Sanders. *The Educated Negro and His Mission*. Occasional Papers, no. 8. Washington, D.C.: American Negro Academy, 1903. Reprint, New York: AMS Press, 1970.

Scott, Darieck. *Extravagant Abjection: Blackness, Power, and Sexuality in the African American Literary Imagination*. New York: New York University Press, 2010.

Sharpe, Christina. *In the Wake: On Blackness and Being*. Durham, N.C.: Duke University Press, 2016.

———. *Monstrous Intimacies: Making Post-Slavery Subjects*. Durham, N.C.: Duke University Press, 2009.

Shaviro, Steven. "The Mad Man." *The Pinocchio Theory* (blog), November 30, 2006. Accessed November 1, 2018. http://www.shaviro.com/Blog/?p=528.

———. "Mad Man Redux." *The Pinocchio Theory* (blog), January 9, 2007. Accessed November 1, 2018. http://www.shaviro.com/Blog/?p=537.

Showalter, Elaine. *Faculty Towers: The Academic Novel and Its Discontents*. Philadelphia: University of Pennsylvania Press, 2005.

Spillers, Hortense J. *Black, White, and in Color: Essays on American Literature and Culture*. Chicago: University of Chicago Press, 2003.

Tobolowsky, Barbara F., and Pauline J. Reynolds, eds. *Anti-Intellectual Representations of American Colleges and Universities: Fictional Higher Education*. New York: Palgrave Macmillan, 2017.

Tucker, Jeffrey Allen. *A Sense of Wonder: Samuel R. Delany, Race, Identity, and Difference*. Middletown, Conn.: Wesleyan University Press, 2004.

Vidal, Gore. *At Home: Essays, 1982–1988*. New York: Random House, 1988.
Wallace, Michele. *Invisibility Blues: From Pop to Theory*. New York: Verso, 1994.
Washington, Booker T. *Up from Slavery: An Autobiography*. 1901. Edited by William L. Andrews. Reprint, Oxford: Oxford University Press, 1995.
Watts, Jerry. *Amiri Baraka: The Politics and Art of a Black Intellectual*. New York: New York University Press, 2001.
———. *Heroism and the Black Intellectual: Ralph Ellison, Politics, and Afro-American Intellectual Life*. Chapel Hill: University of North Carolina Press, 1994.
Wilder, Craig Steven. *Ebony and Ivy: Race, Slavery, and the Troubled History of America's Universities*. New York: Bloomsbury Press, 2013.
Williams, Erika Renée. "A Lie of Omission: Plagiarism in Nella Larsen's *Quicksand*." *African American Review* 45, nos. 1–2. (Spring–Summer 2012): 205–16.
Williams, Jeffrey J. "The Rise of the Academic Novel." *American Literary History* 24, no. 3 (Fall 2012): 561–89. Accessed August 10, 2016. https://muse.jhu.edu/.
———. "Teach the University." *Pedagogy* 8, no. 1 (Winter 2008): 25–42. Accessed August 10, 2016. https://muse.jhu.edu/.
———. "Unlucky Jim: The Rise of the Adjunct Novel." *Chronicle of Higher Education*, November 12, 2012. Accessed August 10, 2016. https://www.chronicle.com/article/Unlucky-Jim-the-Rise-of-the/135606.
Womack, Kenneth. *Postwar Academic Fiction: Satire, Ethics, Community*. New York: Palgrave, 2002.
Woodhouse, Reed. *Unlimited Embrace: A Canon of Gay Fiction, 1945–1995*. Amherst: University of Massachusetts Press, 1998.
Woodson, Carter G. *The Mis-Education of the Negro*. 1933. Reprint, Trenton, N.J.: Africa World Press, 1990.

INDEX

Aberrations in Black (Ferguson), 150–51
About Writing (S. R. Delany), 138
academia, 4, 8, 23, 31, 102; in fiction, 4, 8, 31, 36, 129, 133, 134, 148, 156
academic fiction, 7, 12, 16, 25–26, 30, 32, 34, 37, 42, 46, 48, 59–60, 62, 69, 76, 98, 132, 152, 163, 165, 168; as genre, 131; insularity of, 36
academic film, 6, 165
academic novel (genre): 6–7, 8, 11, 32, 36, 62, 92, 97, 144; black academic novel, 30, 32, 33, 37, 39, 184n3
Adichie, Chimamanda: works by, 41, 174
After Bakhtin (Lodge), 109
AIDS, 153, 155. *See also* HIV/AIDS
Allen, Debbie, 172
Americanah (Adichie), 41, 174
Amiri Baraka: The Politics and Art of a Black Intellectual (Watts), 24
anthropology, 113, 115–16
Atlanta, 59, 100, 103, 105, 123–24
Atlanta University, 52, 59; Atlanta University Studies, 59; in fiction, 52, 103–5
Atlantis: Model 1924 (S. R. Delany), 150
authenticity, 25–26, 28, 71, 88, 127, 138, 140, 145, 147–48, 164

Bakhtin, Mikhail, 109, 137
Baldwin, James, 23, 144, 146–47; works by, 144, 147
Bamboozled (Spike Lee, 2000), 88
Bechdel, Alison, 29; works by 29
Bhabha, Homi, 78
Birthright (Oscar Micheaux, 1939), 26, 41
Birthright (Stribling), 26, 40–41, 82
blackademic life, 7, 10–14, 48, 67, 76, 81, 160; cinematic representations of, 13, 127, 167–74; literary representations of, 7, 9–11, 14, 34, 71, 73, 76, 84, 90, 92, 127, 173–74
Black Arts Movement, 120, 130
black bodies, 8, 10, 16, 47, 56, 57, 89, 103, 116, 149
Black Boy (Wright), 38
black college(s), 15, 16, 19, 37, 41, 48, 49, 69–70, 72, 73–74, 76, 79, 80–83, 85, 91–92, 93, 96–97, 99, 105–6, 120–24, 150, 171
Black Flame, The (Du Bois), 18, 27–28, 52, 60–61, 67, 74, 77–78, 80, 97–102, 104, 106, 108–10, 136, 137
black intellectual, 3, 6, 7, 22–25, 27, 29, 30, 32, 37, 38–42, 46–48, 55, 57, 59, 65–67, 69, 70, 72–73, 76, 78, 79, 81, 84–86, 88–92, 100, 102–10, 112–16, 121, 124, 129, 131, 146, 148, 160–61, 163, 166, 168; black intellectualism, 25, 33; anti-intellectualism, 148, 164, 165–66
BlackLivesMatter, 4, 6, 9, 10, 57, 95, 125
blackness, 27–28, 30, 40, 41, 45, 46, 74, 75, 88–89, 91, 92, 111, 115, 142, 151, 157, 161, 163, 167, 171, 172, 174; antiblackness, 16, 71, 96, 98, 169, 172, 173
Black Reconstruction (Du Bois), 3, 10, 107, 110
Blake, or the Huts of America (M. Delany), 58
"Brooklyn" (Marshall), 113–14
Brown v. Board of Education of Topeka, 13, 69; post-*Brown* era, 15, 70; post-*Brown* novels, 97

campus activism, 6, 15, 52, 95, 119, 126, 129
campus fiction, 82
campus novel, 32–33, 81, 97, 115
capitalism, 8, 9, 97, 106–8, 125–66

197

Changing Places (Lodge), 35, 131, 167
Charleston massacre, 98–100
#CharlestonSyllabus, 99
Chesnutt, Charles, 49
Chosen Place, the Timeless People, The (Marshall), 4, 96–97, 106, 113–16, 119
City University of New York (CUNY): Brooklyn College, 113; CUNY Graduate Center, 4, 11; New York City College of Technology, 174
Coates, Ta-Nehisi, 169–70
college novel, 28, 32–37, 70, 79, 82, 86, 93, 96, 105
color, 82, 88, 102, 104, 138, 140, 148, 150, 158, 165, 172
colorism, 9, 16, 47, 66, 71, 74–76, 104, 171, 180n14
Color Purple, The (Walker), 38, 135
Cooper, Anna Julia, 46–47, 123
Cooper, Brittney, 47, 139, 171
Cosby, Bill, 29, 138, 168–72. See also *The Cosby Show* and *A Different World*
Cosby Show, The, 13, 29, 127, 134, 168–69, 172; as false positive, 172
cotton economy, 55, 59, 63, 64, 66
Crisis, The, 26, 28, 40, 110–11, 167
critical university studies, 164
"Cross" (L. Hughes), 70, 91
Crummell, Alexander, 21
Cruse, Harold, 7, 22–23, 136
culture of dissemblance, 47
culture war(s), 7, 77, 105, 124, 125–30
culture warriors, 7, 126

Dargis, Manohla, 29
Dark Princess (Du Bois), 28, 70, 77–78
Dear White People (Justin Simien, 2014), 165, 172
Dear White People (Netflix), 172, 173
Delany, Samuel R., 4, 13–14, 103, 124, 134, 138, 148–74; works by, 4, 13, 103, 115, 134, 138, 148–58, 160, 171, 173
Different World, A, 13, 29, 127, 168, 172–73
diversity, 13, 15, 18, 23, 34, 42, 95, 121, 129, 134, 137
Dixon, Thomas, 45–46, 49

Double Negative: The Black Image and Popular Culture (R. Gates), 168, 171–72, 188n7
Douglass, Frederick, 17, 59
Du Bois, W. E. B., 26–28, 35, 39–40, 46–47, 49, 51–52, 55–56, 59–67; works by, 3, 10, 18, 19–20, 27–28, 46–48, 52, 55, 58–59, 60–61, 62, 63–67, 74, 77–78, 80, 97–106, 107–10, 136, 137, 170
DuVernay, Ava, 29
Dying Animal, The (Roth), 152
Dykes to Watch Out For (Bechdel), 29

Ebony and Ivy: Race, Slavery, and the Troubled History of America's Universities (Wilder), 8, 42, 56, 116
Edwards, Brent, 97
Ellison, Ralph, 11, 144–46, 173; works by, 16, 21, 23, 40, 48, 53, 70, 74, 76, 83–90, 92, 96, 112, 139, 144–47, 150, 174
embodied discourse, 47, 139, 171
embodiment, 66, 139, 148, 151–52, 158, 172
Erasure (Everett), 13, 28, 39, 87, 89, 137–40, 142, 144, 147–48
Everett, Percival, 24, 124, 138; works by, 13, 28, 39, 87, 89, 137–40, 142, 144, 147–48
Extravagent Abjection: Blackness, Power, and Sexuality in the African American Literary Imagination (Scott), 158

Faculty Towers (Showalter), 31–32
feminism, 47, 66, 76, 104, 119–20, 124–25, 130, 134–35, 172
Ferguson, Roderick, 96, 183n41; works by, 95, 150–51
Figures in Black: Words, Signs, and the "Racial" Self (H. L. Gates), 37, 40
Fields, Barbara and Karen, 29
Finnegans Wake (Joyce), 140
Fisher v. University of Texas, 42
From #BlackLivesMatter to Black Liberation (Taylor), 6

Gates, Henry Louis, Jr., 32, 38, 40; works by, 37, 40

Index 199

Gates, Racquel, 168, 171; works by, 168, 171–72, 188n7
gender, 21, 25, 29, 47, 48, 55, 66, 69, 71, 75, 76, 82, 104, 110, 120, 127, 130, 139, 140, 151, 158, 165–66, 168, 171, 172
Go Tell It on the Mountain (Baldwin), 147
glossolalia, 137
Gramsci, Antonio, 7
Griggs, Sutton, 13, 45, 48–67, 69, 78, 97; works by, 19, 20, 46, 48–53, 55–58
Guess Who's Coming to Dinner (Stanley Kramer, 1967), 139

Hammon, Jupiter, 17
Hansberry, Lorraine, 23
Harlem, 26–27, 53, 59, 75–76, 79, 87, 90, 104, 111, 146, 150
Harlem Renaissance, 13, 27, 69–70, 110–11, 150. *See also* New Negro Movement
Heroism and the Black Intellectual: Ralph Ellison, Politics, and Afro-American Intellectual Life (Watts), 3, 23, 146
Higher Learning (John Singleton, 1995), 105, 127, 190
Himes, Chester, 24, 37, 55, 91, 138; works by, 70, 90–91, 94
Hindered Hand, The (Griggs), 46, 49
historically black colleges and universities (HBCUs), 15, 20, 23, 42, 69, 72, 83, 91, 96, 120, 139, 150, 171, 174
HIV/AIDS, 152, 153, 155; activism, 157
homophobia, 4, 56, 126, 155
hooks, bell, 7
Hopkins, Pauline, 49
Howard University, 16, 18, 22, 69; in fiction, 41, 122
Howe, Irving, 144
Hughes, Langston, 23, 111, 120; works by, 70, 79, 91–92
Hughes, Thomas, 60; works by, 60
Human Stain, The (Roth), 41, 128
Hurston, Zora Neale, 59

I Am Not Sidney Poitier (Everett), 138
Imperium in Imperio: A Study of the Negro Race Problem (Griggs), 19, 20, 46, 48–53, 55–58, 67, 83

integration, 13, 15, 23, 42, 52, 69, 96, 97, 114, 121–24
interiority, 13, 29, 40, 43, 72–73, 75, 76, 90, 163
Invisible Man (Ellison), 16, 21, 23, 40, 48, 53, 70, 74, 76, 83–90, 92, 96, 112, 144, 150, 174

Jacobs, Harriet, 17
Jacoby, Russell, 24
Japanese by Spring (Reed), 7, 13, 37, 48, 77, 120, 126, 128–37, 142, 156
Jefferson, Thomas, 57; works by, 8, 38, 57
Johnson, Mat, 24, 41; works by, 7, 127, 161–63

Larsen, Nella, 13, 27, 55, 70, 91; works by, 16, 27, 41, 66, 70–77, 85, 91, 96, 104, 118, 121, 161
Letting Go (Roth), 149
Lincoln University, 120
Locke, Alain, 23, 69
Lodge, David, 35–37, 151; works by, 35, 109, 131, 167
Lorde, Audre, 130, 159
Lucky Jim (Amis), 31, 35, 130, 149
lynching, 55–56, 100, 102, 160
Lyons, John, 32

Mad Man, The (S. R. Delany), 4, 13, 103, 115, 134, 148–58, 160, 171, 173
Mansart Builds a School (Du Bois), 28, 97, 103, 105–6
Macharia, Keguro, 70–71, 75, 76
Marshall, Paule, 13, 78, 107; works by, 4, 96–97, 106, 113–16, 119
McGurl, Mark, 36
McMillan Cottom, Tressie, 5, 164
Meridian (Walker), 16, 27, 72, 96, 119, 122–24
Micheaux, Oscar, 26
mind-body, 149–61
minority, 29, 35, 37, 70, 78, 95, 108, 162
miseducation, 83, 121
Mis-Education of the Negro, The (Woodson), 18, 22
Mississippi Valley State College, 3

Moon, Bucklin, 40, 79; works by, 41, 79
Mooz-lum (Qasim Basir, 2010), 190
Morehouse College, 3, 16, 53, 123, 138, 173; in fiction, 138
Mullen, Bill V., 77, 136
multicultural(ism), 13, 37, 127, 129, 135, 136, 137
Mumbo Jumbo (Reed), 128–30

NAACP, 25, 110, 111
nationalism, 97, 119; black nationalism, 13, 23, 58, 124, 136; internationalism, 106
Native Son (Wright), 40, 142–45, 147
neoliberalism, 13, 127, 162
New Negro, 13, 48–58, 67, 69–94
New Negro Movement, 58, 69. *See also* Harlem Renaissance
Nigger Factory, The (Scott-Heron), 16, 86, 96, 105, 119–21
Notes on the State of Virginia (Jefferson), 8, 38, 57
"Novels of University Life" (Saintsbury), 34

On Beauty (Smith), 41, 127
Ordeal of Mansart, The (Du Bois), 28, 100–102, 109
Orientalism, 77, 136; Afro-Orientalism, 77, 78, 136, 185n32
over-education, 18–19, 104

Parable of the Sower (Butler), 38
Parable of the Talents (Butler), 38
Passing (Larsen), 71, 72
Philadelphia Negro, The (Du Bois), 60, 170
Pickens, William, 21
Plessy v. Ferguson, 45, 91
Portrait of the Artist as a Young Man, A (Joyce), 89–90
postcolonial/ism, 77, 78, 97, 107, 113, 136
predominantly white institutions (PWIs), 67, 70, 95
"Professor" (L. Hughes), 70, 79, 92
public intellectual, 5, 24
Push (Sapphire), 38
Pym (Johnson), 7, 41, 127, 161–63

queer, 72, 73, 75, 76, 92, 111, 117, 148, 150, 151, 160; of color, 55, 150; fiction, 152; readings, 158; studies, 155; theory, 148, 155
Quest of the Silver Fleece, The (Du Bois), 19–20, 28, 46–48, 55, 58–59, 63–67, 104, 109
Quicksand (Larsen), 16, 27, 41, 66, 70–77, 85, 91, 96, 104, 118, 121, 161

racecraft, 29
racism, 7, 11, 14, 15, 28, 32, 56, 88, 98, 135, 137, 169; antiracism, 136
Reconstruction, 10, 13, 45–46, 51, 98, 100; post-Reconstruction, 15, 28, 45, 49, 59, 97, 99–100
Redding, J. Saunders, 13, 24, 69, 74, 79, 81–82, 97; works by, 20, 69–70, 81–83, 85, 173
Reed, Ishmael, 24, 78, 120, 124; works by, 7, 13, 37, 48, 77, 120, 126, 128–37, 142, 156
Reorder of Things: The University and Its Pedagogies of Minority Discourse, The (Ferguson), 95
representation, 25–30, 34, 39, 40, 52, 77, 78, 84, 86, 87, 102, 107, 143, 147, 173
respectability, 3, 29, 48, 67, 110, 112, 148, 150, 156, 174
respectability politics, 47, 111, 138, 170
Roth, Philip, 40, 152; works by, 41, 128, 149, 152

satire, 13, 31, 35, 40, 67, 137, 162
Scarborough, William S., 21–22
Schomburg, Arturo, 21
School Daze (Spike Lee, 1988), 48, 74, 121, 123, 127, 171
science fiction, 4, 14, 154
Scott-Heron, Gil, 120; works by, 16, 86, 96, 105, 119–21
segregation, 35, 45, 46, 52, 108, 136, 169; desegregation, 36, 83; segregationists, 85; segregationist propaganda, 46
Shorter Views: Queer Thoughts and the Politics of the Paraliterary (S. R. Delany), 149

Showalter, Elaine, 35, 82, 177n28
Smith, Zadie, 24, 78
social science, 113, 114, 183n41
"Some Queer Notions about Race" (S. R. Delany), 151
Something the Lord Made (Joseph Sargent, 2004), 191
Souls of Black Folk, The (Du Bois), 28, 60, 62
Spelman College, 16, 124, 170, 173
Stranger and Alone (Redding), 20, 69–70, 81–83, 85, 173
strategic negativity, 171
student activism, 6, 52, 95, 119, 126
student protest, 13, 95, 96, 121–22, 132

Tale of Plagues and Carnivals, The (S. R. Delany), 152
Taylor, Keeanga-Yamahtta, 4–6, 160; works by, 6
theory, 12; cultural, 15, 138; French, 133; gender, 166; literary, 13, 37, 38, 71, 138; queer, 155, of the novel, 40, 137; race, 98, 140, 166
Third Generation, The (Himes), 70, 90–94
Thirkield, Wilbur, 18–19
Thirteen Ways of Looking at a Black Man (H. L. Gates), 39
Times Square Red, Times Square Blue (S. R. Delany), 151
"Tom Brown at Fisk" (Du Bois), 28, 60
Tom Brown at Oxford (T. Hughes), 60

University in Modern Fiction, The (Rossen), 32, 35, 61, 133
Up from Slavery (Washington), 20–21, 46, 47–48, 86, 135, 150

uplift, 3, 8, 16, 29, 38, 45–48, 63, 66, 69, 74, 87–88, 90, 94, 109
Uncle Tom's Cabin (Stowe), 144

Vardaman, James, 18, 101

Waithe, Lena, 173
Walker, Alice, 13, 72, 119; works by, 16, 27, 38, 72, 96, 119, 122–24, 135
Wallace, Michele, 129–30, 134
War for the Soul of America, A (Hartman), 125–26
Washington, Booker T., 20–21, 46–49, 54, 65, 84–86, 88, 135; works by, 20–21, 46, 47–48, 86, 135, 150
Watts, Jerry G., 7, 11, 12, 23; works by, 3, 23, 24, 146
Wheatley, Phillis, 8, 9, 17, 38, 57, 145
white supremacy, 6, 10, 13–14, 19, 20, 22, 28, 30, 53, 62, 65, 67, 73, 75, 76, 78, 81, 89, 96, 97, 99, 107, 108, 121, 126, 128, 133, 158, 160, 161, 163, 171, 173, 182n8; Christian, 76; cognitive dissonance of, 57; educational policies rooted in, 16; hypocrisies of, 12
Wilder, Craig Steven, 56, 116; works by, 8, 42, 56, 116
Williams, Jeffrey J., 163–64
Without Magnolias (Moon), 41
womanism, 120, 124
Woodhouse, Reed, 149, 153, 157
Woodson, Carter G., 22; works by, 18, 22
"World and the Jug, The" (Ellison), 40, 139, 144–47
Worlds of Color (Du Bois), 28, 104, 106, 108
Wright, Richard, 40, 136, 144, 146–47; works by, 38, 40, 142–45, 147

www.ingramcontent.com/pod-product-compliance
Lightning Source LLC
Chambersburg PA
CBHW032036290426
44110CB00012B/825